THROUGH THE WATER AND THE FIRE

A Swift Boat Sailor's Story

The story of a young man's transition from a wild teenager to a combat-hardened warrior in an unpopular war and his transition back into society, his struggle with finding the meaning of it all, and finally his commitment as a Christian man of God.

D1264418

Charles Hunt

edited by Laura T. Gainsborg

ISBN 978-1-64114-854-2 (paperback)
ISBN 978-1-64114-855-9 (digital)

Christian Faith Publishing, Inc.
832 Park Avenue
Meadville, PA 16335
www.christianfaithpublishing.com

Printed in the United States of America

When you pass through the waters,
I will be with you;
and when you pass through the rivers,
they will not sweep over you.

When you walk through the fire,
you will not be burned;
the flames will not set you ablaze.

For I am the Lord, your God...
your Savior...

—Isaiah 43:2–3a, NIV

A small trickle of blood came from the tiny wound in his chest. He took one last difficult breath and exhaled one final time. The young Vietnamese soldier's body lay motionless and completely relaxed on the engine cover of our fifty-foot patrol boat. Growing up on the farm and hunting, I was familiar with the killing and death of animals many times; now, I had witnessed the death of a human being right at my feet.

Forward on the deck of the bow, Johnson sat with a severely wounded soldier on each side of him and his twin-mount machine guns. He reached into the bloody stump where a leg was once attached to a young warrior before a blast had blown it off. Pinching off the femoral artery was all that stood between life and death for him on this dark and foreboding day.

As soon as the dead and wounded were medevaced by the helos, we maneuvered our mud and blood covered Swift Boat back into the canal where the carnage had occurred to deliver an angry vengeance.

CONTENTS

PREFACE

From time to time during my adult life, I have felt that I should write a book. There were several roadblocks to carrying out this notion. The main one was that I had no idea what to write about. Furthermore, the idea of someone who does not like to read because it is tiring, then deciding to write a book doesn't seem to jive. And even if I were an avid reader fueled by a passion for a specific topic, life had afforded me little time for what seemed to be the massive task of writing a book. But now after raising our children, foster children, and grandchildren, I have found the time to write. More importantly, I have found a topic for which I have a great passion and firsthand experience.

Since serving on Swift Boats in Vietnam, I have grabbed every magazine and book that I had ever come across about the small boat Navy in Vietnam. Recently, I purchased and read (yes, I read) White Water Red Hot Lead *written by Dan Daly. Mr. (LT) Daly writes about his personal experience from training for Swift Boat duty through his tour of duty up to and including his return home. I thoroughly enjoyed reading the book (a rare event for me). It brought back many memories and a few tears. Most importantly, it awakened in me the desire to write about my service on Swifts in Vietnam.*

It may seem a little redundant to do what Dan Daly has already done, but his experience was somewhat different than mine. He was there two years prior to me and he was doing coastal patrols in the most northern part of South Vietnam, termed I corps. By 1969, when I arrived in Vietnam, the US Navy had turned most coastal patrols, termed Operation Market Time, over to the South Vietnamese Navy. My areas of operation were in the most southern part of South Vietnam in the Mekong Delta. This area was termed IV corp. We were engaged *in Operation SEALORDS which is an acronym for South East Asia Lake Ocean River Delta Strategy. The Mekong delta is the rice basket of Vietnam and laced with waterways of all sizes.*

So while Dan and I served on Swift boats and some things were the same, there were other things that were very different—especially the proximity in which we encountered the enemy and the types of special operations that we ran. Therefore, I think it worthwhile to share my experiences which broaden the recorded history of what we "Swifties" did in Vietnam. Beyond that when my great grandchildren ask, "What did Grandpop Charles do in the war?" there will be a record.

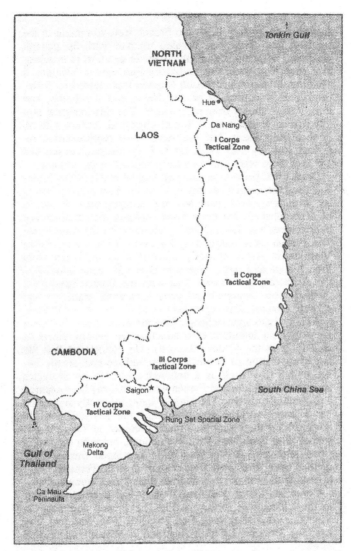

South Vietnam

Shortly after I began to write this book, my wife reminded me that my mother had saved every letter that I had sent home to her and Dad. When my mother passed on, my wife Claire held on to and put away the

11

box of letters. Reading them for the first time since I wrote them over forty years ago was at times funny, at times sad, and at times embarrassing. But they have proven invaluable in aiding my memory in the telling of my story. Throughout the story, I have copied segments from some of those letters.

As I struggled to come up with a title for this book I wrestled with titles that included the word freedom. *My thinking was shaded by my underlying sadness that we, the people of the United States, paid so high a price for another people's freedom and then abandoned the effort. As the mental struggle for a title continued, I came to the realization that my story and life itself is all about choices, and freedom is all about choices—the freedom to choose how we shall be governed, the freedom of what we believe and how we worship, the freedom of speech, and on and on it goes.*

There is a famous saying, "Life is 10 percent of what happens to you and 90 percent of how you react to it." How you react to the things that happen to you is generally your choice. Of course, there are times when natural instincts take control, but as a rule, you have a choice as to how you will react. That is if you are free. But without freedom, you often lose your choice.

The course of history is determined by choices. The fate of nations and their people is determined by government's choices. Woven all through my story are choices. Choices that I made, choices that others made, as well as the results of those choices. This story is about freedom—that idea, that concept, that way of life that we cherish so dearly and all too often take for granted. And this is about the price of freedom and about the loss of freedom only fully and deeply appreciated when experienced as I did firsthand.

ACKNOWLEDGEMENTS

To Laura Gainsborg, my friend and personal editor who volunteered to edit my book for free as soon as she heard I was writing. How can I thank you enough for the untold hours you spent reading, correcting my grammar, suggesting changes and rereading over and over? Thank you even more for your non-judgmental encouragement that kept me going and believing that I could write something of value.

To My Family ...
This book is for you to know:
1. My Experience in Vietnam
2. The Price of Freedom
3. God Loves You

I wrote this book to share with you my experiences in Vietnam, not to have anyone think of me either as a heroic war veteran nor for anyone's pity. I recorded my experiences so that you would get a sense of the precious value of freedom. I want you to get a personal feel for the price paid by me and countless others for freedom, and sadly how that sacrifice was discarded by the American people who decided the price was too high to pay for another people's freedom.

I also want you to know that God loves each one of you, watches over us, and sometimes intervenes in our lives in very special ways. So I will share with you how He taught me that truth by reaching halfway around the world through prayer to keep me safe during a time of great danger.

INTRODUCTION

During the Vietnam War, the US Navy was tasked with stopping the flow of enemy forces and supplies into the country from the coast.

After the US Navy stopped the flow of Communist forces and supplies into South Vietnam from the coast, a strategy was developed in 1968 to destroy the Viet Cong strongholds in the Mekong Delta and take back control of the many inland waterways.

This is the story of a young man who joined the Navy to avoid close up combat, but ended up being a floating target deep in the most remote areas of the Mekong Delta and Ca Mau Peninsula.

From the many letters he sent home, his personal memories, and the memories of his crewmates, he tells the stories of life and death aboard a fifty-foot patrol boat. He shares the emotions felt as the months of boredom are highlighted by moments of fear and high adrenaline. His feelings about freedom, family, and the war protests back home are intermingled with his countdown to when he can go home.

The Vietnam experience did not end for many veterans when they returned home. Petty Officer Hunt's story continues with readjustment to civilian life, emotional reactions to the trial of Lieutenant Calley of the Mi Lai massacre, his own Christian spiritual awakening, participation in the relocation of Vietnamese refugees, involvement in the 2004 presidential election, and the effects of exposure to Agent Orange.

Lastly, he expresses his sadness with how we, the American people, abandoned the South Vietnamese people and allowed the sacrifice that he and all the Vietnam veterans made, for the cause of freedom and democracy, to be wasted.

CHAPTER 1

THE SIXTIES

The '60s started out great but ended up not so great. During that decade Yankee slugger Roger Maris broke Babe Ruth's thirty-four year record of sixty home runs by hitting his sixty-first home run in the last game of the 1961 season against the Boston Red Sox. Pull tabs appeared on cans, and the US postal service introduced zip codes. Beatlemania struck the country when "I Want to Hold Your Hand" and "I Saw Her Standing There" were released in the United States in 1963. Initially I did not like the Beatles—I think mainly because my girlfriend was enamored by them to the point of me being foolishly jealous. In time, they won me over as I came to enjoy the change they had made to the sound and structure of rock 'n' roll music. Eventually, I would be performing a few of their songs during my high school years in a band called the Stags.

In 1964, Ford introduced the Mustang that would become a legendary muscle car. Chevrolet would counter in 1966 with the Camaro and the era of muscle cars began. Pontiac produced the GTO, Oldsmobile the 442, Plymouth the Barracuda, and Dodge the Charger.

By the time I reached the age of seventeen in 1965 and got my driver's license, I had already gone through six "field" cars—old cars that I purchased dirt cheap and used to race around the pasture and fields on the family farm. I would get going as fast as the car would go and then throw it into a broad slide to initiate a sliding turn in order to avoid crashing into the tree line at the end of the fields. I'd then get right back on the gas and straighten the car out for the next stretch and repeat the process again and again until something broke. Here the beginnings of my lifelong career began as I figured out how to get cars put back together and going again with limited tools and resources. Oftentimes bailing wire, solder, wood, and screws or whatever could be found were used to patch things back together. One by one as each car bit the dust, it became the parts' donor for the next four-wheeled victim of my appetite for speed and daring in the field.

Once I became a licensed driver, a whole new and more powerful string of cars fell victim to my lead foot. Drag racing both legal and illegal became a passion. I rigged several of my cars with switches to kill the tail- and stoplights. If I were pursued at night on a dark country road my car would seem to disappear right before the pursuing officer's eyes. The need for speed and the inevitable damage done from burnouts and speed shifting necessitated my learning more and more about the art of automotive repair.

While I was celebrating my twentieth birthday on February 4, 1968, approximately a half million US forces were defending against the communist's major Tet Offensive in South Vietnam. At the conclusion of the offensive, it was a major battlefield victory for the American forces, but the now-slanted reporting by the media turned it into a loss for support of the war.

In 1968 both Robert "Bobby" Kennedy and Martin Luther King were assassinated. The Civil Rights and antiwar protests were raging. Saddam Hussein became Vice Chairman of the Revolutionary Council in Iraq after a coup d'état. Little did anyone here in the United States notice or care about the eventual brutal dictator that we would go to war against years later, eventually capture, try, and execute.

In July of 1969, while I was awaiting orders at Philadelphia Naval Base, Neil Armstrong became the first man to walk on the moon. Woodstock took place from August 15 to 18 in Bethel, New York. Thirty-two acts performed outdoors to five hundred thousand concert goers. As the sex, drugs, and rock 'n' roll were winding down at Woodstock, I was leaving home, traveling to California to begin training for Swift Boat duty in Vietnam.

I graduated from Hopewell Valley Central High School in June of 1966, and that was the peak of the '60s for me. Life was filled with fast cars, parties, rock 'n' roll music (I played guitar), and girls. I had not been a stellar student but had amazingly coasted through high school. My theory was that homework should not interfere with my social life; it all had to get done in study hall. This worked well enough most the time. I did well enough to get accepted to what was then called Trenton State Teachers College (now the College of New Jersey). Believe or not, the tuition for New Jersey residents at that time was only $75 a semester.

All I ever wanted to do was work on cars. Because of this, the high school guidance counselor persuaded me to go to college so I could teach auto mechanics. To my dismay, the course of study for an industrial arts degree only included two classes in auto mechanics and a whole lot more math, history, and English, more than I wanted.

In December of my first semester, a ridiculously huge paper was due for my history class. The professor had demanded that at least seventy-five books had to be used as references and at least four of them were to be read completely. I did not really understand how to answer the question that the report was supposed to address. I do not recall how many pages the report had to be, but I decided that no report was going to absorb that much of my time. I had my motorcycle all apart at the repair shop where I was working part-time while in college. I distinctly remember asking myself, "What do I really want to do with my time? Do I want to go sit in another class, or do I want to get my motorcycle back together?" My motorcycle ran well, but my attendance suffered. The time had come for me to make a decision about continuing college or dropping out. Reluctantly, I went to the dean's office. Initially, I planned to discuss withdrawing from the history class. After a brief discussion in which I related my unhappiness with college, the dean presented me with my options. I made the decision to quit college altogether rather than suffer on and receive a failing grade. The dean's parting words were, "I hope you enjoy (serving) Uncle Sam more than I did." It felt like a kick in the pants to boot me out the door.

Dropping out had one major drawback—the draft. The selective service requires all eighteen-year-olds to register. If a male dropped out of college in the '60s, the draft board was notified. Shortly thereafter, he would be drafted into the Army. Young men who did not want to serve in the military and go to war looked for ways to avoid this such as becoming "career" students, faking a physical defect, or leaving the country, known as draft dodging.

I had no qualms about serving my country but wanted no part of going to Vietnam to risk being killed or wounded. The evening news showed daily accounts of combat actions in Vietnam along with the number of American casualties to date. At that time, I did not really understand what the war was all about. So it seemed the honorable way to avoid Vietnam was to join a reserve unit. Reservists never experienced Vietnam (or so I thought). The problem was that reserve duty had become such a popular way to avoid Vietnam that all units quickly filled and had long waiting lists, which meant a young male could get drafted while waiting to get into a reserve unit. But I thought that I had cleverly found a way into a unit. My graphic representation professor at Trenton State was a captain in the Naval Reserve, and he would arrange for me to join the Navy Reserve. I had few thoughts about sea duty and was not enticed by the recruiting slogan "Join the Navy and see the world." I was only looking for a way to not be walking around in the jungle and getting shot. I envisioned that the worst that could happen would be sitting safely off the coast on a big ship.

The Navy Reserve obligation was one year of drills, two years active duty, followed by two more years of drills, and one last year of standby reserve for a total of a six-year commitment. Army, Air Force, and Marine reservists had much shorter active duty tours, which did not allow enough time to train them and get in a tour of duty in Vietnam. So I dropped out of college, and in February of 1967, I joined the Navy Reserve. I did well on the written tests but had difficulty with the eye test. (I doubt that I would have passed the eye test part of the physical in peace times.) My eye test went something like this:

"Cover your right eye and tell me what you can read."

"E."

"That's it?"

"Yes."

"Cover your left eye and tell me what you can read."

"E."

"That's it?"

"Yes."

"Son, step forward here a few feet, now cover you right eye and tell me what you can read."

"E."

"Cover your left eye and tell me what you can read."

"E."

"Ok, son, step forward a little more and tell me what you can read."

"E, F, aaah, P?"

"Other eye."

"E, F, P, aaaah, T."

"All right now, son, let's step a little bit closer, now what can you read?"

"E, F, P, T, O, Z?"

"Okay let's go back to the beginning location and put your glasses on."

"E, F, P, T, O, Z, L, P, E, D."

"Good enough!"

Once the written test, the physical, and the background check were all completed, it was time to be officially sworn into the United States Navy. It came as a shock to me when taking the oath with my hand on the Bible that I was swearing to defend our country and its Constitution with my life if needed. No one had briefed me on this serious piece of information. I went ahead with the oath, having no idea at the time how close to fulfilling that vow I would come.

CHAPTER 2

YOU'RE IN THE NAVY NOW!

Boot Camp

I n February of 1967, I was off to boot camp at the Great Lakes Naval Training Center and had no idea how cold it would be. Now keep in mind I was a farm boy who had never been farther from home than a couple of family trips to New York City, so I had never been on an airplane or a subway or had to make travel connections. This was going to be a whole new travel experience for me. The Navy had issued me travel vouchers and a sheet of travel instructions. Early one morning in February, my parents drove me to the Trenton train station from whence I commenced with the excitement and stress of making multiple travel connections to a training experience that I was aware would not necessarily be pleasant. So I progressed from train to bus, to bus transfer to Philadelphia airport. Then on to Chicago O'Hare airport to a Navy transport bus to Great Lakes Training Center. Needless to say, I was apprehensive about misunderstanding directions or not arriving in time for the next means of transportation, but every connection of the journey was made in minutes without any wait time. If I had dallied at any point, I would have missed the next connection.

Boot camp is not just for training, it is also a weeding out of those who will not make it in military service as well as the molding of those who will. Therefore, the process requires making life miserable and degrading while coupling that with the frigid temperatures of the Great Lakes in February and not knowing anyone. I was not used to being hollered and screamed at—that was not how I was raised. It was obvious that boot camp was not going to be a barrel of fun. Upon arrival, we were marched off to pick up uniforms, get our heads shaved, and get shots. One man got a hematoma in his arm from his shot and passed out on the spot. The only good part of boot camp for me was that it would only be two weeks for us reservists, who did much of the basic training at the weekly drills as opposed to the nine or ten weeks for regular Navy.

For some reason, I guess because of my towering size, I was singled out to be the recruit master at arms. This gave me a temporary higher rank than the other recruits in our company but saddled me with responsibility of waking a sixteen-man cleaning crew in the wee hours, getting them off to early breakfast, and then returning them to the barracks. I then directed the crew in cleaning and preparing the barracks for inspection while the rest of the company was at breakfast.

In boot camp, every article of clothing had a way to be folded and specifically placed in our locker. Every rack (bed) had an exact location in the room and a precise distance from every other object. There are thirty-six spigots and thirty-six buckets for washing uniforms in the wash room. Every bucket had to be in an exact position. If for some reason a bucket were missing, it would have to be missing from location number 36, not any other location, and a written report had to be filed for a missing bucket. If any spigot had a leak or drip, it had to be tagged as such and a report filed. As the master at arms, I was responsible to know all these details and make sure they were carried out. Needless to say, everything had to be spotless, and there could be no "gear adrift," meaning there could be no unaccounted-for items or items out of place. This all was a lot to learn in a short time and a lot of responsibility for a brand-new recruit. In addition, there were some of the crew that did not like taking orders from someone that was actually as low ranking as they were. One individual decided to give me an attitude and not follow orders. I had to write him up for insubordination. His punishment was an evening of "happy hours", which is doing a couple hours of extra physical exercise in an overly warm gymnasium while wearing a blue wool uniform. Upon his return from "happy hours", his wool uniform was completely soaked with sweat, but he never gave me a problem again and followed orders without complaint! The upside of being on the cleaning crew was that the we were exempted from standing a personal inspection of our uniform or locker.

After morning inspections, a long day of training and harassment began. Outdoor activities meant freezing half to death, and indoor classrooms meant hours of sitting at near attention while fighting off the urge to doze. I don't recall every topic and area of training, but marching, swimming, marching, firefighting, marching, rifle range, marching, and the use of gas masks stick out in my mind. Did I mention marching? After donning our gas masks, we were marched around the inside of a building while tear gas was thrown in. If our masks were not put on correctly, we knew very quickly as the tear gas could seep in. After a few times around the inside of the building, we were ordered to remove our masks in order for us to experience what exposure to tear gas was like. Imagine 120 guys streaming out with burning tearing eyes, coughing and choking all at the same time.

The only physical abuse that I saw happen at boot camp was on the rifle range. We did our practice in a large indoor range with .22 rifles instead of regular issued M14s. The instructions and training were delivered not by Sailors but Marines. It seemed that the Marines liked us even less than our regular instructors. At this point in my story, it would be helpful to explain the use and meaning of one of the many slang words used in the Navy—*drifty*. The *Urban Dictionary* has six definitions of the word *drifty*. Number six seems to fit best with the Navy's use of the word when speaking about a person's attributes: *"A person whose awareness and judgment are lacking."* We heard the word used a lot. I presume that it was used frequently in the Navy due to boat and ship handlers needing to be aware of drifting when not "underway" or drifting off course. The street language explanation of the meaning of "drifty" would be *"a jerk that doesn't have his shit together."* While we were practicing on the range, there was one *"drifty"* recruit who had a problem or question and decided to turn around to speak to the Marine instructor. The problem was that he turned around rifle and all, which meant he was swinging a loaded weapon past everyone on his one side. The instructor immediately knew the danger of the action and proceeded to correct the recruit's position with extreme prejudice. I suppose the instructor believed that anyone who was that "drifty" needed a significant physical and emotional event to help remember to keep his weapon pointed down range at all times. I believe that "drifty" will forever remember after the beating and tongue lashing he received.

The food at boot camp was some of the worst-tasting stuff I ever ate. The safest thing was to just eat bread. I did not eat much anyhow because I became extremely homesick. It is a terrible feeling coupled with the urge to cry, which I fought because who wants to be seen crying at boot camp? I just wanted to go home.

During this time, I developed a cold and was allowed to report to sick bay. Upon arrival, my temperature was taken, and I was assigned to a line determined by my temperature level. There was a line for each level of temperature, which determined just how sick a person was. I was given some APCs (like aspirin) and a cup of salt to gargle with hot water, and then it was back out into the cold. There were rumors of the number of recruits that had died from pneumonia—not a comforting bit of information when you are sick.

These experiences of being away from home, enduring the physical challenges and purposeful belittling of the instructors, learning to obey orders, being put in a position of responsibility to direct others and continue even when sick and homesick were the beginning of the transformation for me from boy to man.

Because we passed our inspections, we were given a twelve-hour pass to go to Chicago. So what do brand-new sailors do with twelve hours in a big city? Not being old enough to drink legally, the first thing was to get a decent meal. I was impressed with how inexpensively one could buy a huge steak dinner in Chicago at that time. A small group of us checked out the USO club, which provided snacks and the opportunity to call home. There were notices about upcoming dances, which would be after we had to head back to base.

On the street, I was surprised at the quantity and crudeness of the pornography that was readily available on display in storefronts.

Eventually, we wound up in a strip club—not so much a club as a dirty old theater with drunks sleeping it off here and there. Half the show was a cheap pornographic movie and the other half a few past-their-prime strippers. Once we were back on the street, we became aware that the purpose of the movie was to allow the girls time to dress and walk down a block to the next strip joint and perform the same routine. This all seemed cheap and crude. And what a rip-off for anyone who paid to get into the next strip joint only to see the same strippers again!

Boot camp had an interesting set of rules for fighting. If a recruit hit someone, he got a week in the brig.[1] If a recruit hit someone back, he got two weeks in the brig. If a third recruit tried to stop a fight, he got three weeks in the brig. I guess the thinking was to prevent an all-out brawl. Men who were in the brig were often seen carrying buckets of rocks from one end of the base to the other. Once all the rocks were at one end, then they had to take them all back to the other end. And of course, the brig was run by whom but the Marines, where they could really let a sailor know how they felt about him.

Training "Cruise"

From boot camp, I flew to Boston's Logan Airport and reported to the USS *Compton* DD705 for a two-week training "cruise". The *Compton* was a destroyer that was built, commissioned, and served in the Pacific during WWII. My two-week cruise was no cruise at all. We did get towed from one pier to another—that was the extent of our "cruise." The Compton was a training ship and had a permanent skeleton crew. It seemed that the crew did not think very highly of us reservists and just used us to do their dirty work. I was still homesick, and remember it now as a dark and dreary time that I just wanted to get through and get back home.

---

[1]   brig is a naval term for a military prison

My duty consisted of cleaning the "bilges" in one of the boiler rooms. Prior to this time, I had never heard of the word *bilge*, but I became intimately acquainted with bilges. It was seriously hot due to the oil-fired boilers that produced the steam that power the turbines that propel the ship. There was also a constant loud noise from the exhaust fans that barely helped remove the heat from the boiler room.

On board this destroyer I learned about having a tiny footlocker and sleeping in racks stacked six or seven high. This meant that if the person above or below me turned over, I probably got bumped and would likely deliver the same to them. A "rack" is simply a rectangular metal frame with a section of canvass stretched inside the rectangle to support a body. On some racks, there are thin mattress-type pads stuffed inside a long sack-like cloth called a fart sack. Some guys just used the "fart sack" like a lightweight sleeping bag. You can figure out for yourself why they are called "fart sacks"! Sailors in the uppermost racks had to climb up using the lower and middle racks to step on. Living in such close quarters, if anyone was sick or had bad gas, everyone suffered. Space was at a premium aboard ship, and I found it interesting how everything managed to fit in so completely.

The food was better than boot camp, but I was appalled at the amount of food that got thrown away at the end of each meal. I was raised and taught to never waste food. Sometimes onboard ship, whole trays of untouched food were dumped into the trash can. It was difficult for the cooks to know how much food to prepare because they never knew how many men would be on board to eat and how many would go ashore to eat elsewhere. Also, every night there was a movie in the mess hall and sometimes ice cream. The movie helped to pass the time and get my mind off being homesick.

There were watches to stand around the clock even though we were in port and not underway. The watches were four hours long, so after working all day, I might get a few hours' sleep and then be awakened to go stand a four-hour watch. Mine was a boiler watch, which meant watching the water level in a sight glass and adjusting the water flow to maintain a proper level.

Once as part of my daytime bilge cleaning, I had to replace a broken lamp globe. In the process, my hand slipped, and I incurred a deep laceration on the base of my right hand. The medic in sick bay cleaned and bandaged it then gave me instructions on how to keep it clean and dry. Upon returning to the boiler room, I advised the Petty Officer in Charge of the medic's instructions to keep it clean. I was told to just clean with my left hand. That proved to be nearly impossible, so every day, I would report back to sick bay with a dirty bandage and get a lecture about keeping it clean. Eventually, as the cut worsened, I probably needed stitches but was too late. I still carry the scar today as a reminder of my time on the *Compton*.

At the end of the first week, I got a few hours' leave to visit Boston with strict instructions to stay out of the "combat zone." The combat zone was a red-light district lined with bars and houses of ill repute. It was notorious for fights and trouble. So once again, I walked the streets, getting something to eat and visiting the USO club. The USO club seemed friendly and peaceful, but there wasn't much to do there. I think I sent a postcard home from the USO club. Being raised on a farm in a rural area, I felt very much out of place in the city.

Reserve Drills

After the month of training, I returned home and went back to work at Housel Brothers Amoco and Mower Shop where I continued to gain mechanical experience. I also attended drills at the reserve center located on Duck Island in Trenton, New Jersey. That center is no longer there as the space gave way to a highway connection. Four of my friends from high school attended drills there also. They were Bill Metcalf, Rich Furlong, Tom Reside, and Ken Wolfarth. Metcalf and Reside wound up serving on bases in Vietnam at the same time I served there. Drills consisted of classes on basic military information and marching. The reserve center was located next to the sewage plant and in the summer the stench was bad.

I applied for and was accepted to a Navy "A" school to become an Electrician's Mate. The school was supposed to be my first duty station, but my father had a heart attack, so I requested and got a deferment from active duty. The deferment caused me to lose my slot in the much sought-after "A" school. I was disappointed to lose the opportunity to go to an A school, but I think now that God had other plans for me in regard to a profession.

In anticipation of my family needing extra money due to their poor health and with the desire to advance my trade as a mechanic, I left Housel Brothers and went to work as a used car mechanic at Coleman Oldsmobile on Olden Avenue in Trenton, New Jersey. I continued to drill for an additional sixteen months past the normal one year before going on active duty. I changed my specialty from Electrician's Mate to Engineman. During my extended time of drilling, I completed all the correspondence courses and requirements with high marks to advance to the rank of 3rd Class Engineman. I found the courses to be easy and got some good fundamental training in engine operations, maintenance, and repair.

CHAPTER 3

SWIFT BOAT TRAINING

Active Duty, Orders, and Counter Insurgency Training

On 30 Jun 69 (that is how military records dates), I reported for active duty at the Philadelphia Naval Yard. I requested to be stationed in New York or Bayonne, New Jersey, in order to be near my parents due to their continuing poor health. While waiting for orders, I was assigned to the "Admiral's Barge." It was easy duty, and I was able to keep my '64 Chevy Impala convertible in the parking lot outside the base. I-95 was not built yet so I used the NJ turnpike to commute back and forth when I was off duty long enough to make the trip. My hot rod Chevy had a 4:88 to 1 ratio differential for quick acceleration when drag racing, but it was killing me on gas mileage making the trip back and forth to Philly. I replaced that differential with a 3:08 to 1 ratio, which helped the fuel economy but killed the acceleration. It was fun to have a convertible but convertible bodies were heavier than hardtops or sedans. The end result was a heavy vehicle with poor acceleration but improved fuel economy. I no longer liked my car.

Basically, all we had to do on the Admiral's Barge was to keep it immaculately clean and occasionally take the admiral of the naval district and dignitaries out for an evening dinner cruise. Before being added to the crew, each one of us was required to sign a statement that we would not reveal anything that went on while dignitaries were aboard. Before boarding our passengers, a group of Filipino stewards would arrive with lots of fancy food and drinks. We would take our guests out on the Delaware River to enjoy dinner and an evening cruise.

When passengers were aboard, our crew had to be wearing dress whites with white tennis sneakers. Everyone except me. As the Engineman, my station was in the engine room, and I wore the normal work uniform, which was blue jeans and light denim shirt. I was not allowed to leave the engine room and be seen in work uniform. That was okay with me; I was more comfortable being in the engine room than being all spit and polish and kiss ass around a bunch of dignitaries.

After about a month, my orders were in. I remember standing in line and stepping up to the counter and being told that I was going to Cam Ranh Bay, to which I inquired, "Where is that?"

"Vietnam," was the answer.

In retrospect, my response at that time seems funny. I said, "I can't go there!" Upon reading my orders, I had a second question: "What is Naval Inshore Operations Training Center and what is a PCF?" The clerk informed me that NIOTC at Mare Island California was for small-boat training. Specifically, I would be in PCF training. PCF stands for Patrol Craft Fast, nicknamed Swift Boats. It was difficult to digest; I had requested to be stationed close to my ailing parents but got orders sending me to the other side of the world.

Back on the admiral's barge, I found one of the crew had been in Vietnam. He explained to me that every patrol boat in Vietnam had to have an Engineman, and the life expectancy was about nine months. (I believe that was quite an exaggeration.) So my working hard to advance from E3 Fireman to E4 Petty Officer, 3rd Class Engineman before going on active duty had helped to plop me smack-dab in the middle of the war. I quickly started the paperwork procedure to request a hardship reassignment.

The Navy gave me thirty days leave before reporting to California for training—a month to enjoy civilian life before my life would radically change forever. A month to languish and wonder what it would be like.

Finally, on August 18, I said my good-byes and flew from Philadelphia to San Francisco Airport, caught a Greyhound bus to Vallejo, and then the jitney over the bridge to Mare Island. Mare Island was the home of a nuclear submarine training school. I later found out that most previous small-boat training had been done at the Coronado base in San Diego. I never found out why the training had been moved to Mare Island.

The walls of the administration building were lined with men's citations for courage under fire. Wow! This was serious stuff! What was I getting into?! So much for being safely off the coast on a large ship. The course was to be ten weeks long and included the following areas of instruction:

Orientation to NIOTC and counter insurgency training
Vietnamese history, culture, and the war
Survival Evasion Resistance and Escape
First aid
Radio communication procedures
Coding and decoding messages
Weapons and live fire
Rules of engagement
Survival swimming
Vietnamese language
Boat handling and navigation
Patrol and board and search procedures
Final-battle problem

The first week was orientation to the war and the Vietnamese culture. They explained why we were in Vietnam, and I bought into it hook, line, and sinker. Communist insurgents from North Vietnam were infiltrating South Vietnam and committing atrocities on civilians targeting village chiefs, teachers, and politicians. Local forces were ill equipped or poorly trained to protect the people especially in the more rural areas of which there were a lot. Our mission was to stop the flow of arms, munitions, supplies, and enemy troops into South Vietnam via the coast through the implementation of

Operation Market Time. Market Time ops were mainly stopping and searching any suspect vessel off the coast of South Vietnam. Carrying out the mission was being done with Swift Boats, Coast Guard WPBs, destroyer escorts, and South VN Navy junks all assisted by surveillance planes.

A newer and second operation was SEALORDS, an acronym for Southeast Asia Lake, Ocean, River, Delta Strategy. The strategy was to disrupt enemy operations and supply lines by penetrating areas long dominated by the enemy. This was accomplished by regular patrols, night ambushes, and special coordinated operations. Other type small boats such as PBRs, Alpha boats, minesweepers, and Mike boats (converted WWII landing craft) had already been engaged with this mission in a task force called the River Assault Group nicknamed RAG. Now Swift Boats were being moved from coastal patrols to join SEALORDS in the rivers and canals. Again, what happened to being on a big ship and sitting at a safe distance off the coast?

I was assigned to PCF class number 29. We had eighteen enlisted men and two officers. Each day started early with physical training led by Navy SEALs. Monday through Thursday, it was calisthenics, obstacle courses, and one-mile runs. On Fridays, we only ran, but it was five miles. Running was really mostly a medium to brisk (double-time) jog. It was done in time and in step, just like marching. The trainer kept a cadence and taught us some gung ho songs to sing, which helped the time pass and kept us going. The main song was

I wanna be a riverboat sailor, I want to go to Vietnam.
I wanna be a riverboat sailor, I want to kill old Charlie Cong.

Then there was the old stand-by:

My pack is heavy, my belt is tight
My balls are swinging from left to right,
So sound off: 1, 2
Sound off: 3, 4
1, 2, 3, 4, 1, 2

We took great delight in running around the nukey pooh (that's slang for nuclear power students) barracks and loudly awakening them singing:

Nukey, Nukey, don't be blue, we will fight the war for you
Nukey, Nukey, don't be blue, Tinker Bell was a fairy too!

The nuclear power students were typically geeks—mostly skinny, frail, timid-looking kids that had scored very high on tests to get into the school. If one of our Swift Boat classmates stopped running due to fatigue or illness, the rest of us had two choices: we could run around him in a circle until he got up, or we could drag him along with us. We had one guy who occasionally felt the need to stop running. Rather than have to do any extra running around him in circles, two of us would grab securely on to his shoulder areas of his uniform and drag him along, his legs weakly attempting to keep the pace. His face would sequentially display the patriotic colors of first red, then white, and at times a shade of blue.

Excerpt from letter of September 25, 1969 to my parents while in training:

I've been lucky. I haven't gotten any blisters at all. I'm getting pretty used to running and it doesn't tire me as much anymore. I guess they figure if we can't out fight the Viet Cong then we'll have to out run or out swim them!

I've been doing a lot of thinking since I've been in the Navy. Thinking I didn't take time to do before, because I was always running around somewhere. I really want to make something of myself when I get out of the Navy. I want to make myself an extremely diversified person. Only problem is I don't know exactly what I want to make of myself, but I've got plenty of time to think about that. Besides I'll probably lose my ambition for all this when I get out anyhow.

After our early morning PT, we had time to catch a fast breakfast and had usually worked up a decent appetite by then. Classes commenced immediately after breakfast. If the day's class was a lecture in a classroom, the effects of our early morning PT and big breakfast would set in. So dozing off became a problem in spite of the fact that we were continually admonished to "listen up because what you are about to learn could save your life someday." And it was true, what we were being taught would make the difference between life and death for one of us or one of our crew members.

Our first aid instructor had a very effective way to address the problem of dozing off. He kept a .45 loaded with blanks under the podium. If he saw eyes closed or a head bobbing, out came the .45 caliber, and he fired it. I believe a .45 fired in a closed-up classroom is capable of waking the dead. It certainly did the job of gaining our full attention while dozing or daydreaming.

During orientation in the first week, we were informed that we would be going to SERE training at Whidbey Island in the Puget Sound area of Washington State. SERE is the acronym for Survival, Evasion, Resistance, and Escape. Out of the classroom, the stories of physical abuse and deprivation we were hearing from sailors that had been through SERE were cause for some consternation, perhaps even fear! In addition, we were instructed that there was no such thing as failing the course. If a man got the idea that he could do poorly and get out of going to Vietnam, he was sadly mistaken. If one failed to perform well at the survival or POW portion of the training, then he had to do it all over again. That would be like purposely sending yourself to hell a second time. If we failed the second time through, we would be given a dishonorable discharge as unfit for military service.

My first letter home included this line: *"You'd be amazed at the number of guys that volunteered for this. Wow! They gotta be nuts."*

Survival Evasion Resistance and Escape

Early on a Monday morning, we were flown to McChord AFB in Washington state. The next four or five days were spent in the woods. Sitting on benches, we attended daily classes in a crude cabinlike building. The topics were about how to set small animal traps, what kinds of plants and roots were edible, how to construct a shelter, how to evade capture, how to resist the enemy and conduct yourself as a prisoner. Every morning when reporting to the classroom area, there was a huge caldron of water on an open fire. It had coffee grounds tossed into the bottom. No cream or sugar. This was just about the only nourishment provided for us for a week. At the end of each day's classes, we were turned loose to try out the survival training we had received in the classroom. In other words, go try to find some food. We had wire snares set throughout the woods and caught one or two rabbits for a about a hundred men. Once the rabbits were gutted and skinned, that amounted to a fraction of an ounce of meat per man if one was fortunate enough to find a piece of meat in the broth. So basically, we got some water that a rabbit had been in.

Being on an island, we were near the water. We had been taught how to make fishnets out of parachute cord. Let me digress here to express that I think this particular part of the training was a little ridiculous. Where would a Swift Boat sailor find a parachute? Was that going to be part of the equipment on a patrol boat? Maybe we were to count on finding a downed pilot while evading the enemy. Now to continue this silliness, we were given part of a parachute to use as a sleeping bag for the frigid nights of Puget Sound in September, as well as instruction on how to use a parachute to trap the smoke while smoking strips of meat into jerky. But in all fairness, this was an aviator's survival school.

Anyhow, back to finding food. Spears were fabricated from branches. So a few fish and clams were to go into a giant cauldron with lots of water to provide soup or broth for about a hundred men. That made for very little meat and much broth. Unfortunately, someone managed to get a small sand shark. We thought, "More meat!" Not knowing that a shark must be skinned, the shark went into the big caldron. The shark skin ruined the soup. I had had very little food and the expectation of some nice warm broth. It was very disappointing to find out it tasted awful.

As our rabbit snares produced very little, we were provided with a rabbit for training, shown how to kill it by breaking its neck, and how to detect a diseased rabbit. Our instructor informed us not to waste any edible parts of a healthy animal. Stressing how high in protein the eyeballs were, they taught us how to neatly pop them out. Then he asked, "Who wants to try an eyeball?"

He got no takers. Then perhaps to create some incentive or just to check out our hunger level, he presented this verbal challenge, "I will eat an eye ball if someone else will eat one."

A young Hawaiian raised his hand and volunteered, to which the instructor gloomily exclaimed, "DAMN, there is always one in every class," which made it clear that he really did not want to eat an eyeball and had not expected that anyone else would want to. Chewing does not accomplish much, so one must swallow it whole, which they did to the mix of laughter and disgusted facial expressions of the rest of the class.

During this time in survival school, I survived mostly on berries, but they were pretty scarce as week after week, classes scoured the area for food. The nights were very cold in Puget Sound. We slept on the ground, and after some experimentation, to my surprise I discovered that they were correct in instructing us that we could stay warmer by taking our clothes off and putting them under our sleeping bags (parachutes). One thing that really sunk in was how important it was to have a knife in a survival situation. A knife is a multipurpose tool with which one can do all the following:

Kill, gut, skin, cut, slice, and eat food.

Cut firewood, shave kindling to make tinder for a fire, strike a flint or rock to start fire

Split wood by striking the knife with a section of limb

Hammer, dig, build a shelter, cut clothing into strips for bandages

Fight, defend yourself

Therefore, I wore a Ka-Bar Navy-issue knife whenever on board our boat in Vietnam.

Early on the morning of day five, we were given a compass and a compass course to navigate through a heavy growth of timber with lots of trees felled along the course to make the hike a little more challenging. There were checkpoints along the course. One of them was manned by Charles Law. On December 1968, the crew of the USS

Pueblo (reportedly a spy ship) was captured by the North Koreans and held for several months before being released. Crew member Charles Law won great respect among all servicemen for the reputation he gained while in captivity. Not only did he work to keep up the morale of the crew, he often took beatings to protect his fellow shipmates. In a group photo of the captives, he flipped the bird and told the Koreans that it was a Hawaiian greeting. When they found out the true meaning, he received even more beatings. His experience as a POW was used to help structure the training we were receiving. I was honored to meet him.

It took all morning to complete the compass course. Then we were given an evasion route with the goal of reaching a particular road by 3:00 p.m. While attempting to reach the road, trainers dressed as NVA soldiers and armed with Communist-style automatic weapons searched for us in the woods. It was our task to use the skills we had been taught to evade capture. At one point, the "enemy" passed within ten or twelve feet of me while I hid behind a log covered with leaves. If we managed to reach the road in the allotted time, there would be an apple or orange as reward. I was just a little short of reaching the road and food when the signal was given for everyone who had not been captured to report to the road for transport to the POW camp. We were loaded into trucks and driven off to an experience like nothing any of us had ever had in life. For I was now a "POW."

Upon arrival at the POW camp, we were ordered to get off the truck and strip down to our underwear. Then we had to crawl in the dirt on hands and knees and through a small hole in a building much like the opening of a chicken coop. Once inside, the interrogations and harassment started immediately. Those who misspoke were targeted for the most intense treatment. We were removed from the building and lined up one in front of the other. Bags were yanked over our heads, and we were told to hold on to the shoulder of the prisoner in front of us to be led away in a column. This was like nothing I had ever experienced before, and there was a battle inside me between fear of what was going to happen and the fear of showing fear or weakness.

In our training classes, we had been told to passively resist the enemy—do anything that would make his day more difficult without getting ourselves killed. As chance would have it, I was the first person in our column. So when the guard grabbed my hood to lead us away, I decided it was time to resist and stand my ground. After being slapped about the head and face a few times, I decided I had fulfilled my duty to resist and obeyed when I was commanded to move the column forward. We shuffled on "nuts to butts," as the expression goes.

The next stop was in front of a row of three-sided compartments much like a barn stall that housed a horse or cow. The bag was removed from my head, and I was ordered to lie on my back in the dirt in one of these cubicles. My tee shirt was pulled over my head so I could not see the water coming as it was poured into my nose. Of course, my natural reaction was to cough and spit and sputter and turn my head to the side to avoid the water. When I turned, I was kicked in the side and told not to turn. After my torturer determined I would not talk and I had had enough, I was ordered to stand up with which I gladly complied.

Today, I can laugh at what happened next, but it was not funny to me at the time. My boondockers were returned to me less the laces, and I quickly bent down and slipped them on. As I straightened back up the effects of the water I had gulped down during the torture caused a bubble in my stomach that needed to escape. This resulted in my belching directly in the face of my adversary. He immediately erupted in a tirade of words and slaps, demanding an apology from the "dirty American pig" in front of him. Feeling rather embarrassed by what would normally be a gross error of etiquette, I quietly began to apologize but got pissed off with the next slap in the head and determined I would not apologize—no way, not happening! So after my tormentor felt he had sufficiently punished me for my indiscretion, the bag was put back over my head, and I was led off to the compound.

Now forty-some years later, when there has been so much negative press about the water torture of detainees at Guantanamo Bay, I feel like screaming! Hey, we were water tortured as part of our training and testing. So it was okay to water torture us but not our enemies?!

The compound was a large fenced-in area of dirt devoid of any vegetation. The fence was very high maybe twelve or more feet high, with a high guard tower next to the main gate. In one corner of the yard was an outhouse. We got our shirts and pants back but no belt, shoelaces, or eyeglasses. If we needed to use the outhouse, it would have to be called out loud to the guard tower in the manner, "Camp teacher in the tower, one political prisoner requests permission to urinate" (or defecate). Generally, permission was granted, but if the request was not properly worded, permission was denied until we got it correct.

There was no part of our person, our mind, body, spirit, or bodily needs and functions that was not being put to the test. It was both testing and learning. Learning that one can endure much more than he thinks he can and testing to sort out those who cannot hack it before they cause someone else's injury or death. In the small crew of six that we would be operating with in Vietnam, we needed to know that we could count on each other in the most extreme situations. Now was the time to find out, not in life or death circumstances.

The guards were dressed in Communist style uniforms and spoke English in a broken style with the same linguistics and syntax that an Asian with little experience with the language would speak. We were continually berated and belittled and regularly addressed as American pigs along with some additional superlatives.

Whenever a guard or enemy officer approached the gate to enter or to leave, he was to be properly identified and announced. This meant we "political prisoners" were to take turns standing gate duty to make these announcements. In our previous classroom training, we had been taught the importance of maintaining the chain of command even as prisoners. Even as prisoners, there are duties to be performed such as hygiene, sanitation, care of the sick or wounded, resistance, and escape planning. Our Officer in Charge (OinC) was a full commander (an 05). Due to my not being allowed to have my glasses, I had requested of the commander and received his permission not to be assigned gate guard duty because from a little distance, I could not clearly see the insignia on our captors' uniforms soon enough to announce them before they entered the compound. Punishment was dealt out for incorrect or late announcements. Eventually, the commander and I were questioned as to why I did not stand a watch. The commander told them that without my glasses, I could not properly determine their rank in order to announce them on time and correctly. With that the enemy officer turned to me and asked, "What color is the insignia on my collar?" When I answered correctly, he immediately turned and slapped the commander and screamed in his face, "You lied to me, you lying American pig!" I felt bad about that and thought maybe I should have lied and said I could not tell the color.

Throughout the remainder of the day and into the night, various groups of us would be removed for more types of torture and interrogation. When this occurred, those who remained had to maintain the chain of command. We were supposed to attempt to escape, and if we did, there would be a short rest and a snack and then be returned to the compound as if we had been captured. Only two men managed to escape. We were also to continue to passively resist. Passive resistance meant making things more difficult for the captors. But we were to stop short of doing anything that would get us killed in a real-life situation. If we did do something that would get us killed, we were temporarily taken out of the program, explained what we did wrong, and made to do push-ups. Repeat actions would get us sent through the whole week again! There was no way I was going to get myself sent through this punishment again.

The only information we were to give was name, rank, serial number, and date of birth. Persons who slipped or broke and gave more information of any type got even worse treatment. I think after a while, they left me alone because I would not give any information other than what was allowed.

Eventually, it was my turn to be in one of the groups for torture in a small box. This box was so small that I had to get down and bend over into a sort of fetal position to fit. Then the lid was shut and latched. After a short time, my right foot went numb. I don't know how long they left us in there. Time stood still. I think about twenty minutes, but it seemed like hours. These boxes were arranged in a large circle so we could hear a little of what was going on outside the box. One very large sailor would not fit into the box, so he was required to crawl around in the stones on his hands and knees. He was very verbal and agreed to go in the interrogation room and talk. When he got there, he would not talk, and they would beat him and send him back out to resume crawling on the stones. This repeated several times.

When they finally opened my box, both of my legs were so completely asleep from lack of circulation that I could not walk. So two guards dragged me to the interrogation room. I was placed at a small desk with my interrogator across the desk from me. Throughout the questioning, I gave only name, rank, serial number, and date of birth. A pistol was cocked and placed to my head threatening to shoot me if I did not talk. (Prior to the start of SERE training, we had been given made-up, "secret" information) I remained silent. I have to confess that even though I knew they were not going to shoot me, it was very unnerving to have a gun cocked and stuck to my head!

Then I was shown a written confession, stating that Americans had committed various war crimes. I was told to sign or I would be killed. I picked it up to look at it and placed it back down. Again, I was told to sign it or I would be killed. I did not sign. I don't know if it is just me or if it is a common reaction in other people also. But there comes a point where I get more pissed off than scared, and it reinforces my determination not to comply no matter what they do. The interrogators were angry, hostile, and continued to threaten. Then suddenly, it was over. I was led out and returned to the compound. By this time the blood was circulating in my legs, and I could walk with a bit of a limp. It took a year to regain feeling in my big toe. In our debriefing the following day, I learned that picking up the confession was the only mistake I made as a POW. I should not even have picked it up because the action could be manipulated on video to look like I was cooperating.

During the evening, we were taken to another area where there were large, upright, wooden boxes approximately three feet wide by three feet deep and five feet high, much a like an outhouse. Each of us was placed in a box that was much too short to stand up straight in. We were not allowed to sit or sleep, so I stood bent over leaning back against the rear wall of the box. Every half hour, a guard came around to check that we did not sit down or go to sleep. There was a number 10 juice can in the box in the event that nature called. We spent the entire night in the boxes.

I guess it was part of our passive resistance that led to someone starting to sing Christmas carols in the middle of the night, and many of us joined in. Our singing managed to irritate the guards, who in turn came around shouting, threatening, and beating on the doors of the boxes. After a bit of quiet someone started singing, "I wanna be a riverboat sailor, I wanna go to Vietnam, I wanna be a riverboat sailor, I want to kill old Charlie Cong!" The guards came and dragged out our older enlisted man we called Pappy. Pappy had one more year of a twenty-year military career to go and got orders for Swift Boats in Vietnam. A bit of bad luck, but now he had another bit of misfortune. He received some corporal punishment for a song he did not sing for they had grabbed the wrong man. Later we all had a good laugh over this one.

I managed to get a little sleep while standing in a slumped over position but awakened if a guard checked on me. Horses and cows sleep standing up, and so can we humans if we are tired enough. It was so great when I finally started to see some morning light creeping through some tiny spaces in the walls of my box. At that time, I thought I had never been so glad to see daylight come. However, in the year to come, spending nights on the rivers and canals of Vietnam, there would be more daybreaks that I would be even more thankful to see.

Once morning had fully arrived, we were freed from our cells and again returned to the compound. We were allowed to have fire in the compound, and one of our officers burnt the back of his hand in the fire. He had a large blister covering most of the back of his hand. The guards tried to get him to sign a confession before they would treat the burn, but he would not sign. To my amazement, they let it fester for several hours before treating the burn.

The torture continued. Several men were made to hang by their fingers on a chain-link fence. Others were placed in fifty-five gallon drums of water. These were the guys who had slipped and talked to the enemy, so they were really being put to the test now to see if they would break. At some point, they gave us some watery rice broth to keep our strength as we were kept busy moving rocks from one side of the compound to the other side.

Late in the morning, we began to hear gunfire and yelling. The guards ran away, and the next thing we know, the Viet Cong flag was taken down, and the American flag started going up. A hundred and some men stood silently watching with tears in our eyes. Yes, it had only been a training exercise, but it had been a very real lesson. For just a very brief time, we had experienced the extreme opposite of freedom. That flag—our flag, the American flag—meant freedom from the torture and harassment. None of us would ever look at our nation's symbol of freedom again quite the same as we had previous to this week.

Our rescuers entered the camp and led us out to get an apple or orange and our belts and shoelaces. Next we were trucked to an enlisted men's club for the first real meal in almost a week. We were warned to be careful as to how much we ate because our stomachs had shrunken and would reject overeating. After lunch, it was an afternoon of debriefings as to what we had done right or wrong during our POW experience. We had learned valuable lessons in the event we were ever to become separated from our crew or boat. Then and only then were we informed that the guards and interrogators (the trainers) were allowed to inflict whatever pain or damage to us as long as they did not break a bone or cause any permanent damage.

We returned to Mare Island with a deep sense of what we were fighting for: the cause of freedom not necessarily for ourselves but for the people of the Republic of South Vietnam. And having survived the week of hell, we had a somewhat overinflated confidence that we could survive almost anything. I would sooner be killed than become a prisoner of war was one thing prominently established in my mind. Therefore if my capture were ever to become imminent, I would try to get the enemy to kill me first. I believe some of my classmates felt the same way. This kind of thinking makes a fighting man extremely dangerous to an enemy trying to subdue him.

Of course I was glad that SERE training was over, but I was also thankful to have gone through it. Aside from teaching us how to survive, we were introduced to a simulation of the shock of surviving a POW situation. Shock is an immediate problem in a survival situation so it was important to experience it, recognize it, and know how to rely on our training to get us through. So you could say we were somewhat desensitized to the shock of finding ourselves in a survival or POW situation.

A darker side of the experience was the shutting down of my emotions, like someone had flipped a switch. I suspect it is a natural inner self-defense. In there, in this place inside me, it was like novocaine to my feelings, and it was a dark and hollow place in my mind. From in there I could watch life go by like a television show but it did not hurt me. Nothing could reach me—a place void of pain. It was a place where I would return at various times in the coming months in Vietnam—sometimes briefly, sometimes for a spell of time, and sometimes with part of me in each world. The problem is when one returns home, he has to learn not to go there anymore. That learning is not something one has much control of. It seems to be a function of the subconscious experiencing that he doesn't need to go there anymore. Some have to fight to remind themselves that they don't have to retreat there any longer to survive. Evidently, some of us never learn and some lose the fight.

In a letter home on September 1, I wrote,

> *Well, Survival school is over and I'm glad of that. ... To sum up survival school I would say that it was a tremendous strain on everyone physically, mentally and emotionally. It was a very valuable school to anyone going to Vietnam. There were hundreds of things that we learned that could save our lives.*

Patrol Craft Fast "Swift Boat" photo courtesy of pcf45.com

Small Boat and Counterinsurgency Training

I do not recall the exact chronological order the remaining classes came in. As the weeks of training progressed, it became apparent that we needed to take good care of our boat so it could take good care of us. This twenty-ton, fifty-foot aluminum hull boat, its weapons, its speed, and its communications were all essential to our staying alive. Therefore it was important that we be as familiar with our boat and its systems as possible. Each crew member was selected for his specialty in order for a crew to operate as a team, a unit. But beyond that, in the event that one or more of us were to be killed or incapacitated, the others needed to know how to handle the missing crew member's responsibilities. Hence, we were all cross trained. So all crew members needed to know how to rig emergency steering, decode messages, operate bilge pumps, clear jammed guns, navigate, make minor engine repairs, and on and on.

The quarter-inch aluminum hull was not going to provide much protection, so speed and firepower would be our best defense against attack. The speed was delivered by two 12V71 Detroit diesels together putting out close to a thousand horsepower and providing for a top speed of thirty knots. Thirty knots is about 34 mph. Each of the three 270-gallon fuel tanks provided enough fuel to run close to full speed for eight to ten hours or stay on station for days on end.

Overhead view of forward gun tub

Aft mount 81 mm with .50 caliber on top

The firepower was awesome. In the top forward gun tub were twin .50 caliber Browning machine guns. In Vietnam, we had the ammo cans doubled in size to carry 1,200 rounds of belted ammo. Aft on the fantail would become my battle station on the 81 mm trigger fire mortar. A single .50 caliber machine gun was piggybacked on top of the mortar. In Vietnam we had what we called "super shooters", custom built 400 round ammo cans to replace the original 100 round cans. We kept 3 extra cans loaded at all times to increase our ability to rapidly throw another can on the mount and continue firing. The .50s have a range of two miles and the power to penetrate eleven inches of concrete.

M60s with 3,000 belted rounds each.
Aft .50 caliber in foreground

In addition to the fiftys, we had two M60 machine guns which fire 7.62 x 51 mm cartridges. "In country"[2] we kept 3000 rounds belted together in a large ammo can. Usually one crew member sat on the peak (very front of the bow) of the boat with an M60 and one sat on the one side of the fantail with the other M60. The M60 had an

---

2. "In country" means in Vietnam

effective range of 1,200 yards and could fire at a rate of 500–650 rounds per minute.

In Vietnam, when two boats pulled up, turned broadside to "prep the beach," and opened fire, we mowed down everything in sight. Leaves flew off the trees, limbs blew off, mud flung up, and whole trees fell over.

Cartoon in *Stars & Stripes* Newspaper, cartoonist Corky Trinidad

In addition to the machine guns each boat carried two M79 grenade launchers which fire 40 x 46 mm grenade cartridges that exploded on contact releasing three hundred fragments with a lethal area of about five yards. The launcher looks like a twenty-nine-inch break open, large-bore shotgun. The range was about four hundred yards. Sometimes we would carry one of these unloaded while doing a "board and search"[3] because the peasants were in awe of the large bore. No automatic weapons were carried during a board and search in case the crewman were disarmed and the weapon fell into enemy hands, so we usually just carried a .38 Smith & Wesson police special at these times.

The list of weapons carried continued with five M16s, two pump action shotguns, two Smith & Wesson .38 caliber police specials, various concussion grenades and smoke grenades, pop flares, two Ka-Bar knives, several M72 portable rocket launchers and, of course, the 81 mm trigger fire fixed mount mortar on the fantail. The mortar

---

[3.] "Board and search" is to come alongside another vessel, send one or two men aboard the suspect vessel, and search for weapons or contraband.

had a range of about two miles. We carried about a hundred mortar rounds in an ammo box secured to the rearmost part of the fantail. There are various types of mortar rounds: high explosive, white phosphorus, illumination, and flechette or "beehive." The flechette round was filled with tiny little arrow shaped pieces of metal and designed for maximum area coverage at close range. Sometimes we would load a flechette round in the mortar before entering a small canal if we were expecting the likelihood of enemy contact. In summary, you could say we were "armed to the teeth," and we needed to be— given the missions we were sent on in some very remote and dangerous places. To be perfectly honest, I loved the feeling of power I had firing a .50 caliber machine gun. It is a rush. It's a kick! It's something like putting the throttle to the floor on a high-powered muscle car and burning rubber down the road on and on and on!

Occasionally in Vietnam, we were called upon to provide indirect fire support to ground forces. This required a good "fix" on where we and our target were located to compute the distance between the two. Getting a "fix" is determining the longitude and latitude. Then the distance and direction can be computed to our target. A chart is used to find the elevation and charge required to hit the target. Then the number of degrees relative to the boat's heading is computed. All this computation was done by our officer and relayed to us who were manning the mortar. Then we set the elevation, direction, and charge. If a "VT" fuse[4] was used, we also had to set the timer on the fuse. Mortar rounds came with seven small charge bags attached just above the finned portion of the round. There is a charge two built into the round, so a complete round is charge nine. If the officer called for a charge five, that meant we had to strip off four bags.

---

[4] VT is short for variable proximity. These fuses could be set to the desired distance from the ground when they would detonate. The air burst spread the burst of shrapnel in a larger pattern and caused more casualties than an impact detonated round

White phosphorus, called willie peter,[5] was used to mark a location either for the spotter to use to give corrections to our computations or it was used to mark an enemy location for aircraft to target. Generally, on a firing mission, once we were on target, the spotter or ground force would radio a request for a given number of "HE," meaning high explosive. Providing accurate fire support was critical so our rounds would not land on the "friendlies" requesting the support. This is especially difficult if firing from rough water, and the trick is to fire on the upswing when the deck of the boat is level with the horizon.

In the rear of the engine compartment were two banks of batteries—four 6-volt batteries in each bank for a total of 24 volts used by the engines starter motors, the radar, and most of the boat's lighting. A 110-volt power was supplied from a two-cylinder Onan generator. The generator provided power for one of the three radios, the small "reefers" (refrigerator and freezer), a few outlets, and the cooker. The quality of meals and life on board depended on the generator, but unfortunately it, was very finicky and often let us down.

Diesel fuel must be clean for diesels to start easily and perform correctly. Whether we got good, clean fuel in Vietnam depended on what type of facility we got it from. If it came from a support base or repair ship, it was good because it was centrifuged and filtered before we got it. If the fuel came out of a pontoon or fuel barge, it was usually bad. So bad in fact that our large fuel filters would clog long before regular replacement and cause the engines to quit.

> *There are so many conflicting reports about what's going to be happening with the Navy in Vietnam that the best thing is to just sit tight and see what happens. This is the "Brown Water" Navy that I'm speaking of. Brown Water Navy is a nickname for the part of the Navy operating on the rivers and canals because the water there is brown and dirty. I'm*

[5.] White phosphorus rounds explode with a brite white flash, burn through any material they contact and cause a lot of smoke.

pretty sure I'll be spending a year in Vietnam one way or another, but there is a very slim possibility of getting out of there early.
(Letter, September 21, 1969)

A week was spent learning the electrical and mechanical systems of the boat. A big portion of this was devoted to training called systems tracing. Given the number of electrical circuits, fuel lines, bilge pipes, coolant tubes and hoses, etc., this was important for all members to have a basic knowledge of. This systems tracing experience served me well after getting out of the service in my occupation as an automotive technician.

There was also a full week of survival swimming. I have never been a good swimmer. I don't even float well. I think it has something to do with body density. If that is the case, then I must have a lead ass. Early in the week, I failed to complete the required number of laps, so I had to go back at night for additional training. The key is to become comfortable in the water, and that requires a certain level of confidence in your ability to stay afloat without getting exhausted. The extra training helped me gain a little more of that confidence.

We were taught how to swim with a limited number of functional limbs (such as one arm and one leg or two arms and no legs or two legs and no arms) in the event we were wounded. We learned how to use our clothing as flotation devices. One unique bit of training was evasive swimming. We were all lined up on the edge of the pool in flak jackets. Our instructors would randomly run and push one of us into the water. While waiting, we were not to look back to see if we were next. The point was to recreate the surprise of being blown or knocked into the water during combat. Once we were in the water, we had to remove the flak jacket while underwater and allow it to float to the top while we swam underwater away from where we went in. When air was needed, you popped your head out momentarily, gulped in some air, and went back underwater, heading in a different direction than your previous swim so that the enemy could not determine where you might surface again and be ready to shoot you. It was an exhausting week with PT in the morning, swimming classes all day, and extra training at night.

The longer I stay here the more I believe in the war in Vietnam. Maybe I'm getting gung ho or brainwashed, I don't know.
(Letter, September 1, 1969)

Vietnamese language was a crash two-week course taught by Vietnamese instructors. We learned common phrases and how to count in Vietnamese. Most importantly, we learned how to summon persons to us, examine their identification cards, and question them. In Vietnam, we usually had a Vietnamese trainee on board and left the communication to him. Our trainees usually spoke some English and could serve as our interpreters. On the street, in a small town or city, it was common to use slang that was a combination of Vietnamese, French, and English. A fair number of Vietnamese could speak French due to Vietnam having been a French colony for many years until their defeat by Ho Chi Minh in 1955. Every thing or person could be numerically ranked from "numba one" to "numba ten" by the Vietnamese—and of course, we picked up on using that system also. I actually never heard anything get ranked in between number 1 and number 10. Number 1 was very good and number 10 was very bad. To "butterfly" was to be unfaithful to your spouse or lover. To "crocodile" was to kill. "Dinky dow" meant crazy. "Ti ti" meant small or short. "Boo coo" meant large or many. "Di di" meant go, and "di di mow" meant go fast. And finally—"fini" meant finished.

The F-Word

I have always found it interesting how people who have moved to a different region of our country sometimes acquire the accent and speech mannerisms of their new location. Likewise, in the Navy, most men develop new speech patterns and use of words. In addition to nautical and military terms and slang, most men quickly learn the art of inserting the four-letter F-word into every sentence at least once if not multiple times. It is often used quite creatively joining it with other words. The artfulness of it makes me think of the narrative in the perennial holiday movie *The Christmas Story* in which Ralphie describes his father's use of obscenities in this manner: "In the heat of battle, my father wove a tapestry of obscenities..."

When I returned to civilian life, I had to reduce my use of the word lest I sound like a cretin. It was not until several years later when I accepted Jesus Christ as my Lord and Savior that God put it on my heart to get the word out of my vocabulary. With His help, I was eventually able to break the old habit, but I confess that on some occasions of great anger or duress it pops back out again.

Write often—letters are like gold to servicemen I've learned that.
(Excerpt from Letter, Sept. 8, 1969)

We usually had weekends to ourselves unless there was travel or special training scheduled. This time could be used to do laundry, write home, and unwind a little. And a fair amount of time was spent in the enlisted men's club usually drinking. It also had a decent menu of typical fast foods like hot dogs, burgers, fries, grilled cheese, and chili. During happy hour, beer or mixed drinks were only ten cents, which meant a sailor could get wiped out for a dollar or less.

One Sunday one of our classmates, who had the not-so-masculine nickname of Poopsie, spent the afternoon at the club drinking beer and then switched to tequila shots of which he had a great number in a very short time. On the short staggering walk across the street and parking lot, he managed to get into a shouting match with a couple of guys from another barracks. This ended up with them coming out and kicking his ass.

We had a fellow last night that had way too much to drink. Ajax and I carried him to his rack (bed). But he flopped out and split his head open on the floor. Then he just went sorta

half delirious and half into a fit. It took five of us to hold him down and wipe up the blood and keep a pillow under his head so he wouldn't bang it again. We had someone call the ambulance, but they took 10-15 minutes to get here. Meanwhile he kept fighting to get up and yelling and screaming. He was like some kind of mental case, but he's really a nice guy. Boy, some of the things that he came out with were something. It was like his subconscious was talking or he was having bad dreams or something. One minute he would scream that he didn't want to die, next he'd moan for someone to help him, then he'd beg to be killed and then he (would) fight and struggle and scream that he was going to kill us all. He was really bad. Then he started puking. When the ambulance came we carried him out and he fought us all the way. They put handcuffs and leg bracelets on him and strapped down in the stretcher. What an experience! And he doesn't remember it today.
(Letter, Sept. 15, 1969)

During the middle of the night, the shore patrol returned him stitched up and extremely sick from all the drinking. They deposited him in the utility room of our barracks where we found him in the morning. He was one hurting puppy or Poopsie. The whole incident was actually kind of scary as I had never seen anyone so drunk and act so insanely wild. He was probably on the verge of alcohol poisoning or was experiencing it. From that day on, I resolved to never urge someone to drink more than he should. I had experienced that the results can be very dangerous even deadly.

We were allowed to go off base on leave most weekends. David Ajax and I became good friends and went on leave together usually with several others. We used Greyhound busses to go to San Francisco, Sacramento, and Reno, Nevada. One time in San Francisco, we rented a car, possibly a 1967 Chevy. To minimize our mileage charges and show off my mechanical skill, I reached behind the dash and disconnected the speedometer cable to avoid the seven-cents-a-mile charge. We then spent the day driving around seeing the sights in San

Francisco and Berkeley. We even drove through the beautiful bayside town of Sausalito. Only now do I acknowledge that disconnecting the speedometer was actually theft and very wrong.

> *You just wouldn't believe all the hippies out here. There is one whole section of S.F. with nothing but hippies and Berkeley is just about all hippies.*
> *P.S. When I get "in country" I'll be making more money than I'll know what to do with. Besides saving I want to send money so Georgie can take guitar lessons, but don't say anything to him. I want it to be a surprise.*
> (Letter, October 11, 1969)

One Saturday, Ajax and I set out for Reno on a Greyhound bus. We bought round-trip tickets just in case we did not do well gambling. The scenic ride through the Rocky Mountains was worth the trip. The combination of mountain streams through the rocks and trees was picturesque. The first thing we did was rent a room and eat just in case we lost all our money so we would have a place to sleep and not be hungry too long. Then it was off to the casinos and shows. Blackjack was our favorite game, and initially, we were winners and enjoying the thrill of the game. At some point, we took a break from gambling to go to a topless show. It actually was a little tame after having spent a few nights at the topless/bottomless clubs in Vallejo.

Sometime during the wee hours, exhaustion forced us back to our room for a few hours' sleep, and then it was back to the tables where we eventually wound up losers. We had a little change, which we lost playing slots in the bus terminal. But we each held on to twenty-five cents to pay for the jitney from Vallejo back to the base. So we returned to the base penniless on Sunday evening. We really did not need money. The Navy provided all our real needs, but the money orders I had tucked away in my locker served to fund our trips to the enlisted men's club until payday.

The weekends were a great opportunity to see a few things on the West Coast. I was impressed with how spread out things were as compared to the old cities of the East Coast. Of course, my experience of East Coast cities was based on an extremely limited number of trips to just a few cities, but West Coast cities seemed cleaner and brighter.

Late one Friday afternoon a few weeks prior to our graduation, we received all our immunizations required before going overseas. The gamma globulin shot hurt like crazy, and my butt and hip hurt for days ruining that weekend. I was told that it was made from ground-up duck embryo. The vaccine was really thick and took forever to get out of the syringe and into my body.

For a week, we were trained on the arsenal of weapons we used. Daily we disassembled, cleaned, and reassembled weapons until it was second nature. Then we were sent to Camp Roberts, a reactivated Army firing range farther south in California, for a week of live fire. The training started early in the morning and went into the evening. We fired all the same type of weapons that we had become extremely familiar with the previous week. I only managed to qualify as marksman with M16 and did not qualify with the .38 caliber police special. From an elevated location on a hill, we fired .50 caliber machine guns and the 81 mm mortar at old vehicles down below. There were large tarantulas on the firing ranges. These black hairy scary creatures can jump from six to ten feet. In spite of their frightening looks and reputations, some of the men were chasing them around with a stick to see them jump.

Having grown up on the farm with ready access to guns and the freedom to roam the woods and fields to hunt, this weeklong shooting was all good with me. One training session that I excelled at was "quick kill." We practiced turning and firing from the hip at little tin human silhouettes. For safety's sake, this was done with BB guns. Years later at home, I learned that quick kill should not be done with a weapon that has a hammer. While I was carrying a twelve-gauge shotgun at the hip, a ground hog attempted to evade me by jumping into a hole in our old chicken house. The ground hog was quickly dispatched as my "quick kill" training immediately kicked in. As I inspected my kill and checked for any other varmints, I realized my right hand was wet. Looking down I saw it was covered with blood.

For a moment, I was puzzled as to how that had happened. Did a pellet ricochet off the chicken house foundation? Then I figured out that the hammer of the shotgun had rammed through the web of my hand between the thumb and forefinger. As the doctor applied the butterfly dressing, he explained that he had seen this a number of times but usually from a .45 caliber handgun.

Only a week or two prior to graduation, I received a final answer on my request for hardship reassignment. It had been denied based on the premise that active-duty service personnel were required to be able to be assigned to any location at any time.

> *You speak of* (name omitted) *as if Vietnam effected him adversely, mentally. On the contrary I think it's going to make a much better man of me.*
> (Letter, October 13, 1969)

Near the end of our training, we finally got on the boats to get experience at boat handling. This started out learning how to cast off and pull away from a pier and then come back alongside the pier and tie up. Next we transited out into San Pablo Bay and got used to navigation skills heading out to San Francisco Bay and back.

> *Thursday morning we took the boats out at about 10:30am. We proceeded on a 75 mile trip that took us 17 miles out to sea for firing practice. (note: entering the Pacific Ocean from San Francisco Bay is some of the roughest water on earth.) Guys were vomiting all over the place. I felt ill but didn't get sick. A 50 foot boat doesn't give a very pleasant ride at sea.*
>
> *We ceased fire at nightfall and proceeded to our respective patrol areas along the coast. We practiced patrolling and sending in reports until dawn, when we headed back in. It really wasn't any fun at all and we had to stand look out watches up in the forward gun tub and it was freezing cold up there. I got two hours sleep.*

It was beautiful though coming back under the Golden Gate Bridge and seeing all the picturesque things in that particular area. It (the weather) was beautiful at that time. Most of the time it was rainy and foggy. We got back in around ten and had to clean up the boat and had to clean the weapons. We had just enough time to get a decent meal (you eat C-rations at sea, if you feel well enough to eat) and then were off to the dispensary to get a great big needle in the rump.

The letter goes on to describe the usual weekend routines of washing clothes, reading mail, writing letters, hitting the bars and clubs, fights, clowning in the barracks, and then resting up from it all. Then the letter proceeds to describe the week coming:

This week we'll be out from Monday morning til Wednesday morning. This our final battle problem where we go out and play war games, search boats, etc. Thursday we have classes and Friday we have graduation, take a class picture and check out. We leave Monday at 10:30 or 11:00pm from McChord AFB in Washington.

I think you should know how I feel about everything before I leave. I'd rather not go to Vietnam. Of course I'd rather not be in the Navy either, especially this kind of Navy. But in life we don't always get our drothers. I've got to go and I'm going to do my best and keep a positive outlook as I have been doing.

I believe in what we're doing in Vietnam, even though I may not agree with how we're doing it. But it's all a very complicated situation, so maybe our country is doing what's right the right way. I'm not afraid to die, because once you're dead its all over with, there's no more pain or worries. I'm not afraid of being wounded as long as I'm not maimed. I am afraid of being captured, because that's constant hell, but even that can be endured...In conclusion

*I might add that in a way I'm proud of the unit I'm in and
the work they do.*
(Letter, October 19, 1969)

The final battle problem was conducted in the sloughs which
are low land winding waterways north of San Pablo Bay. The sloughs
are similar to some of the waterways we would operate in Vietnam.
Our class of twenty men manned three Swift Boats and commenced
patrolling our assigned portions of the sloughs with guns fully loaded
with blanks. Occasionally, a sampan would come through out patrol
area for us to practice our board and search procedures. We were to
practice coding and sending reports.

Suddenly, all three boats received instructions to proceed to
a particular canal and extract a SEAL team. Once all three boats
were in the canal, the extraction was cancelled. On our transit out
of the canal, we were attacked (by our trainers). They fired blanks
at us with M60 machine guns from hidden locations on the canal
banks. They also tossed smoke grenades at us. We returned fire and
attempted to make a full-speed exit from the canal but found a wire
had been strung across its mouth. All three boats came to an emergency stop, nearly colliding with each other. The Officer in Charge
(OinC) ordered our forward gunner to shoot down the cable. Now
this seemed a little silly as all our weapons were loaded with blanks,
so how could we shoot down a cable with blanks? Hey, but orders are
orders, so fire away he did. Eventually, the cable was dropped (and
pulled away) as if shot down.

We had been advised at the start of our "final-battle problem"
that there could be an occasional civilian craft transiting our patrol
areas, and we were to leave them alone. They should be easy to
identify in American pleasure craft as opposed to foreign sampans
or junks. One night as evening approached and visibility declined,
we were slowly patrolling through a winding set of S bends when
we viewed a small craft slipping around the bend ahead. Following
procedures as we had been taught, we sped up. Our officer got on
the loud speaker and issued the order to come here in Vietnamese,
"Lai day! Lai day." But the small craft just sped up a little. The next

warning step is to fire three warning shots in the air. To this, the suspect craft increased to full speed to evade us. In response, the order was given to the forward gunner to open fire. The evading craft was under fire by our twin .50s but outran us. We broke off pursuit once we got to the end of our patrol area and radioed in a report of the incident. Now during the final-battle problem, we were to practice sending reports every so often, and they could be fictitious or factual. Therefore headquarters was never completely certain as to actual or made up events. About twenty minutes, after our suspect craft had outrun us, there was a message sent to all units inquiring as to "who fired on the civilians." None of our three boats responded. Minutes later, our boat received this inquiry: "Reference your report of (time), did you fire on civilians?" Upon reflection, it became evident that the elusive craft was not a part of our "final-battle problem," so a sheepish "affirmative" was our reply.

All units were then informed that the exercise was temporarily suspended as we had some extremely frightened civilians that would be returning through our patrol area and we were to leave them alone. I can imagine how scary this must have been for them. First, a boat much larger than theirs speeds up and blasts some foreign words over a loud speaker, then shots are fired. Although we were firing blanks, they were still loud, and in dim lighting, there was still a bright muzzle flash. So being pursued by a large boat with twin .50 caliber machine guns blazing away had to have scared the daylights out of those folks who were just out for a little pleasure cruise.

Our training ended with the debriefing of what we did right and wrong during the final-battle problem. There was a graduation ceremony where we received the certificates for completion of Coastal Patrol and River Incursion Training and for Survival, Evasion, Resistance, and Escape.

I had never attended a military awards ceremony before. I was deeply moved by the experience, especially during the portion when sailors who had already served in Vietnam were receiving medals for their combat actions in Vietnam. Little did I know that one day I would be on the receiving end of such a decoration instead of the spectator.

Graduation was on a Friday with orders to fly out of Washington state the following Monday evening. Originally, I had not planned on spending the money to fly from one coast to the other and back again for only two days at home. The desire to see family and home for possibly the last time overpowered the cost. This decision also opened up the possibility of "missing movement" if a flight were delayed or missed. Missing movement is an extremely serious offense in a time of war and is subject to court martial.

The two days at home were spent visiting friends and family to say my final good-byes. Ten weeks of training had transformed me from a disinterested, apathetic civilian into a gung ho sailor with a mission to accomplish with my Swift Boat brothers. Amazingly I remember saying that even if the Navy said I did not have to go now, I would go anyhow because I did not want my classmates to be there without me. This feeling of everyone taking care of each other grew even stronger while patrolling, living together, and doing combat together in Vietnam.

I do not know if I can really imagine the worry and pain my parents were experiencing knowing where I was going and what I was going to be doing. Had I any idea of their feelings at that time, I surely would not have written home some of the things that I did. At the time of my writing to them, I thought because I was not telling about direct attacks or damage to our boat or casualties on our missions that writing about the rest should not upset them. Now reading my letters from the viewpoint of a parent and grandparent, I am very aware of how naive I was at that time. To make it worse for them, every day, the television evening news was filled with major events of the war including the number of US casualties. This daily tallying of casualties served to fuel the antiwar sentiments of the country and for parents it was a daily, agonizing reminder of what might happen to their child.

My best friend Dick Rogers always drove me back and forth to the airport as Mom and Dad could not deal with the trip and traffic. While Dick waited, the time came for my final good-bye in the back-yard. If a person wanted a visible sign of whether they were loved, or not I certainly saw it. My father could not even speak'; he just stood and cried while my mother tearfully managed a few words.

In their retirement years, Mom and Dad had a time of devotions together every morning, during which they read from the Bible and from a devotional and spent time in prayer. Every morning during their devotions and every evening when grace was said before dinner, they prayed for my safe return.

I don't like to get into long winded discussions about Vietnam, but I'll try to explain in a few words. To start with South Vietnam is a country trying to be free and set up a working democracy. North Vietnam has tried to stop this by killing public officials (terrorism), blowing up schools full of children, hospitals, slaughtering village leaders and leaving them as a gory spectacle. All this is to try to scare the people in going along with Communists. Now there are two ways to look at this when it's happening on the other side of the world. You can ignore it and say it's no skin off our noses or you can say as Americans who believe in democracy we can't allow this to go on. Also we had signed a treaty or pact or something like that saying that we would help particular countries in case of communist aggression. It's the old story of putting the shoe on the other foot. What if you were one of those Vietnamese people? So now people say (I was one of them) that we are not fighting the war right. Well this is a hard kind of war to fight. It is not a group force type of war, There is no line that marks which side is yours and which side is the enemy's. Also we have to keep from getting ourselves into a world war. Even if the military wanted to step up things, I don't think the American public would stand for it. They would say we weren't going along with a withdrawal situation. So we're kind of stuck with fighting the war just the way we are. About the only thing I can see is for us to have better trained men, more improved weapons and more improved techniques of warfare. (And we are about the best right now.) I think there are several reasons why a portion of the American public is against the war:

1. *They don't know enough about it.*
2. *It's on the other side of the world.*
3. *It's a race of people we're not found of.*
4. *There was no initial act of aggression against the U.S. to set the country together against the enemy. For example: bombing Pearl Harbor or sinking of the Lusitania*
5. *It is difficult to accept the fact that the conflict has to be fought the way it's being fought.*

In conclusion I will say that I don't like the war in Vietnam, I don't even like talking about it, I just want to put my time in and get out of there. But I do feel that we are right being there and should stay there. Maybe my mind will change, but this is how I feel now.
(Letter, September 11, 1969)

CHAPTER 4

VIETNAM – MONTHS 1 & 2

I t seems that I have blocked out the emotions experienced and most of my memory of the flight from Philadelphia to Washington State to then begin the twenty-three-hour flight to Vietnam. Now reading my letter home of October 29, it sounds like the alcohol and clowning may have been partially responsible for the memory loss.

Well, I sure have put some miles on since Friday. It is Wed. night here in Cam Ranh Bay and as best as I can judge it is probably sometime Tues. at home. My flight to Seattle stopped in Detroit and St. Paul. I caught the bus at Seattle to McChord AFB. I arrived 1/2 hour early. Then we had a 3 hr. wait. There were 19 of us sailors and over 100 Air Force men. And we for the most part were in true Navy style and spirit (that is half drunk and raising hell). It seemed as though we were the center of attraction and kept everyone in stitches. The first part of our flight took about 3 hrs. We stopped in Anchorage, Alaska at which time the Navy took over the bar in the terminal. An hour later (all refueled) we were on our way on a 7 hr flight to Japan. We stopped in Japan and had a 3 hr. wait there, but there was no bar there. Then it was about a 5 hr flight to Vietnam...

Civilian airplanes were used to transport us to and from Vietnam. It looked like they recruited all the older stewardesses for these flights. In all the previous flying I had flown, the stewardesses were young and good-looking. There was a northern route and a southern route to Vietnam. We took the northern route as described in my letter. It is amazing how tiring it can be just sitting in a plane for nearly a day. I do not recall the revelry during the first portion of the flight, but I do recall being extremely tired and uncomfortable at the end.

> *We landed around 11am this morning. We had a briefing, exchanged our money for "military payment certificates (MPC)," and went through customs. We are on the west side of the base. The base is really big. Like it was about an 8 mile ride to our barracks. I guess tomorrow we'll find out where we're going or the next day. The word is that almost all Swift boats are operating in the rivers now.*
> (Letter, Oct. 29, 1969)

It was my first time seeing sandbagged buildings, armed checkpoints, and lots of barbed wire that was not intended for the same purpose as back on the farm. The beach and water of Cam Ranh Bay were beautiful, and we enjoyed swimming and sunning while we awaited orders.

> *I'm still at Cam Ranh Bay, but by the time you get this letter and answer it I'll be in Cat Lo. I'll be attached to Costal Division 13. The first month or so is supposed to be further training. Until further notice, our boat crews will stay together for the most part.*

Note: The last two sentences did not prove to turn out for me. Due to the shortage of enginemen and the rotation of personnel back to the "world" (world meaning back to the United States), I was assigned to an established crew and put to work right away. My "further training" was doing it firsthand!

Cat Lo is located south (SSE) of Saigon (now Ho Chi Minh City) in IV corps, which encompasses the Mekong Delta. In addition to being the headquarters for Costal Division 13 (COSDIV 13) it was also the headquarters of Coastal Squadron One (CosRonOne). About five miles south of Cat Lo was the city of Vung Tau, which had been a French resort during the colonization period.

> *Cat Lo is supposed to be about the best place to be, all the way around. Sooner or later though, as we become proficient we most likely will be sent to An Thoi for 4 or 5 months. That is where the action is… Boy! is it hot!!!*
> (Letter, Oct. 30, 1969)

Maps and Charts

Vietnam Coastal Map and Swift Boat Bases
(Courtesy of the Maritime Museum of San Diego)

There are five coastal divisions of Swift boats in V.N.

CosDiv 11 - An Thoi   *CosDiv 14 - Cam Ranh*
CosDiv 12 - Da Nang   *CosDiv 15 - Qui Nhon*
CosDiv 13 - Cat Lo
CosDiv 15 was just turned over to the V.N. Navy yesterday. CosDiv 12 is supposed to be turned over in about 3 or 4 months and CosDiv 14 several months after that. The trouble is they're getting the regular areas and we're staying in An Thoi (CosDiv 11) which is really bad and CosDiv 13 which is O.K. It's their war and I think they should be in An Thoi instead of us. But the feeling is that they just don't usually make as good of fighters and sailors as we do. So once again the U.S. must pay for the honor of being No. 1...

To fly anywhere in IV corps required first flying to Saigon and then getting a flight to our destination. Like the old saying "All roads lead to Rome," in the Delta, all flights lead to Saigon, and then you hope to catch a flight to your destination. When we received orders, we got a mimeographed stack of a dozen or so copies. The orders authorized us to use whatever military transportation we could find. We also were given three to five days to get to our destination in case we encountered difficulty making a flight or connection.

It is difficult to attempt to relate the sights, sounds, and smells of Saigon. We had been briefed and warned about cultural shock. Obviously, the people look different and talk fast in a strange language. Fish is a staple, and it is abundantly fresh, dried, or rotting. In some areas of the city, sewage was also a problem.

Traffic was like nothing I had ever experienced even in New York City. All types of conveyances scurry and weave in and out with little regard for lanes or safety. The most common vehicle was the two-cycle motor scooter. There were also bicycles, cars, trucks, rickshaws, military jeeps, and Lambretta taxis. The Lambretta taxi was used to transport both people and goods. It was a motor scooter in the front with dual wheels in the rear. It had a small roof over the driver and a small cart mounted over the rear wheels. The cart had low short benches on either side so passengers sat facing each other, and it also had a low roof overhead. With the overwhelming majority of vehicles on the street being powered by two-cycle engines, the racket of rip-bip-pip-pip-pip-pip went on almost continually.

Leaving the main gate of the airport, we were immediately converged upon by taxi drivers offering to take us in town. This was my first lesson in the art of bargaining. Whatever price the driver says that the fare is, you disagree and offer less. He acts angry and counteroffers, to which we firmly state our last offer, which is close to what he really wanted anyhow. I am not sure which increased my pulse and blood pressure more—my first Lambretta taxi ride into Saigon or the first time I was shot at!

Boy transportation in V.N. sure is poor. We got up at 3a.m. Monday morning. We didn't get a flight out of Cam Ranh until around noon. The flight was to Saigon. When we got to Saigon we couldn't get a flight to Vung Tau until the next day which is today. So Sandoval and Weekly and I went into town. We kept looking for "downtown" Saigon or what you might call the good part of town. Well either we didn't find it or there just isn't a good part of town. The streets are crowded. Most people in the street are riding bicycles or motorbikes. Very few cars. Mostly Army jeeps and small taxis. In many places they throw their garbage right in the street. Some of the people even shit in the street. None of the servicemen wear dress uniforms. Everyone wears fatigues. A lot of servicemen carry their rifle or machine gun right in town with them. Some places are surrounded with barb wire and have bunkers built right out front and sandbags all over. I've never seen an Am. city slum area anywhere near as bad as this. When you walk into a bar, the whores are right there to sit on your lap and try to get you to spend all your money. They know enough English to get what they want. And they know all the tricks. The mistake made now

70

is that Americans start to think that all Vietnamese are like
this, which isn't true…
(Letter, Nov. 3, 1969)

Once we checked into a hotel, we headed to the club on the top floor. Prior to leaving for Vietnam I had decided that I would stay sober and fully alert at all times so as to be ready for any danger. Well, here I was, only about three days "in country," tossing them down. So much for any resolve to stay sober and alert. Prostitution was rampant in every city in Vietnam, and every hotel had its regular bevy of young girls. I sincerely wish I could say I abstained, but that would be untrue. I thank God that He has forgiven my sins. I hope that family and friends that read this take into account my youth and circumstances. It's kind of backwards; in a time of life when I would soon be facing the possibility of quickly facing my Maker, I should have been living as far from sin as possible instead of taking a "devil may care" attitude.

The next day we caught a flight to Vung Tau and a truck to Cat Lo. In addition to being the base for Costal Division 13, it was also the Squadron headquarters. Cat Lo was a small base, a little rural but not way out there.

Well we finally made it to Cat Lo around 3:30pm this
afternoon. Even though I haven't seen much of the base,
there's something about it I think I like. Maybe its because
there's a lot of Swift Boat sailors here or maybe it was seeing
the Swift Boats. Just as the service builds a respect and love
for your flag and country, training for so long for Swift
Boats builds a respect and love for the boats. … We are
presently in Quonset huts but are supposed to move into
regular barracks.

71

Row of Swifts tied up at base.
Note the newer Mark 3 Swift with the taller pilot house

Well things have been happening fast now. Wednesday I got assigned to the crew of PCF 63. The rest of my class is getting further training, but they (PCF 63) needed an Engineman right away so here I am. Tomorrow morning we leave for 12 days we'll be stationed at a PBR base camp on one of the rivers in the Delta...

The 9th Infantry used to be in that area. Now that they've moved out, there are (reportedly) 5 divisions of North Vietnamese troops in the area. So I may see some action real soon. Here in CatLo the Army moved out also. There are some ARVN troops here to take their place though. You can hear mortar and artillery fire quite often, but I don't know who's firing it. It's pretty far away though. You can see fire fights at night in the distance too. Our forces fire illumination rounds and the helicopters come in and fire on whatever or whoever they see. It's really pretty to watch at night. Don't get the wrong idea, there's an air base up the road about 5 miles and its all a pretty secure area.

The girls in Vung Tau are definitely better looking than the ones in Saigon. The food is good here. We have good food on the boat too, no C-rations. The mosquitoes have just about eaten me alive... Time seems to be going along fairly fast. Maybe it will be a short year, I sure hope so.
(Letter, November 6,1969)

When I reported to my boat I met the OinC (Officer in Charge) LTJG Jack Burke. One of the first pieces of information he asked for was my blood type, which he then added to the rest of the crew's name and blood types on a side window of the pilot house. That was a sobering bit of necessity in case a blood transfusion was needed. Eventually, I met the rest of the crew. Bill Hogan. who planned on going to seminary and becoming a priest; Steve Johnson, our Gunner's Mate from California; Neil Hirsch, and a Vietnamese trainee.

Hogan, Johnson, Hirsch

Our first assignment was to report to Binh Thuy on the Bassac River to participate in riverine operations. This required a few hours of transit out into the South China Sea and down along the coast and into the mouth of the river. About midway, our port 12V71 Detroit Diesel engine cracked a fuel line. So my first repair as Engineman was reflaring the end of a fuel line while continuing our transit on just the starboard engine.

The naval base at Binh Thuy had Swift Boats and PBRs that patrolled the river and ran special operations with a US Navy SEAL detachment and local forces. Across the street was a Naval Air base. These two bases provided support for Navy patrol boats and planes in that area. Binh Thuy is right next to Can Tho.

VN trainees watch row of Swifts underway in Vung Tau Bay

Well we left CatLo yesterday morning and got to Binh Thuy (pronounced Bin Too wee) at about 9pm. We refueled and went out to our patrol section. There we anchored and set up a watch...

The Engineman that was on this crew before certainly didn't do a very good job in my estimation. I've all kinds of things to fix and an awful lot of cleaning to do. [Now] We have 6 Americans and 3 Vietnamese sailors [on the boat]. We are supposed to be training them as we patrol but it isn't easy for many reasons. Number one is the language barrier.

They speak a lot more English than we do Vietnamese but it is still difficult. Also in a situation like this you want things to be done right and you'd rather trust yourself than someone else. They are young too. Also sometimes you wonder if they want to learn. They are about 19 years old, but are about Georgie's [my thirteen-year-old nephew] *size. We're supposed to make combat forces out of them?!? But besides all this, as I get accustomed to the boat and it's routines, I want to try to teach them too. The one that is striking[6] to be an Engineman is named Kim. They are usually bright and smiling. I keep getting the feeling though that we're sort of taking them along for the ride. Some of the American sailors don't like them, they think they are lazy and stupid. I am trying to keep an open mind.*

I think yesterday I drank more water than any other day in my life. Boy was it hot…

We can wear whatever we feel like wearing while we're on patrol. Bathing suits, shorts, sandals, t-shirts, no shirts, bare foot, just about anything.
(Letter, Nov. 8, 1969)

***

Well we laid our night ambush last night. Boy was that hairy. We went in and tied up to a tree about 20 foot from the shore and waited. Talk about nerve racking! Three hours of waiting in full battle dress, no talking, no moving, and no smoking; just laying dead in the water. Engines off. We were sitting ducks if the VC were waiting for us, but on the other hand if he tried to cross and didn't see us, we had him dead to rights. About midnight a fire fight started across the river and their stray rounds were coming pretty close to us. That lasted about ten to fifteen minutes. At

---

6. striking is a term used in the Navy which means that a sailor is working towards a particular skill rate/rank

about 12:45 we saw a signaling light on the bank we were next to. We waited but nothing happened and we're not supposed to fire unless fired on. Finally we left.

This morning we had a big operation. Five Swift Boats picked up 300 ARVN troops and took them up river and beached and inserted them. We had 2 Coast Guard boats laying back for cover. Before we beached 8 helicopters shot the place all up, then we 5 boats moved in and we chopped the beach up in little pieces as we did. We received no return fire. We were supposed to stay in the river to give fire support if needed, but our boat was called to meet another boat with troops aboard and insert them at another location. We did so and then moved into a real small canal and moved parallel to them. We received no fire. We took them back to their base.

Tomorrow at 5:30am we are supposed to conduct a roundup operation. There will be 3 or 5 Swifts rounding up all the boats in the area and taking them to a Coast Guard boat to be searched. It's supposed to be about 15 hours long. Then we may get a day off in Binh Thuy.

So you can see we aren't giving the enemy much rest. He is in the area but he's hard to find. We are only a part of the operations going on around here.

That's all for now.

(Letter, Nov. 9, 1969)

As my letters indicate, one of our functions was to pick up various types of ground forces and transport them to an insertion point then stand by to provide fire support or extract the ground force. Eventually we became familiar with the various types of irregular forces. They varied in their effectiveness and dedication. The really good units were paid by kill, capture, and intelligence gathered. Provincial Reconnaissance Units referred to as PRUs were one of the good paramilitary units. They were controlled by the local province chief but paid by the CIA. Every airport in the Delta had at least one

Air America place which was a civilian-type-looking small plane used by the CIA.

Air America plane on "Marston Mats"[7]

Other good units we worked with were the Montagnards, Chinese mercenaries, and of course the best of the best—US Navy SEALs. The Montagnards came from remote tribes in the Central Highlands. They were usually a little darker skinned than most Vietnamese and smaller in stature. But what they lacked in size, they made up for when it came to fighting.

What can I say about Navy SEALs that has not already been said in numerous books and portrayed in movies? My initial exposure to SEALs was limited. During my early months in country, I never heard of one being killed. They were mysterious, and every one of them appeared to be in top physical condition. While I was at Sea Float, we had two SEAL teams and occasionally worked with them.

---

[7]. Marston Mats were developed in WWII to quickly create a landing strip for planes. The steel sections interlock and can be quickly replaced if the air strip receives damage. Marston Mats were used by the U.S. all over Vietnam.

It appeared as time went on that the standard of physical conditioning had been lowered, and I heard that the training time had been shortened in order to provide enough SEALs to handle all the operations going on. I actually saw a SEAL with a bit of a belly! In time, the SEALs did start to take some casualties. I also learned that one of the reasons they could go on some really wild missions and survive was because they aborted a good number of missions if they were detected or things went wrong.

There were two types of militia units and they were the worst. Regional forces and Popular Forces nicknamed Ruff-Puffs. That nickname says it all. Once inserted, they would head off in a direction opposite of the last-known enemy positions and return with chickens stolen from the civilians. On one such occasion, we forced one of these local forces to throw the chickens overboard once we had gotten back underway. This angered the chicken thieves and scared the heck out of the chickens.

At the end of the mission, we disembarked these troops at the location we had been told to take them. It seems that this was not where they wanted to be left off. Still angry over our insistence of freedom for the stolen chickens and now further irritated with where we had dropped them off, several of them vented their frustrations by firing a few shots over our boats to demonstrate their frustration. Our officer was so angry at this that he got on the radio and threatened their Commanding Officer that if they fired again, we would open fire with our .50 calibers. The full firepower of two Swift Boats would have killed every one of them as they were standing out in the open on an empty muddy river bank.

Well we got relieved yesterday afternoon. We didn't have to finish the roundup. We're in Binh Thuy now, but are going out at 6:30am tomorrow morning. All I've done is repair things on the boat since we've been in Binh Thuy. There are so many things that need fixing, but when I get everything in shape it should be easier. Tomorrow morning we have to insert troops again. It is very hot during the day, I'm getting a nice suntan. When I go down in the engine room for any length of time I soak my clothes with sweat.

I probably won't get any mail or pay until we get back to CatLo, which will be 8 or more days yet. I'm really getting impatient for mail now. If another boat comes up here from CatLo while we're here, it may bring us some mail. Actually I think it's a pretty poor set up being based at CatLo and spending most of our time somewhere else.

P.S. 349 days to go.

(Letter, Nov 11, 1969)

When a boat returns from being out, the boat must be made ready to go back out before food, showers, or sleep. This is in case of an emergency or call for help; everything must be ready to go back out immediately. If the base had limited water hours, we sometimes missed out on showers. If the chow hall closed before we were done, then we missed a regular type meal. At the end of a long day or night, or days and nights, this was a severe test of discipline. Guns had to be cleaned, decks scrubbed, charts filed, log updated, munitions replenished, fuel tanks refilled, and engine maintenance completed.

Engine oil and filters got changed every one hundred hours of operation. Oftentimes returning to base for me meant first cleaning the aft .50 caliber and then changing oil and filters. Each engine held nine gallons of oil. So changing oil in two engines meant humping four jerry cans of oil from a base repair shop to my boat. There was no environmental protection agency in Vietnam. Dirty oil was just drained into the bilges, and the bilge pump just pushed the filthy slick out into the river. Likewise, empty ammo boxes and packing went over the side into the river. The peasants would retrieve the mortar boxes and build shacks out of them. Usually, one of my crewmates would help me because the engine maintenance took longer than the other tasks.

**Vietnamese troops disembarking from Swift
Boat into mudbank at low tide**

*Sorry I haven't written lately, but the fun and games are
over and its* [sic]*a lot of hard work and long hours now...
Our last two days we were really busy. Picking up troops
and inserting them on the beach, providing mortar fire
and picking the troops back up day and night. It's good
to see you're accomplishing something. The troops have
captured several VC, medical supplies, ammunition and
killed 3 VC. That is 3 we know of for sure, we may have
killed or wounded more with our mortar fire...We're
going out this morning on patrol again. There is a rumor
that we may be detached here from Binh Thuy for another
couple weeks. I sure hope not. This is a PBR base. It's hard
to get parts for Swift Boats here, the food here is lousy, the
barracks are lousy and many other reasons why I'd rather
be in CatLo.*
(Letter Nov. 16, 1969)

***

Well, we were just relieved from our patrol and we're heading back into Binh Thuy. The first day of our patrol was pretty good, we just rode around looking for males crossing the river. We took two people in who didn't have proper I.D. Neither turned out to be VC so they were released. That night we fired 34 rounds of mortar at a spot where 150 VC were spotted. I haven't heard any official report, but the spotter said he thought we did some real damage. The next day we rested during the day and didn't do much.

Last night we fired some mortar rounds at Dung Island for harassment purposes. Dung Island is in the middle of the Bassac River where we have been patrolling. It is a favorite crossing point for the VC. Most of our operations are directed at Dung Island. Around 4 am this morning we got a call that an outpost was under attack. So we stormed up the river to assist. When we got in the vicinity we received a few sniper rounds. They sure are poor shots. You could hear them hit the water around us. But they were nowhere near. First we opened up on the spot where the fire came from with our twin .30 caliber machineguns. We stopped—received a few more rounds. Then I opened up with our after .50 caliber machinegun and the sniper fire ceased. Either I got him or he decided to quit while he was ahead. He probably just ducked down in a hole somewhere. After that we supplied mortar fire for the outpost. Shortly after that the attack ceased. As we were just about finished we spotted a large sampan. We came up on it and illuminated it with flares. It seemed deserted so we fired a few rounds of M16 at it and threw a few grenades to make sure it wasn't booby trapped or mined. Another Swift towed it away.

Around 9am this morning we inserted troops in one of the canals on Dung Island. While waiting to pick them up we spotted a small abandoned junk, which I cut to pieces with my .50 caliber. The darned thing wouldn't sink. So we fired M79 grenades at it but missed. So we pulled up closer to it and dropped a grenade in it. That made splinters out of it.

**Concussion grenades exploding and
destroying a captured sampan**

The reason we sink or take junks and sampans is because no one is supposed to be on the waters at night and during[sic] *the VC abandon them when they hear us coming. They use them to cross the river. Actually we don't have much trouble because unless the VC are ready and waiting for us, they don't want to mess with us, they'd rather just sneak away than fight us. The only exception to this is sniper fire, which they use to harass us occasionally. When they are ready and waiting for us, that's when we're in trouble.*

I'll say one thing, I feel like I'm really doing something in VN, instead of just spending a year here sitting on some base like some people.
(Letter, Nov. 18, 1969)

Occasionally, we would be sent on a psyops (psychological warfare operation) mission. We had a cassette tape player connected to our loud speaker system. The loud speaker was extremely loud. We would go to areas known to have enemy activity and play tapes that urged the Viet Cong to surrender. The message told them that if they surrendered, they would be treated well; but if they did not surrender, eventually, they would be killed or captured. Evidently, the VC did not like the message as quite often it resulted in them responding with rockets and automatic weapons fire. I hated it for a number of reasons. First, it was painfully loud; second, it was in Vietnamese, which meant we did not have any idea what was being said in spite of our two weeks of language classes; and lastly, in order to be heard, we were traveling dangerously slow and close to the riverbanks, making us an easy target for an irritated enemy.

Our usual location for psyops missions was around Dung Island. This large island located in the Bassac River was a known VC sanctuary where enemy contact regularly occurred. So psyops missions were like going out to jerk the tiger's tail.

We started out on patrol this morning but the saltwater pump on my starboard engine crapped out. So we're headed back in to try to get parts.
(Letter, Nov. 20, 1969)

***

I finished repairing the engine…We got back on patrol early yesterday evening. Someone spotted a large number of VC carrying heavy weapons, so we went into the area and had the biggest shoot'em up I've seen yet. Every gun on 3 boats was blazing. Funny thing we weren't shooting at anyone or anything in particular, of course we never are, because we never see the VC hiding in a hole or in the bushes. But we just shoot to make sure no one is there. We beached and fired mortar rounds for a while and then pulled out again once again destroying the wild life on both sides of us. This morning we inserted troops and then went up a canal that was so small that when we turned around

the bow was on one bank and the screws were churning up mud about 2 feet from the other bank. We found two sampans which we destroyed. Our officer got hit by a piece of shrapnel from our own guns. It hit him in the leg, not bad though. So we're going in off patrol a day early, that's pretty good anyhow.
(Letter, Nov. 21, 1969)

Bac Lieu

On November 24, 1969, we were deployed to a place called Bac Lieu with another Swift and the Coast Guard WPB, Point Monroe. The WPB is a larger boat at a length of eighty-two feet. The purpose of the WPB was to serve as a supply and support boat for our two Swift Boats. They carried extra fuel and ammunition to supply us as Bac Lieu was extremely remote and had no resources to supply us. The transit took us out of the Bassac River into the South China Sea and southwest to the mouth of the Thanh River and on to a remote base. The only other Americans in Bac Lieu were thirteen Navy Seabees building a base and a US Army advisor to coordinate the local forces with us. We stayed there about a week. Every day, we loaded up Vietnamese troops and set out to a different location where the troops would off load and sweep the area.

US Coast Guard WPB

Well this morning we're on our way again. Only this time for something a little different. Us and another Swift and a Coast Guard patrol boat are going down south a little farther to another river. We aren't certain how long we'll be there, maybe a week or two. I don't know when I'll get to mail this letter. We're supposed to be going on an old fashioned Sea Lords raid. The kind where you shoot up the whole countryside. It sounds like fun and everybody is always talking about the old Sea Lords raids. Now days we're not allowed to shoot at anything that moves like before. We are loaded for bear too. You wouldn't believe the amount of ammunition we loaded on this boat this morning. 11,000 rounds of .50 caliber and 12,000 rounds of .30 caliber. We plan on doing some shootin'.

(Note: .30 caliber were not issued to Swift Boat crews but our Gunners Mate had done some trading to get two .30 caliber machine guns and consequently at times we had difficulty obtaining ammo for it.)

This place is supposed to be way out in the boon docks where nobody but the VC go.

Last night the 34 boat took some AK47 rounds. (That's a communist fully automatic rifle.) One of my buddies (Sandoval) from my class at NIOTC was on it, but nobody got hurt. One went right through a can of .50 cal. ammo that the Engineman was sitting on, one through their fuel tank and 3 through their mortar box and through some mortar rounds, but the mortar rounds didn't go off. They were kind of lucky. But that's the way it usually goes, the VC are just plain lousy shots. I guess by the time I get to some place to mail this, I'll already have in it how our Sea Lords raid went. That's all for now.

(Letter, Nov, 24, 1969)

***

We got to Bac Lieu on the night of the 24th. The next day we took some troops out and inserted them. Five of them were injured by booby traps. I mean to tell you we were in VC territory. There were little VC signs here and there that the VC left and bunkers all over. We didn't get any VC, but we burned a few houses and sunk some sampans and blew up some bunkers. The 26th we went back to the same canal and destroyed everything in sight. That was kinda fun. I forget exactly what all we did yesterday, but we came back in early and the Coast Guard boat cooked Thanksgiving dinner for all of us. It was really good too. Today we took a special kind of troops out and they killed 2 VC. We caught a lady in a boat with special documents and records, and she turned out to be a VC Lieutenant. How about that. We also took two VC suspects who didn't have I.D. cards.

(Letter, Nov. 28, 1969)

We came across the two VC suspects mentioned in the letter on our way out one morning. They were two military age males traveling in a small sampan. Seeing males in the age range between sixteen and thirty-five that were not in uniform always aroused suspicion. So we stopped them to search and check their papers. The irregular troops we had on board took over the interrogation, and things did not check out. The two were separated, and they told two very different stories. This resulted in the interrogators using the old "good cop, bad cop" routine. They yelled, threatened, and beat the crap out of suspect number 1 while talking normally to the suspect number 2. I could see the fear in the captives' eyes. Eventually, they tied up one with one of our lines and threatened to throw him overboard and drag him into our screws. At this point Lieutenant Burke intervened to prevent an inhumane act and the fouling of our propellers. I was relieved that the cruelty had ended as it was not easy to stand by and watch. We later turned the two over to local authorities.

> *This morning was cold for Vietnam. We took special forces almost to the mouth of the river and then up a small canal and dropped them off. They weren't in there five minutes and we had a call that one of the V.N.s had been killed. We heard some shots and a lot of explosions. [Their objective was to free a POW comp that has 44 prisoners.] Five minutes later we were told to pick them up. As far as we know right now, they walked into a mine field. Not to mention a few VC. Our boat took on the casualties, there were two dead and seven wounded, one of the seriously wounded ones died so we've heard. The war becomes very real when two dead men are laying [sic] next to your feet and you are putting dressings on the wounded. We pulled out and transferred the two seriously wounded ones to a helicopter, the others we put on the Point Monroe which is much bigger. Then believe it or not we went back into the canal and shot up the whole place. Then we went back into the river and put a whole bunch of mortar rounds into the area. And then as we left we shot up everything in sight. This, I guess, is poor retaliation for three dead men, but what else is there to do?*

*I think tomorrow is our last day here, I kind of hope so.
My estimation of V.N.s as fighting men is rather poor
because of what I've seen of them on our operations, but the
V.N.s we had with us yesterday and today are called PRUs
which stands for Provincial Reconnaissance Units and
these guys are really good. They are out and out professional
killers and they hate VC with a passion. They even wanted
to go back in again today after all that happened to them.*
(Letter, Nov. 29, 1969)

The events and particulars of the above letter require some further explanation. As I had stated, the mission was to locate a POW camp. The type of POW camp we were after was not the typical POW camp that comes to mind. Movies and pictures of POW camps during WWII are usually a stationary complex with several buildings and a large perimeter fence holding a large number of prisoners. The VC and NVA had another system in place in South Vietnam. A POW camp could be several guards holding several prisoners temporarily in a makeshift hut or huts until the prisoners could be transported to another such camp eventually getting them up into North Vietnam to the more permanent-type POW complexes. These small camps could easily be moved to avoid being found. In some cases, in very rural VC controlled area such as the U Minh forest or parts of the Cau Mau Peninsula, camps could be larger and hold prisoners for much longer periods. We learned about these camps months later when a SEAL team freed Vietnamese prisoners in the Cau Mau and the prisoners told us that they heard the noise of our diesel engines out in the river for months.

The troops we worked with in Bac Lieu turned out to be very good and had been active and successful all week. Although I do not recall at this time which type they were, I believe based on their performance that they were PRUs. A web search of "Provincial Reconnaissance Units" reveals multiple sources revealing the use of the PRUs by the CIA to carry out Operation Phoenix, which was to target the Viet Cong infrastructure.

It was a dark and ominous day when we transported and inserted them at the suspected location of the POW camp. We exited the canal after they disembarked and then stood by in the river, monitoring radio communication for whatever assistance the ground force might need. It was only a short time before we began to hear all hell break loose with explosions and automatic weapons fire. Within minutes, we received a call to extract the troops. They had walked into a mine field and ambush. Once in the mine field with multiple casualties, they were pinned down and had to fight their way out. We immediately proceeded to the extraction point and waited. Soon they emerged from the mangrove forest. All the wounded were loaded onto our boat because our Gunner's Mate Steve Johnson had mistakenly been sent to a medical corpsman school earlier in his time in the Navy. Steve manned his custom-built twin .30 caliber machine guns on the peak of the boat. Two severely wounded were laid in the cramped space on either side of Steve and his guns. Another severely wounded was laid on our port engine cover. Although he had only a small wound showing in his chest, I watched him draw his last painful breath. The commander of these men was so distraught at the casualties they had received that he stood in the muddy water crying while pounding his fist on the bow of the boat. It was a powerful emotional scene. The event was surreal.

One of the wounded with Steve had lost a leg at the hip and was spurting blood from his femoral artery. There was not enough leg left to apply a tourniquet, so Steve reached into the bloody stump and held onto the pulsing artery with his fingers. Once all the men were aboard our two Swift Boats, we exited the canal and marked a safe LZ (landing zone) with smoke for a medevac to land and remove the seriously wounded. The noise level was very high so the helicopter crew could not hear Steve screaming to hold the femoral artery, which resulted in the man bleeding to death in the helicopter.

This scene was also unreal and would have made an amazing picture as just a short distance away were two water buffalo watching as the last bits of colored smoke were beaten away by the whirling helicopter blades. The boat's exhaust flappers rattled to the pulse of the multiple twelve-cylinder engines, and men were shouting and crying as the helo was loaded. There was so much blood on our boat that it ran down the deck along the side of the gunnels.

We transferred the remaining wounded to the Coast Guard WPB and then reentered the canal. We took the area under heavy prolonged machinegun fire. It is unknown whether we inflicted any damage on the enemy as we had no idea how far into the jungle he was located. It just felt good to strike back. Then we went back out into the river, beached, and mortared the area. This was not one of those days we celebrated afterward.

Monsoon Storm

We left Buc Leiu yesterday morning at 9 a.m. We got a report that the seas were okay. Well they definitely were not. Once we got into the ocean it was really rough. Too rough to turn back into the river. So we had to fight our way back to Binh Thuy. After four hours of hellacious seas it was too rough to make it into the mouth of the Bassac River. We then had to try to make it to Vung Tau. By now almost everybody on the boat was sick.

The peak tank (which is the most forward part of the boat) was completely flooded, two windows were broken in the pilot house and the main cabin was starting to flood. Needless to say we were all kind of scared. We had to keep pumping continuously to keep the water down and the seas were almost bad enough to capsize the boat. I'll tell I was really scared. More scared than I've ever been in any canal or river, day or night.

It took about 8 or 9 hours to get to Vung Tau and we couldn't get in there either so we had to go to Cat Lo. Which took another hour or two. You will never know how glad I was to get out of the ocean. It took 3 hours to pump all the water out of the boat. I'll tell you I'd rather go into any river or canal with any number of VC in it than go through that again.
(Letter, Dec. 1, 1969)

With our time in Buc Leiu completed, we headed back out to the South China Sea to make our transit back to Cat Lo. Once we had gotten to a little wider (which means safer) part of the river, I cooked up a batch of chopped hot dogs with baked beans, which we all devoured. Along the way we made a radio call for a sea and swell report. The report came back for three- to five-foot swells. But we were experiencing three- to five-foot swells a mile or so upriver. I was quickly becoming concerned as I had hated the rough water and seasickness that I had experienced in San Francisco Bay. Johnson and Hirsch told me it was nothing to worry about saying, "Don't worry about the weather until we get worried." That did not take long to happen. As we headed out into the South China Sea, the weather quickly got worse. Soon we were plowing through eight- to twelve-foot swells. Eventually, seasickness set in, and unsecured gear started flying around inside the main cabin. I was wishing I had not eaten so many hot dogs and beans. During our operations in Buc Lieu, one of our crew had fired an M82 LAW rocket from the bow of the boat, not thinking about the back blast from the rocket tube. The back pressure had blown out one of the pilot house windows. Now despite the temporary patch we had installed, every wave that engulfed the pilot house sent water around our patch, and we were slowly flooding. As the Engineman, I was the crew member most familiar with and responsible for the bilge pumps. So as the storm continued to worsen, it was my job to regularly crawl out the rear main cabin hatch, lift an engine cover, crawl down into the engine room, and switch the valves to pump from one flooding compartment to another. This had to be accomplished while hanging on for dear life. After each trip back and forth to the engine room, I returned to sit on the gun locker that housed all our small arms. Within minutes, I became nauseous, crawled to the large garbage can on the other side of the main cabin and vomited into the garbage can that we all were using for that purpose.

Lieutenant Burke drove for nine of the approximate fourteen hours we battled the storm. Bill Hogan took the wheel for most of the other time. A few times I ventured up into the pilot house to watch our boat get swallowed by the next monster swell and come out the other side of the swell to drop with a crash to the low side of the swell. I could see the next one coming like a towering wall of water. We had ridden into a monsoon storm with swells at times reaching twenty feet high.

By now, Johnson and Hirsch were worried, and I was way past worried. I was sure that one of these monster waves would eventually flip us, and we would be trapped inside the boat as it sunk. Even if we managed to escape the boat, I would not last long with my below-average swimming skills. Sometime during the night, we threw all our extra ammo overboard to lighten the boat. By design, Swift Boats were nose-heavy, which increased the boat's tendency to surf on a wave and then nosedive under the water.

We had to maintain a very slow speed, and as we entered the next swell, we could hear the engines strain and slow. Then the bow of the boat would poke into the swell rather than ride over it, and the windows around the whole pilot house would be solid water outside like being in a big fish bowl. The missing window with the patch would gush water around the sides of the patch. After a second or two that seemed like an eternity, we came out the other side of the swell, the engines now relieved of their load raced as we were briefly suspended in midair with no water around the propellers. And then we dropped twenty tons of boat, fuel, guns, and ammo came crashing down with so much force that I thought the hull would break.

Exhaustion sets in quickly from bracing yourself against the violent rolling and up and down banging and crashing. Eventually, we came to the end of the fear-induced adrenaline flow; and despite everything, we dosed off even if only momentarily. Again and again, Lieutenant Burke would call out from the pilot house, "Hunt, switch the bilge pump." I would again make my way out and crawl into the engine room, closing off one set of valves and opening another set, then crawl back to my seat on the gun locker, vomit within minutes, and then just start to drift off but not make it. Johnson, Hirsch, and our VN trainee spent most of their time in their racks.

At some point, we lost our radar, which was an important aid to knowing where we were. There was no GPS. We had to keep track of our compass headings and keep the lights of the other two boats in view without getting too close. Getting too close meant risking a collision of two boats.

One might ask why we simply did not turn and head into one of the rivers and wait out the storm, but that could have been disastrous. To keep control of a boat or ship in heavy seas, the boat must ride into the swells. Ideally, you "tack" into the seas at a slight angle. If the angle is too sharp, the boat can get turned over or "broached." If you attempt to turn around and get caught while turned broadside to the swell, the boat also may become broached. If turning around is accomplished, the waves will either pound the fantail down into the water or the boat will surf on the swell or the wave. Surfing is a scary sensation because the swell catches and lifts the back of the boat. Then with startling power it pushes the nose down into the water. In the worst-case scenario, it pushes the nose down and the tail up, flipping the boat upside down. Given the nose-heavy design of our boat and the number of Swift Boats known to have succumbed to this fate, it was determined by all three boats not to attempt entry into a river mouth until the seas were calmer.

Needless to say, during those harrowing hours, I spent a fair amount of time praying. You may have heard it said that there are no atheists in a foxhole—I doubt that there are any atheists in small boats riding out monsoon storms. I was sure I was going to die that night. It is one kind of fear when a person is in danger and he has the option of "fight or flight." It is entirely different when the danger drags on for hours and he can't do anything about it.

****

Finally, I did doze off; and when I awoke, I heard the engines' speed was up and felt no bang or crash, so I thought we were once again suspended in midair and about to come crashing down. And then I realized that it was daylight and we were running in smooth water. Praise God! Thank you, Jesus! We made it through the storm and were in the channel back into Cat Lo. The feeling of peace and relief were beyond anything that can be put into words. Years later I heard a song released by Andrae Crouch titled "Through It All." The first half of the second verse goes like this:

I thank God for the mountains and I thank Him for the valleys,
I thank Him for the storms He brought me through.
Chorus:
Through it all, through it all, Oh, I've learned to trust in Jesus,
I've learned to trust in God.
Through it all, through it all, I've learned to depend upon His Word.

My having ridden through fourteen hours of a life-threatening monsoon storm gave special meaning to this song. Additionally, I can identify with the following verses from Psalm 107:23–31:

Others went out on the sea in ships;
they were merchants on the mighty waters.
They saw the mighty works of the Lord,
his wonderful deeds in the deep.
For he spoke and stirred up a tempest
that lifted high the waves.
They mounted up to the heavens and went down to the depths;
in their peril their courage melted away.
They reeled and staggered like drunken men;
they were at their wits' end.
They cried out to the Lord in their trouble,
and he brought them out of their distress.
He stilled the storm to a whisper;
the waves of the sea were hushed.
They were glad when it grew calm,
and he guided them to their desired haven.
Let them give thanks to the Lord for his unfailing love
and his wonderful deeds for men.

During the long hard transit, anything that had not been tied down or put into a locker was strewn across the main deck. One of our communications radios that had been bolted to the shelf was ripped off. The ammo box that houses all the mortar rounds had ripped completely off the deck of the other Swift Boat that was traveling with us. The Coast Guard *Point Marone* had little difficulty with the trip as it was much larger than our Swift Boats. Evidently, they trailed us and kept track of us like a mother hen.

CHAPTER 5

CHAU DOC & BINH THUY

Binh Thuy and Chau Duc

The crew of PCF 63 with cases of ammunition required to re-arm (author and OIC not in picture)

After our harrowing experience battling a monsoon storm, we spent a few days in Cat Lo resting up and getting the boat back into shape. Of course after each day's work, we would catch a Lambretta taxi for the approximate five- or six-mile ride into Vung Tau. Vung Tau had been a French resort area during the colonization period. Many of the buildings showed the influence of French design. It had beautiful beaches and was also used as an in country R & R center. R & R was the acronym for "rest and relaxation." The draw for servicemen was the bars and the women. No need to expand on that subject.

On December 5, we made the transit from Cat Lo back to Binh Thuy. We stopped at the naval facility in My Tho on the Mekong River to refuel before continuing on to Binh Thuy on the Bassac River.

My letter on December 6 contains the one topic that is common in almost every one of my letters: talking about mail—whether I had gotten mail or not, who wrote, who did not, where to send future mail as I moved about the Delta and, on occasion, a request for certain items I could not get in Vietnam.

The letter continues:

> *Right now we are on our way out on patrol. I think we are going to be standing by for a MedCap team. This is a group of medical people who go into the villages and give aid to all the people. We stand by to protect them and get them out in case of enemy attack.*
>
> *On the river we can do just about as we please as long as we do our job. Take now for instance, I'm laying in my rack writing this letter in a pair of dungaree shorts, stocking feet, green t-shirt and wearing my Christmas hat. Like last night on our way to Binh Thuy we were eating popcorn and drinking beer. That's one thing I like about this duty, they eliminate the picayune military bullshit. Just do your job and do it right. Like right now I've got a mustache and long sideburns. Who's gonna come out on this river and tell me to shave them off? Nobody else wants to be out here!*
> (Dec. 6, 1969)

***

Well here we go again. We're on our way to patrol at the Cambodian border. We're supposed to be there a week, but it will probably be longer. I had Steve draw a map of the Mekong Delta so you can see basically where I am. Chou Duc is where we are headed now. It is a province next to the Cambodian border.
318 days to go.
(Letter, Dec. 13, 1969)

Boy this Cambodian border patrol is great. We are on 3 days and off 1 day. But when we're on, all we do is sit anchored in the middle of the river. We get up anytime from 8 to 9 in the morning, eat breakfast around 11 we find some excuse to go to the support ship [YRBM] *down river. We spend a few hours there, come back to our patrol area, anchor, and go swimming for a couple hours. Eat dinner, sit around and read. And hit the rack around 9 or 10 o'clock. Of course one of us has to be on watch night and day. But compared to what we have been doing, this is a real vacation.*

Christmas tree on the radar mast

I've got Aunt Mae's Christmas tree [that she mailed to me] *mounted on top of the radar mast, which is the very top of the boat...*

I'm glad to hear that Danny is home safe and sound. [Danny is Dan Breese a high school buddy and saxophonist from our rock'n'roll days in our group "the Stags." Dan served as an Army MP escorting convoys up north near the DMZ.]

Searching a motorized junk

On the right is our crew's Vietnamese trainee checking a junk.

Note the .38 caliber pistol sticking out of his holster on his right hip. At the rear of the junk the operator adds fuel to his engine. This engine is about a 10 HP Briggs & Stratton mounted on a pivoting base and fitted with a long shaft allowing the small prop to be raised and lowered into the water. Most of the engines found on sampans had a label on them with the words *Helping Hands* and I think *US* also.

These engines were provided to the Vietnamese through a US Helping Hands program, much like buying a house. The recipient agreed to pay a given amount at agreed upon intervals.

We were deployed to the Chau Duc area to check water traffic for infiltration of enemy personnel or supplies across the border from Cambodia into South Vietnam. We did not stop and search every vessel. The larger ones were better able to hide contraband, so we concentrated on them most. We could also tell if a vessel seemed to be avoiding us. Searches were relatively simple unless the vessel had a lot of cargo. If there were floorboards, they were lifted to check underneath. Each passenger had to provide proper identification. If a person was at all suspicious, we would bring that person onto our fantail to search them.

We were taught in NIOTC how to forcefully do a body search on a detainee as if he might turn and attack us at any point. This search entailed having the detainee stand with legs spread wide and body leaning way forward with hands on a railing or wall stretched way out. If the person to be searched failed to position his body as instructed, we kicked his feet into the position we wanted them. In this position, if the detainee offered any resistance, it was an easy push to drop him flat.

Our search procedure required a full-body frisking—not a pat-down but squeezing the entire length of each extremity and rubbing the entire trunk front and back, including the crotch and butt crack. Our instructors had never said anything about being gentle. In most cases, the persons we searched did not need to be treated in this manner. To start with, they were usually humble terrified civilians wearing only two pieces of clothing—a lightweight, loose-fitting, button-up short-sleeved shirt with one pocket and a pair of lightweight shorts. They either wore no shoes or wore sandals. I started off my first body search in Vietnam as taught and was quickly ordered by my officer to ease up.

Searching junk of Buddhist monks dressed in bright-orange robes

While deployed at Chau Duc, our support base was a YRBM. YRBM stands for Yard Repair Berthing and Messing. For those not familiar with the Navy's terms, *yard repair* refers to repairs normally done at a Navy yard, *berthing* means a place to sleep, and *messing* means a place to prepare and serve meals. YRBMs are not self-propelled. They are basically large barges that look like repair ships and are towed to a strategic location and anchored. When I was there, YRBM 20 was anchored in the Bassac River and YRBM 21 was anchored in the Mekong River. Each was located a few miles from the border.

The YRBMs supplied us with food, fuel, ammunition, and some repairs. As we were only there on a temporary basis they did not provide berthing so we slept on our boat. Our boat had become our home, and we were more at home in it as opposed to sleeping in a strange place shared by others. The YRBM also served as the forward command center for all the riverine craft operating in the area. At any given time, a collage of various types of boats were tied up alongside the YRBM, resembling a mother hen tending her multisized chicks.

At this location on the west side of the country, the Mekong and Bassac Rivers are very close to each other, and there is a canal that connects the two rivers, so we could quickly go from one river to another by means of this interconnecting canal. There was a very strong whirlpool or eddy at the confluence of the canal and the rivers, which had to be navigated with caution.

Floating Shell gas station in the Bassac River across from the town

Floating Esso gas station. The small engines mounted on the back of the sampans and junks had very little fuel capacity. The gas

stations had fifty-five-gallon drums to refuel these vessels when they came alongside.

This view of the city of Chau Duc from the Bassac River shows a triple level of living structures. The structures to the rear of this picture are built on the ground. The buildings on the bank are built on stilts to protect them from high water levels during the regular flood times. Right on the water are floating homes, and next to them are junks and sampans. This is one those heavily populated areas where we absolutely could not return fire unless we were in severe danger of losing personnel or the boat. Enemy contact at this location was extremely unlikely, and if it happened at all, it would only be sniper fire, which would not justify killing or wounding large numbers of noncombatants. I cannot speak for the actions of every Vietnam veteran, but I can speak of our understanding of and adherence to the rules of engagement. We fully understood the lethal capabilities that were in our hands. I enjoyed firing machine guns. I got a kick out of seeing the rounds tear things up. But neither I nor anyone of my crew members ever knowingly fired on noncombatants. If we were attacked and in immediate danger, we returned fire. During my service, an attack never occurred in a populated area where we would cause collateral damage.

There were areas where we had to obtain the permission of the local province chief to open fire if not in immediate danger. This caused a delay in responding to enemy contact as radio communications did not always get accomplished in a timely manner.

Stories of careless control of firepower and the resulting civilian casualties blackened the eye of everyone who served in Vietnam. Those types of stories were grossly contorted and never put into proper perspective. I once heard it said that the news only reports on the house that burned in a given city but says nothing about the tens of thousands of homes that did not burn. The point is the burning house is news, and the ones that did not burn are not news. Likewise, thousands of combat operations were carried out with disciplined control of firepower. They were not news. The heartbreaking mistakes, accidents, or outright carelessness were news; but unfortunately, they gave the public a distorted idea of how American fighting men conducted themselves.

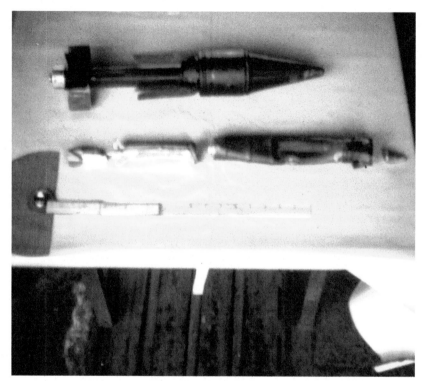

Undetonated B40 RPG rocket at top (retrieved from inside a damaged Swift Boat). Below are the pieces of a detonated rocket next to a scale.

On one occasion, later in December when we were back operating out of Binh Thuy, a B40 rocket (a type of the Russian-made RPG rocket–propelled grenade) was fired at us from the tree line at the river's edge. It was the first time I had been directly shot at. It was the first time I had seen a B40 rocket coming at me. What really impressed me about this rocket and others I would see in the months to come was the rate at which it accelerated. To say it "traveled fast" is not enough to accurately explain it. It kept going faster and faster the farther it traveled. I was able to witness this speed and acceleration in addition to the distance it could travel as the rocket was fired from a distance of about 120 yards and cleared the pilot house by about three to five feet. The rocket had a whooshing, whistling sound as it traveled and left a white smoke trail. Was it cause for alarm and excitement? Absolutely!

We returned fire briefly, beached at a safe distance away and mortared the area of the attack. Our officer called for air support. The planes came and fired rockets, etc. Then we made a firing run on the area of the attack. We requested permission of the province chief to insert the troops to sweep the area to assess the damage, but for some unknown reason, the province chief would not give his permission.

For most of us on the crew, it was our first time being shot at and returning fire, and we had earned our "combat action ribbon"!

One day while on the border patrol a small raft came floating down river. We could see a Viet Cong flag on the raft and a few other unidentifiable items. Wisely fearing that the flag was there to lure us souvenir-hunting Americans, we attempted to determine if explosives were attached by firing a grenade at it.

Getting no secondary explosions but still not discounting the possibility of a booby-trapped explosive being connected under the float,[8] a new plan was devised. We took the tow lines from both Swift Boats and tied the lines together. The line was fed out as the two boats carefully separated and spread out from each other.

---

[8] The first Swift Boat lost in Vietnam was sunk when a mine was detonated as the crew attempted to take a Viet Cong flag as a souvenir. Four men were killed and two were wounded. *Brown Water, Black Beret* page 370.

A detailed account of the incident can be found in the Swift Boat Crew Directory at Swiftvets.net

Once the line was drawn tight, the two boats gradually strad-dled the raft, each keeping a safe distance. The line caught the raft and flipped it over as was the plan. After securing the tow lines, we carefully approached the overturned raft to inspect the underside. Determining it to be safe, we retrieved the VC flag and a bundle of Viet Cong propaganda pamphlets.

Souvenir Viet Cong flag we recovered from the raft

Well, I thought of something I really need for you to send me. I brought a can of spray stuff to VN. for athletes foot and its almost empty. The name of the stuff is ATHA-SPRAY…Please send 2 or 3 cans. I can get medication for athletes feet but this stuff works much better. Also please send a whole bunch of Kool-Aid and Ice Tea mix.

Skin irritation was a big problem in Vietnam given the heat and humidity and our limited opportunities to get to showers. Nursing athletes foot and crotch rot was a constant battle. Despite several trips to the sick bay when we were near one, Steve could not get rid of a severe case of crotch rot. Logic told us that if Atha spray worked really well on athlete's foot, then it should also work well on crotch rot. Now the spray did burn a little when applied to the red cracked spaces between the toes, but we failed to accurately calculate the sensitivity level of the crotch area when deciding to apply the miracle cure to private areas. So Steve dropped his drawers and sat back spread-eagled on the rack; careful aim was taken on the red raw target areas, and like firing our machine guns, one of us opened fire. *Fire* now became the message instantly sent from the nerve endings of Steve's crotch to his brain centers and vocal chords. No doubt somewhere in the jungle the VC heard his screams and suspected us Americans of torturing one of their comrades. We were correct about our premise! The painful experiment was successful, and in a couple days, Steve's skin irritation started to heal.

Another day while we were anchored watching water traffic near the border, another Swift Boat approached us. I did not recognize the hull number as being one of the boats operating from Coastal Division 13. They came abreast of our boat close enough for Lieutenant Burke and the skipper of the other boat to yell back and forth. I did not know any of the crew on the other boat, and they looked strangely different. It was something about their faces aside from the dark tans from hours of sun exposure. It was the eyes and the facial expressions. More accurately, the lack of facial expression and eyes that looked like they were seeing us but gazing far away. I came to know this as the "thousand-yard stare." The stare was developed from hours and hours upon day after day of intently studying the riverbanks to catch that first muzzle flash, puff of smoke, or rocket launch so the enemy's location could be quickly determined so one knew where to direct his firepower. Evenings were not different for the eyes. While on night ambushes, our eyes searched the darkness for any motion that might be that of the enemy. I believe the lack of facial expression was the result of emotions that had been suppressed so tightly that the face ceased to show emotions. This is not to say that they never smiled or frowned, but smiles and frowns were the exception not the norm.

It turned out that this crew and boat had just made the journey up a river and through a system of canals from Ha Tien on the Gulf of Siam to our location in Chau Duc. They had spent many months in Coastal Division 11, and their appearance showed the signs of how difficult it had been. I still had that experience ahead of me.

Emotions

After submitting the first part of my book to my gracious volunteer editor, she advised me that I should tell more of the emotions. That drew a blank for a while. I thought that I had told some of the emotions. I guess the first part of the problem for me recalling emotions is that I am a man. Emotions take a backseat to logic and function and a number of other things. Secondly, life's bad experiences forced me to shove emotions aside or turn them off to get through tough times. Finally, finding more emotions than I had already written about was a task I did not know how to begin.

Eventually I discovered that past emotions are best found when I wake up at two or three in the morning and cannot get back to sleep. Then as I think back over what I have written or have yet to write, some emotions are recalled like items hidden in an old black box. A mysterious black box that I cannot see the bottom of, but it's scary to think what I might find in there. I cannot just reach in and get them, but they might come out if I set the stage.

There are other emotions that I have a difficult time keeping in the box. There are random times on certain topics when tears come. Sometimes the tears are quite unexpected, and take me by surprise. I find the tears embarrassing. I don't want them. It is frustrating to me when I try to stop it from happening and I cannot. I have wrestled just to state here those topics that at times will hit me hard. The sensitive topics usually relate to patriotism, heroism, lives lost in combat, and the resulting effects upon widows and children of service men that died in combat. These topics cause sadness. One day I can handle the news of these topics matter-of-factly, and the next day I will be struck with sadness or even tears. Discussion of the price paid in Vietnam only for the effort to be abandoned is also a topic that triggers emotions ranging from anger to tears to disgrace.

After our week in Chau Duc, we returned to Binh Thuy and joined back into the rotation of patrols and operations with the other riverine craft at that location.

Small village in canal south of Binh Thuy

Swift Boats in the canal cause the villagers to stare

Vietnamese irregular forces aboard our boat stare back. Note the hooches on stilts and sampans high on muddy banks indicating low tide.

Homes on stilts in flood season

Village children waiting for candy and snacks

Christmas Eve on the Bassac River was colorful. There were small outposts every so many miles along the river, usually near a small village. On Christmas Eve, it seems that many of the outposts celebrated by firing tracers into the sky. The tracers burn red as they fly through the sky. Radio procedures and etiquette were largely ignored as men sent Christmas wishes and clowned around.

On Christmas Day, as the rest of the world had a holiday and the day off with a big Christmas dinner, we sat in the middle of the river eating turkey loaf. Turkey loaf—yuck!

> *I'm fine, I hope everyone's O.K...*
>
> *I am finding it very difficult to right* [sic] *lately. It's hard to find time to stop and concentrate just on writing and there really isn't a whole lot to right* [sic] *about sometimes...*
>
> *Right now we are anchored in the middle of the Bassac River preparing our turkey loaf dinner...*
>
> *306 days to go*

(Letter, December 25, 1969)

Chieu Hoi (pronounced *chew hoy*) was a program that encouraged the enemy to surrender and come over to our side. Pamphlets delivered in a number of manners communicated to the enemy the details of how he would be treated and served as a note for safe passage. Many of those who came over to our side were retrained and then served as what was known as Kit Carson scouts assisting the South Vietnamese in locating and fighting the enemy.

On Christmas Day as we sat anchored in the river, a sampan approached with a man in it. When he came alongside, he spoke to our Vietnamese trainee in their language that he wanted to surrender. When the translation was passed on to us, the man handed his weapons up to us and surrendered. We searched him and listened to his story as relayed to us by our trainee. This man was tired of living in the jungle with little to eat and wanted to take advantage of the benefits promised in the propaganda. We radioed in the reception of our surprise Christmas gift and transferred him back to the base for processing.

Well, boy have things been happening around here lately. On Christmas night we got a radio message to return to Cat Lo for reassignment to Cos Div 11 in An Thoi. Needless to say we were somewhat less than happy to here [sic] *that. An Thoi is the division that has the most action and casualties.[9] We went to Binh Thuy and refueled and stayed the night. The next day we returned to Cat Lo. When we arrived the word was that we were definitely going to An Thoi but not with our boat...*

[When you live and fight on and take care of a boat for two months, an attachment develops along with pride of ownership even if we did not "own" it.]

Another crew has taken over the 63 boat. Neil (Hirsch) has been transferred to the 74 boat. (Instead of saying PCF

[9.]   Costal Division 11 An Thoi awarded 163 Purple Hearts from late 1968 to early 1969. Hill, Lt.Bill, "Swift Boat Sailors Made Naval History", *Pacific Stars & Stripes, [Saturday December 5, 1970]* page 30. print

74 or PCF 63, we say the 74 boat etc.) Mr. Burke is going to An Thoi with the Da Nang crew. Steve (Johnson), Bill (Hogan), John (Bullwark) and I will probably be split among the other boats here in Cat Lo. I sure would like to stay with Steve as he and I have become real good friends.

There must be something really big going on in An Thoi because they've taken 12 boats and 14 crews from the other divisions and sent them to An Thoi. I think they are going to put a big push on the U-minh (spelling???) forest. It is the oldest, biggest and strongest VC stronghold in South Vietnam. Also we've been putting a big push on Dung Island lately and we're gonna push a whole lot more.

Before my year in Vietnam is finished, I'll probably have to go [sic] An Thoi, put (sic) better later than sooner. Maybe things will cool down before I have to go.

They took Steve's .30 caliber machine guns away from him because they are unauthorized equipment on a Swift Boat. We tried everything to keep them, including hiding them on another boat, but we had to give them back. It was a real shame, because they were Steve's pride and joy. He has had them for 6 months and was attached to them. He was madder than a wet hen and really hurt too. Besides all this, they are better protection than 1 M-60 machine gun on the bow of the boat. I say "protection" because fire-power is your only protection on an aluminum boat. And also we were the only boat in the division with twin .30's on it.

(Letter, Dec. 28, 1969)

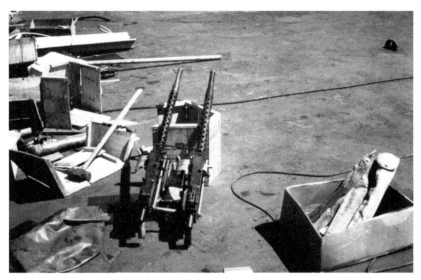

Twin .30 caliber machine guns

]

Well, Guess what? Things are switched around again. Mr. Burke, Hogan and I are going to An Thoi with 3 of the guys from the Da Nang crew. We'll be leaving here tomorrow morning…Don't worry about An Thoi, things are never as bad as people make them out to be. I am not worried about going there at all. Steve is staying here, but I'll probably see him again, because of the way Swift Boats get around the countryside. He still may get transferred there yet.

An Thoi is where they have "Sea Float" which is in one of the articles I sent you, I think…Soon there won't be much of this country I haven't seen.

I sent $200 home this morning. Set 30 or 40 aside for Georgie's [guitar] *lessons and take what you need and bank the rest.*

(Letter, Dec. 29, 1969)

S&S Photos and Story
By JOC Jim Falk

ON THE CUA LON RIVER, Vietnam—Just over a year ago fast patrol craft (Swift boats) of the U.S. Naval Forces in Vietnam made their entrance into river warfare with a blazing sortie through enemy-controlled waterways flowing into the Gulf of Thailand.

It was quite a change from their usual task of seeking out Communist infiltrators on the open sea with Operation Market Time.

And it marked the first time in three years in the combat zone that the 50-foot aluminum-hulled craft had ventured into the more restricted narrow waterways.

Today the Swift boats are still patrolling the southern portion of Vietnam's rice-rich delta with Operation Sea Lords.

The mode of operation has changed greatly from those first missions of ripping through uncharted areas to virtually shoot up everything in sight.

Charlie has been driven further back into the woodwork and forced to ply his trades of murder, extortion and terror in a less open manner.

With the Swift boats have come psychological operations teams, a unique floating support base called Sea Float, Navy Seals and tough Montagnard troopers to establish a government presence where none existed before.

And with the relative security brought by these forces, the Swift boats have switched to carrying psyops teams to points along the waterways in the southern tip of Vietnam where they set up check points, making contact with local residents to pass the government word and gain intelligence on the enemy.

This often brings information on where Charlie is collecting "taxes" and where he might be building up his strength.

When enemy presence is confirmed, the fast, sturdy little craft load up with reaction forces and head for the suspected area, ready to rip through the waterways again with their arsenals blazing.

The article that I sent home was published on November 18, 1969 in the military's Stars & Stripes newspaper and written by JOC Jim Falk

119

CHAPTER 6

AN THOI – COASTAL DIVISION 11

Travel from Cat Lo to An Thoi again was done with a handful of copies of my orders that served in place of a ticket for transportation, whether the transportation was a plane, helicopter, truck, or jeep. Again, to get anywhere in the Delta required a flight to Ton Son Nhut air base, located next to Saigon, and then transferring to a plane headed to our destination.

When I landed at Ton Son Nhut air base, I set out to locate my cousin's husband who was stationed there. As I walked across the base, I was amazed. This base had sidewalks, paved roads, green grass, movie theaters, clubs, and by all appearances could have been mistaken for a base back in the States. Stationed at most street intersections was an AP (Air Patrol—the Air Forces equivalent of the Army's MP, military police) dressed in clean pressed green fatigues. After two months on the rivers, my style of dress was not up to the standards of the spit and polish of this oasis in the middle of a war zone. I was wearing my grubby tailored "tiger" greens I had bought in Vung Tau, no "cover" (hat), and had a Ka-Bar knife strapped on my hip. I was stopped at nearly every corner and asked where my cover was, told I could not have a knife, and then asked what unit I was attached to. As they had no idea who, what, or where Coastal

Squadron One or Coastal Division 11 was, they therefore did not know to whom to report me. After receiving a bit of scolding about my being "out of uniform," I was on my way again marveling at the amenities that these guys had in comparison to the life I was living out in the boonies.

Finally, I located my in-law sitting behind a typewriter in an air-conditioned office. A short walk took us to the rather modest building where he lived with a small number of other airmen. He had a mama san that cleaned for him and did his laundry. We went to a nearby club that evening for a steak dinner with baked potato and were entertained by a Filipino band that did a fairly good rendition of American rock 'n' roll albeit with a bit of an accent. I spent the night in his hooch and was on my way in the morning to catch my flight to An Thoi. Months later, when my cousin's husband returned home, he received a Bronze Star. It was unbelievable to me. How on earth could a guy sitting in an air-conditioned office on a base with all the amenities get a Bronze Star? Allegedly, it was for how well he had typed up the reports. Give me a break. Men are living in the filth and heat with the bare necessities of life, risking their lives on the waterways and in the jungles, and he gets a Bronze Star! Just unbelievable.

Well, I've made it to An Thoi O.K. I had my doubts at times. I don't mind flying at home on big airliners, but flying around Viet Nam on troop transport planes, I don't like. We had a little trouble landing, the air currents over the island gave the pilot a lot of difficulty the first time we tried to land, so at the last minute he decided to bring the plane up and try it again. That's kind of shocking when there's a mountain ahead of the plane. The second time was a little rough, but we made it okay.

The flight from Ton Son Nhut air base on a C123 transport plane to Phu Quoc Island was routine until the landing. There was no normal seating on the plane. We sat on a cargo net suspended from the bulkhead and attached to a lateral pipe about eighteen inches from the wall and the floor forming something like a very wide-webbed lawn-chair-type bench. My "seat" was near a window that was missing its glass. Just outside and slightly above the hole where the glass used to be was the starboard (right) engine hanging beneath the wing. Every change of engine speed or workload was right there next to me along with whatever contortions of the wing that might occur. Hey, but the open window provided nice air circulation!

The airstrip on Phu Quoc Island is located between two mountains. One mountain was situated at either end of the airstrip. I sure wish they could have laid out the airstrip in a different location because between two mountains, there is strong air turbulence. Worse yet, in order to clear the first mountain and then get low enough to land required the pilot to drop quickly after clearing the first mountain. This dropped us right into the turbulence. The plane proceeded to bounce around like on a carnival ride. The challenge now for the pilot was to keep the plane stable enough to touch down without the plane tilting left or right, or having its nose too high or low.

On his first landing attempt, he could not get his aircraft stable enough—and that meant guess what? What is fast approaching at the other end of the airstrip? The other mountain! At the last second, he decided to abort the landing. As he put the power back on and pulled back the controls to climb, the engine just outside the window strained for all it was worth. Now shaking and vibrating were added to the bouncing up and down and left and right. I had already resolved myself to the possibility that I might die in combat, but I had not thought about being killed in a plane crash. I figured that if we crashed, my body would be strained through this cargo net like dough through a pasta maker.

We cleared the second mountain and circled around for another attempt at getting onto the ground in one piece. Once again as we dropped down over the first mountain like we were on the carnival ride. It became a struggle between pilot and nature. As the ground grew closer, it seemed that all at once, the pilot must have decided that it's now or never. He dropped us out of the air in a manner that felt closer to a crash than a landing. As we bounced and sped down the temporary airstrip, the pilot reversed the engines, attempting to slow and stop before running into mountain number 2. Once again, the deafening roar of the straining engine just outside the missing window and the contortions of the wing materialized. Finally, we slowed down and rattled across the metal mats that formed the temporary airstrip and taxied into place. Ah land! Sweet, sweet land. The sea had given me cause to love the land, and now the air had doubled that love. When the motion stopped and the engines wound down, the fear dissipated, and there was peace and relief.

Things around the air strip in An Thoi looked pretty barren and remote. Later on, I learned that there were over twenty thousand North Vietnamese and Viet Cong POWs imprisoned on the island. The notoriously barbaric "tiger cages" were used to torture prisoners. The tiger cages were constructed of barbed wire and just large enough for a man to fit inside. Once inside, any sudden movement would cause the prisoner to be jabbed by the barbed wire. Responsibility and guilt for the construction and design of the tiger cages can be placed upon the French in the 1940s, but the South Vietnamese carry the blame for the extensive use of them during the Vietnam War.

The media has made a loud outcry about the United States' mistreatment of prisoners detained in the Abu Graib detention center, and well, it did need to be decried, but I think it pales in the face of the long horrible tortures inflicted by the peoples of Southeast Asia on one another and on our US servicemen. Additionally, the waterboarding of terrorist detainees at Guantanamo Bay has come up numerous times in the news and has been a debate within our government. Overall the living conditions, food, and medical care at Gitmo make it look like a resort compared to the conditions endured by so many in Southeast Asia.

The awful things that mankind will do to each other is hard to grasp and even harder to stomach. Yet Vietnam was no different than all of human history. The United States is no exception. If one delves into the military prisons of the Revolutionary and Civil Wars of our country, there are numerous accounts of horrible conditions and torture leading to thousands dying of starvation and disease. Consider the millions tortured, used as human experiments, and put to death in the ovens under the Nazi regime. Consider the atrocities now going on in Syria and several nations in Africa, and one can see that the human race has not advanced much. These are just a few of the millions of atrocities mankind has committed. Watch the television news and it is filled everyday with shootings and other acts of violence we commit. No wonder that those of us of the Christian faith proclaim, "Come, Lord Jesus, Come."

In the scriptures, the prophet Jeremiah laments over God's people failing to obey the Lord and delivers these words from God, "The heart (of man) is deceitful above all things and beyond cure. Who can understand it?"[10] None of us likes to hear the words of the prophet, but all too often they are true. Lofty as our evaluations of ourselves may be, how do we know for sure in what manner we would act in the conditions of war with the knowledge of friends or loved ones lost to the struggle? How far would any of us go to attempt to extract information that would save a fellow countryman, friend, or family member? Would we begin with lofty excuses for our actions and then become callous? It is easy to think better of ourselves, but do we really know? War can sometimes grind away on our spirit and erode our morality.

From the air strip in An Thoi it was a short walk to the admiral's barge that would transport us to Coastal Division 11's floating base anchored in the Gulf of Siam a few miles south of Phu Quoc Island. Coastal Division 11 really did not have a conventional base. The division was based in the barracks ship APL 21 affectionately called the Apple and the repair ship USS *Tutuila* ARG-4. AMMI pontoons were tied alongside the repair ship. On the pontoons were cradles to set boats on when they were lifted out of the water for repairs.

---

[10]   Jeremiah 17:9 Life Application Bible

It was a short boat ride to my new duty station. Soon I could see the repair ship in the distance, and as we approached, I could see a Swift Boat out of the water sitting in a cradle for damage repair. When we got up close to the several Swift Boats tied up alongside, I could see that the level of combat action in CosDiv11 must be true. Many boats had plywood where main cabin windows had been blown out. Every boat had square or rectangular patches welded on the hull— evidence of the damage received when the enemy's rocket propelled grenades found their mark. What was in store for me in the coming months?

Most of CosDiv11's boats were deployed to two ATSBs (Advance Tactical Support Base) at distant locations. One was located at the mouth of the Giang Thanh River next to the town of Ha Tien which is located at the top of the Gulf of Siam. The other ATSB was the notorious Seafloat anchored in the middle of the Cua Lon River about four or five hours southeast in the very southern tip of the Ca Mau Peninsula.

> *The setup here is sorta* [sic] *complicated to explain from what I know of it so far. An Thoi is on the island. We stay on the APL which is about a mile from the island.*

This is really a desolate area, but very pretty. Seafloat is in the middle of one of the rivers on the tip of Vietnam. We operate out of Seafloat for 2 weeks to a month. We also patrol the coast and the border here...

It's twelve midnight. They just blew a siren and shot off about 20 flares. Big celebration, Huh!

Happy New Year!

Love, Charles

(Dec. 31,1969)

***

Well we got a boat yesterday. The 40 boat. It's in a little better shape than the 63 boat was when we got it, engineering wise anyhow. Otherwise its not exactly in great shape. We worked on it all day today. Tomorrow we're going out and test fire the guns and make sure it runs okay and everything works. So far the crew seems to be getting along real well with each other.

Time will tell...

Crew of PCF 40 January 1969

Klaus Loquasto QM2, PA; Jesse Church RD3, Wyoming; Bill Hogan RD2, NY; Jack Burke LTJG; Tony Amoruso GMG3, NY; Charles Hunt EN3, NJ.

I'm not sure, but I think it will be a good crew. [And it was a good crew]

Jesse got shot in the back in DaNang. Anybody that's been shot and still has his wits together in a river, should be a good man. Hogan and Loquasto are two I'm not sure of. Amuroso is nicknamed Ammo...

Cos Div 11 is due to be turned over to the V.N.'s on either June 1st or July 1st. I hope I get out of here by then. I don't want to stay here as an advisor. I don't trust the VN's enough to ride rivers with them.

(Letter, Jan. 5, 1970)

Seafloat

I suppose that over the course of the United States Military history, there have been an unknown number of operations or logistics that few people have ever heard about, nor will the history books mention. Some of these operations are more unbelievable than fiction. The daring of the planners to conceive they could even be successful would border on lunacy. Compared to the number of Americans involved in a given conflict, only a few ever operated in these little-known places, yet the danger faced, the courage displayed, and the heroics performed challenges the stuff of legends and action movies.

Slightly more than three thousand American sailors served on Swift Boats during the Vietnam War. During the early years of the war, Swift Boats only patrolled the coast so probably only about half of Swift Boat sailors ever operated in the rivers and canals.[11] Seafloat was only a US operation for slightly more than a year starting in

---

[11.] "November 5, 1968, the Navy formally approved river patrols for Swift Boats." *Swift Boats at War In Vietnam p. 127*

June 1969 until it was turned over to the South Vietnamese in 1970. So the number of Swift Boat sailors that experienced this unique slice of combat history in this sometimes apocalypse-like setting may number somewhere around three hundred.

The name Seafloat is somewhat misleading as the only time it floated at sea was as it was being towed through the South China Sea southward along the coast of South Vietnam on its way to its eventual midriver anchorage smack-dab in the middle of enemy-controlled territory in the Ca Mau peninsula. But to those sent to operate in the remote rivers and canals of the Ca Mau, the name *Seafloat* had a very ominous meaning. Rather than the relative safety of a coastal patrol in open water or the routine boarding and searching of water traffic on the larger rivers, *Seafloat* meant regularly going into the enemy's backyard and running various types of special operations. I doubt that the higher-ups ever thought they could totally remove the Viet Cong and NVA from every nook and cranny of the Ca Mau. Their goal was to inhibit the enemy's ability to transport men and munitions, and prevent the enemy from collecting taxes and goods from the few local civilians. Being at Seafloat also meant depending on a highly vulnerable base located far away from any major military assets that could assist quickly in a time of attack. In other words, Seafloat was out in "Injun country."

In Thomas Cutler's book, *Brown Water, Black Berets*, Admiral Elmo Zumwalt, Chief of Naval Operations, is quoted with this description of the Ca Mau penisula where Seafloat was situated:

> *A place of streams and mangrove swamps, hard to get to and even harder to get into, at the extreme southern tip of Vietnam. For years the Viet Cong had been using the peninsula as a sort of surge tank, taking sanctuary there when our forces in the neighboring areas of the delta had the upper hand and sallying forth when the fortunes of war shifted. The U.S. command had regarded the peninsula as so irremediably enemy country that it had evacuated as many of the inhabitants as possible and then bombed it with B-52s.*

My fellow Swift vet Weymouth D. Symmes authored his chronicle of the battle for the Mekong Delta in 2004. In *War on the Rivers,* he describes the Ca Mau Peninsula this way:

> *Within the Ca Mau Peninsula were great waterways slithering through the dense mangrove swamps. One entered the Ca Mau with a sense of foreboding, to be swallowed up by the sluggish brown rivers and lush green of the jungle, engulfed with a helpless sense of the remoteness of the area.*
>
> *It was desolate and deserted by the people who had lived there before. A few still scratched out an existence by fishing or cutting wood, but they were often pressed into service by the Viet Cong, who made the villagers feed them, provide their troops and build bunkers from which the enemy assaulted boats. In the early 1960s the enemy had driven the Vietnamese Navy from the Ca Mau, and had destroyed the region's capital, Nam Can.*
>
> *To the west was the U Minh forest…an almost impenetrable jungle, where in 1952, 500 French paratroopers dropped into the area and were never heard from again. Farther to the west was the Rach Giang Thanh Canal, which skirted the border between South Vietnam and Cambodia.*
>
> *Prior to 1968 the enemy virtually had its way in the U Minh forest.*

Weymouth goes on to describe the details and results of a number of the initial forays into this area and concludes with this description of the enemy stepped up tactics:

> *By the end of 1968 the enemy had begun moving heavier weapons and better-trained forces into the area and changed their tactics by concentrating their fire from one bunkered position before escaping into the mangrove or bush. Generally ambushes came from river bends or along narrow canals where PCF maneuverability was limited.*

Rocket attacks became more numerous and accurate. In addition, the VC began mining rivers and constructing barricades. To counteract this, Swifts began night ambushes and inserting SEALS and Special Forces.

Seafloat courtesy of John Yeoman

***

Well, on the 7th we left An Thoi for Sea Float which is in the middle of the Cua Lon River. SeaFloat is a complex of 13 plontoons [sic] which support about 15 Swift Boats, 1 zippo (which is a boat which shoots flames) 2 monitors (another type of river boat which is heavily armored) and 3 helicopters. There are about 120 VN troops in an outpost next to us on the beach. There are 2 seal detachments here also. (Seals are Navy special forces, like the Army's Green Beret, but much better.) Other than that there is no one else around here, except the V.C. The Army and Marines gave up on the area because of the terrain.

Yesterday we escorted the Division Commander up the river. Today we escorted a tug boat out to the ocean.
(Letter, Jan. 8, 1970)

Tugboat towing a housing barge in for RMK-BRJ construction workers that were building a permanent base for the Vietnamese Navy next to Seafloat.

PCFs always operated in at least pairs. Some operations were done with more than two Swift Boats, but as a rule, we always operated with two boats. The officer with the highest rank and time in grade would be the Officer in Charge (OinC) of the operation for the two or more boats. This meant that we always had a cover boat. The only time we separated was on night ambushes. Even then, we were not too far apart, and we knew we had another boat with us. At times, a lone boat would make a coastal transit as there was little chance of enemy contact off the coast.

One of our regular tasks was to escort tugboats in and out of the river to and from our location. The tugboats towed barges in with supplies for us and for the land base, being build next to Seafloat. Top speed for the tugboats was about eight knots at best, which made for a slow, boring ride in the oppressive heat. If it was monsoon season, it rained on and off during the trip. One minute I would be putting a poncho on and trying to keep my ammunition covered up, and the next minute the rain would stop and the humidity would be like a sauna. For a number of months, I was under the mistaken belief that the enemy would not ambush us when it was raining, but eventually, they proved that theory incorrect. Likewise, for many months, I thought they would never ambush us from a defoliated section of the riverbank, but eventually, we were ambushed from a low-built bunker that was hard to see in the remains of a mangrove forest.

When escorting a tug or any other craft, one Swift would lead the way and one would follow with the tug and its tow in between the two Swifts. This provided the best ability to protect the tug boat and its crew. When ambushed, we were not able to use our speed to exit the ambush. Our job was to protect the tug, but we used our speed to make ourselves a little more difficult target to hit. When shots were fired, the two boats commenced a circling action around the slow-moving tug and its tow. The trailing Swift would open fire and go to high speed as it was positioned between the tug and the ambush site. At the same time, the lead boat would make a high-speed turn heading back to the rear of the tug on the side opposite the ambush site and then make a second high-speed turn to move into position between the tug and the ambush site, keeping machinegun fire concentrated on the enemy position while the other Swift duplicated the same circling action.

On one of our tug escorts in January, I do not remember which one, we were returning from escorting a tug from the construction site back out to the coast when an enemy rocket was fired at our cover boat. The rocket missed, and there were no further rounds fired at either boat. We mortared the area that the rocket came from, radioed in the action, and continued on our way.

Well on the 10th we escorted another tug out. That night we had an operation but it was cancelled. Last night we were a standby reaction unit in case the boats on another operation needed help, [sic] *they didn't. This morning we took about 40 Montagnards up a small canal near Seafloat. They searched the area for hours, but made no contact.*

The disembarked troops have just left the boat as evidenced by the footprints in the mud. They are entering the trees but already are camouflaged so well that without zooming into the picture and studying it carefully they are not seen.

> *Montagnards are Vietnamese mountain people. They are supposed to be the meanest, most blood-thirsty Vietnamese fighters over here. They're detached* [sic] *here for 1 month to help protect Seafloat in case it is attacked during the Tet offensive...*
> (Letter, Jan. 12, 1970)

Well, yesterday we escorted a tug at 4 a.m. and one at 7 p.m. No enemy contact. Last night we shot up some places where we saw signal flares that are usually V.C. signals to inform the other V.C. that boats are in the area. This afternoon we got a call to rush troops to an area where a VC unit was believed to be seen headed toward Seafloat, it was a false alarm.

Often we have to wash our clothes in the river... While at Seafloat...

Wash

Rinse

Dry

Between the muddy water and the stains from the medi-
cation I use occasionally for crotch rot, my underwear are
getting pretty bad looking. I can't get anything but baggy

Navy underwear here, so please send me 8 pair of size 36 jockey underwear, and I'll discard my old ones.
(Letter, Jan. 15,1970)

***

Yesterday they found brand new clay-more mines in the canal we were in several days ago. We were supposed to go up the canal this morning with troops and a UDT team (underwater demolition team). But they cancelled the operation at the last minute. We still don't know why. I don't like going up little canals, but after you have an operation all planned and get all ready and get underway and then they cancel it, it kind of irritates you. I must be developing a taste for adventure (or danger) as usually one would thank God that such an operation were cancelled. I know one thing when I get home, either the 4th of July is going to be dull or I'll be jumpier than a cat in a room full of rocking chairs. I'm curious to find out which. Actually watching a display will be the dull part. It's those unexpected firecrackers that will get me. I've taken pictures of boats firing at night, I don't know if they'll come out. I hope so. In a way, its really pretty.
(Letter, Jan. 16, 1970)

In January of 1969, I was able to buy a portable cassette tape player recorder at the ship's store of the USS *Krishna* for $25.25. My parents and I started sending audio cassette tapes back and forth. According to my tape on the evening of January 17, we inserted two Navy snipers and five Montagnards to set an ambush at the mouth of a canal to watch for Viet Cong coming out of the canal or crossing the river. The Montagnards serve as security for the snipers in case things go wrong. I was never aware that the Navy had snipers as I suppose few other people were aware either. The snipers had M14s that were custom fit for them. We had a sniper on board for several days at a different time and he was a strange character. It is one thing to return fire when attacked. It is quite a different thing to just sit and wait to kill someone who doesn't even know you are there.

Leaving the ambush site, I heard a dull thud come from the engine room; soon after hearing the noise, I began to smell a burning odor. When it was safe to leave my battle station behind the aft .50, I opened the hatch to the engine room and smoke came pouring out. Further investigation revealed the smoke blowing out of the back of the port engine. We shut the engine down and continued back to Seafloat on one engine. Each engine holds nine gallons of oil, this one was two gallons low.

We left Seafloat on January 19 and traveled west back out the Cua Lon River into the Gulf of Siam. Our destination was the USS *Krishna* ACL-38, a Navy repair ship anchored a short distance from the mouth of the river. We had blown an engine and the Krishna had it replaced with a new one by January 20. (On the tape, I mentioned that the cost of a 12V71 engine was $2,500. The price for a reconditioned 12V71 diesel today starts around ten times that price.)

In addition, we were able to get hot showers on the repair ship. The *Krishna* had the capability to make potable water. All the potable water at Seafloat was brought in by barge, such as the ones that we had to escort in and out. Showers at Seafloat were on one hour in the morning and one hour in the evening. We missed the showers if we were out on a mission. Sometime if we were anchored in a safe location near the base, we just jumped in the muddy river and washed off. Most of the water flowing in the Cua Lon even way upstream was salt water because of the strong currents and radical tide changes. Regular soap will not suds up in salt water. It just creates sticky little grease-like balls tangling your body hair on your skin. We used salt-water soap also called sailors' soap.

In order not to be swept away by the current, we would hang on to a rope secured to the boat, or the current would take us away. The currents in the Cua Lon reached eight knots at times, more than any of us could swim against. I had seen the SEALs jump off the ammo barge at Seafloat and swim in place, not being washed away and not making any forward progress, just swimming in place for exercise and conditioning. With my weak swimming ability, I would have been carried away and picked out of the water a few miles downriver by the Viet Cong.

On January 20 (or 21?) we escorted an Alpha boat, also called an ASPB for Assault Support Patrol Boat, from the *Krishna* in a northerly direction to the Ong Doc River where Operation Breezy Cove was underway, challenging the Viet Cong stronghold in the U Minh forest. Like the Swift Boat, the ASPB was fifty foot long, powered by the same 12V71 diesels and had lots of firepower. Unlike the Swift, they were much heavier and slower as they were steel hulled and had minesweeping capabilities.

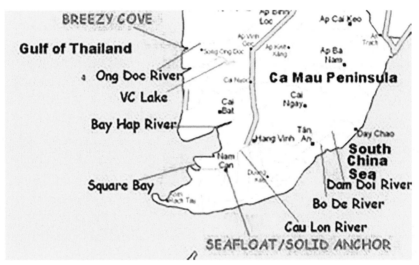

Map: Mobile Riverine Force Association website

We returned to Seafloat and on the 21st [or 22nd?]. That night we went out at 7pm up the Dam Doi River to act as a blocking force. Seals and Montagnards were sweeping the area. We waited in ambush along the river for any VC that were evading across the river. It turned out to be a real real good operation. Our boat and the 12 boat were the first Swifts to go into the Dam Doi River in over a month now. The last boats that went up there were the 50 boat and the 3 boat and both those got hit with B40s which are Chinese

communist built anti-tank rockets. We went up at night and we didn't have any trouble at all...
(Audio, January 1970)

- This audio goes on to describe the activities of the night which resulted in twenty-five enemy killed by the ground forces with no friendly casualties.

The Dam Doi River was notorious for a recent number of attacks that had inflicted heavy damage and casualties on the Swifts. It was especially dangerous for the following reasons. First, it was a long way from Seafloat, meaning that help was not nearby. Second, it was narrow and winding and had thick vegetation on either side. It was the perfect place for the enemy to attack us as they had lots of cover, and our maneuverability and speed were inhibited by the size and shape of the river.

I had a feeling I was going to be in great danger last night. I thought I was going to be in some real danger going into that Dam Doi River. That's a bad bad place to go. Evidently we had them on the run so bad last night they didn't have time to stop and try and mess with us.

This is a good story, wait until you hear this. We had a VN supply ship that was supposed to bring our food in for us [and] resupply Seafloat and these jerks broke the lock off the freezer on the ship so they could go in and get something to eat out of it. Which they are actually stealing our food and somehow by leaving it open it spoiled all the meat and now we're eating C-rations everyday instead of getting a regular meal. Just another incident to help dislike the Vietnamese. I think very little of their military conduct and their thoughtfulness as a person to do anything like that. That's next to a declaration of war around here to steal our fresh meat, it's a wonder that we didn't go out and sink their ship.
(Audio, January)

139

Black Ponies

Black Ponies were the Navy's close-support fixed-winged aircraft that we could radio for help. A high school classmate of mine, Tom Reside, who also drilled at the reserve center with me, would eventually be stationed at the Naval Air station in Binh Thuy where he worked on these aircraft. Later in my tour, I would get the opportunity to visit with Tom on the air base.

The newly formed squadron called themselves "Black Ponies." Their aircraft consisted of fourteen OV-10A Broncos. The OV-10 is a twin-engine, propeller driven aircraft with a very high twin-boomed tail and a 40-foot wingspan; it usually operated at speeds in the 180–200-knot range with a patrol endurance of two to three hours. The Black Pony version was painted dark green for Vietnam service and had been adapted to its close-support, attack role with a variable weapons configuration of M-60 machine guns, 20-mm gun pods, SUU-11 Gatling-type mini-gun pods, 2.75-inch rockets, 5-inch Zuni rockets, and paraflares for night work.
(p. 195 *Brown Water, Black Berets*, Thomas J. Cutler)

***

They (Black Ponies) have turned out to be one of the best fighter planes over here as far as firepower…these things are fantastic. We used them—ah—they don't have them down here, they can get them. They'll fly down here from Binh Thuy, it takes about 20 minutes. If we need 'em or figure we're gonna need 'em…They carry all kinds of weapons… everything in the book. These guys are really good. They really can handle a plane. Usually every time we go on an operation, if they are going to be along they come right down over the boats and buzz over top of us and let us know they are going to be around. Which kinda gives you an extra feeling of protection. And they'll just about risk their neck for a Swift Boat cause they're Navy and we're Navy. And they think were crazy, just outright insane, some of the places we take a 50 foot boat. And we think they're just about insane the way they drive their planes. So we get along real good together because we both think each other is nuts.

(Audio, January)

***

Things may get real interesting around here in the next couple of weeks. I think last nights and today's operation and the operation still hasn't ended yet it's gonna go on until tomorrow morning and God knows when it will end. This might be just the thing we needed to hold them down, we're putting the strike on them first before they put the strike on us. I don't think they are going to be in too good a shape to pull much of a Tet offensive down here on us after what we've done to them the last couple days.

Yesterday's operation was just an outstanding operation - chalk one up for our side. I hope that some of these people that they got were from the anti-boat team. Intelligence says that the VC have an anti-boat team down here. It's a group of approximately 22 men (VC) that are trained and outfitted and supplied specifically for the purpose of destroying boats, American boats. And ah oh about 3 weeks ago the Seals killed about 4 of 'em. We're all hopin' that some of these people they got last night and today are some more of them.

The mosquitoes around here are bad at night, this is about the worst place, the mosquitoes all over Vietnam are bad…but they're bad around here—real bad. I was coated in insect repellant last night while we were out on ambush. Even then they won't leave you alone. They buzz around and buzz around and play around your ears.

That's a real experience (the boat) sitting in the middle of a known VC area at night, standing by waiting for someone to come across the river so you can rip them to shreds or waiting for them to rip you to shreds. It sure is comforting to see the sun come up in the morning. It's very interesting sitting to watch and watch. The sun didn't come 'til 7 o'clock this morning. It was a real moonlit night, real bright out, full moon all night long. I guess there will be boats out there again tonight sittin' there waitin'. We're going out tomorrow morning to relieve them.

It was about 5 o'clock this morning—oh—the whole time we're sitting on a night ambush you can't smoke, can't turn any lights on, have to stay as quiet as you possibly can be. You're (the boat) up as close to the beach, you've got the boat up as close on the beach as you can get it, your engines off. So that if somebody comes along you're as unnoticeable as possible. This is kinda hard to do if you can imagine 6 guys on a boat wearing boots trying to be quiet walking around an aluminum boat—tippy toeing all over.

About 5 o'clock this morning Hogan came over and whispered to me. He's the one that started the thing about the angel on my shoulder bit. He whispered to me to take a look at the tree line and there was my angel. I looked over the tree line and just—you know how at night the trees will make different shapes and clouds will make different shapes and this one bunch of trees—the outline looked just like an angel with its wings, ah with a trumpet up to its mouth. Just kinda struck me funny.

Hogan is super, super, super religious. He's Catholic and he's considering very strongly going into the ministry when he gets out of the Navy. He volunteered to come over here. Strange? He wanted to do his part in Vietnam. This is his second hitch in the Navy. When he gets out this time he wants to—he's already been accepted to two schools. He's thinking very seriously about going into the ministry and being a Catholic priest. And you should hear the discussions

142

that come up between him and I, well between everybody on the crew. Believe it or not religion is a big topic of discussion around here with him around.

We had some real good discussions on the 63 boat because Neil is Jewish; Steve is sort of nothing. He knows more about everybody else's religion than anybody else does. This is a fact. I'm not kidding or saying he's a big mouth. He has studied all of them. He's traveled around the world. He's been behind the iron curtain. He's been to Egypt, Israel. He knows about as much about anybody else's religion as they do themselves. He can tell you things about your own religion but he professes to no religion himself. He's not an atheist, he's not saying he doesn't believe anything. He believes part of this religion and part of that religion and part of another religion. He's got his own religion I guess you might say.
(Audio, January 22, 1970)

At that time, I was very impressed with Steve's eclectic view of religion. I was raised in the Presbyterian church, and Steve's view seemed to me to be very intelligent and freeing—freeing people to believe whatever was comfortable for each person. Later in life as I studied God's Word, I discerned that Steve's "pick and choose" belief was contrary to what the Bible teaches. I came to believe that there is only one way to be reconciled to God and that one way is through belief in the saving work of His Son Jesus Christ on the cross.

For God so loved the world that he gave his one and only Son, that whoever believes in him shall not perish but have eternal life. For God did not send his Son into the world to condemn the world, but to save the world through him. Whoever believes in him is not condemned, but whoever does not believe stands condemned already because he has not believed in the name of God's one and only Son. (John 3:16–18, NIV)

Salvation is found in no one else, for there is no other name under heaven given to men by which we must be saved. (Acts 4:12, NIV)

See to it that no one takes you captive through hollow and deceptive philosophy, which depends on human tradition and the basic principles of this world rather than on Christ. (Colossians 2:8 NIV)

For the time will come when men will not put up with sound doctrine. Instead, to suit their own desires, they will gather around them a great number of teachers to say what their itching ears want to hear. (2 Timothy 4:3)

The following are excerpts from audio about a coordinated multiday operation that involved numerous assets operating out of Seafloat in the Ca Mau peninsula.

The Cua Lon and the Bo De and the Dam Doi Rivers all intersect at one point, actually the Dam Doi looks on a map like it's just the rest of the Cua Lon…we came back to the intersection of the 3 rivers and beached to stay the night for an ambush…this whole operation that's been going on for the last couple of days was planned by the SEALs and they're the people that have been getting most of the (enemy) KIA's too.

I guess it was around 12 or 12:30(pm) they came up, pulled alongside of us. They come up big as day, we're trying to be quiet, no smoking, no lights, they come up big as day talking, laughing, smoking, carrying on. Their officer came on board to talk to Mr. Burke to explain what they were going to be doing. They pulled away and proceeded up a canal that was just a short distance from us, just merrily putting away as if nothing was happening there, having a good old time, going up into a real, real bad canal.

Shortly after that we went into a 2 section watch. Half the crew stayed up and kept their eyes open and waited for anything to happen and listen to the radio, and the other half goes to sleep. I was on the first watch from 12 (midnight) to 3:30 I guess it was and nothing much happened. There was some shootin' going on in the area the Montagnards were in but not much happening there...it was shortly after I went to sleep the other half of the crew took over on the watch...around 4 or 4:30 from the area the SEALs were in they saw small pop flares go up in the air which are small flares that you hold in your hand and you put the lid on backwards and pound it and it shoots a flare up in the air and illuminates the area. They [the second watch] *said that they saw a pop flare go up and heard a mini-gun fire and another flare went up and the mini-gun fired again. This went on for a little while and there was a little return fire and that was about the end of it. There was no radio report saying what happened.*

I guess it was around 6:20 they woke me up; they woke up the whole crew to go to general quarters. We had to go get the 02 boat which is a Vietnamese Swift Boat with a full Vietnamese crew with one American advisor on it. They were beached about a mile up the Bo De from the intersection. They called up and were high and dry on the ground because the tide had washed out. The water level had gone down and they were stuck on the beach and couldn't get off. They had one engine that wouldn't run, and this is typical for the way the Vietnamese do things. They - just—I don't know where their brains are sometimes. Anybody that would sit there and not realize that the tide was going out and their boat isn't going to be able to get off the bank— you know as the tide goes down you have to—even though you try to be quiet you have to start your engine up and back off the beach a little bit so that you don't wind up high and dry. So anyhow we had to go down there and pull them off, give them a line, and pull them off the bank.

As we came back up to the intersection, both boats come up to the intersection out in the middle of where the 3 rivers meet. There was a sampan about half sunk, floating around all by itself. So we went over and threw a grappling hook on it and drug it onto the beach. We beached the boat and pulled the sampan up on the boat. It was just riddled with bullet holes, big hunks of wood were missing out of it and holes all through it, a couple spots of blood here and there, fish nets and rope and things like that and baskets. We called up and reported what we had and they said that the Seals had shot two people in the sampan but they had lost the sampan and evidently this is what we had found. So we unloaded all the junk out of it, fish nets and all on to our boat, pulled it out in the middle of the river, tossed a few hand grenades in it, and sunk it and proceeded on our way back to the base here, to Seafloat.

We came out to one of the buoys out here down river from Seafloat, tied up and cleaned our guns up. There was a lot of dew last night, real heavy dew and all the guns were wet, and you have to clean them up or they will rust up on you. So we cleaned our guns and cleaned the boat up a little bit and then we took a, well a couple of us including I, took a nice dip in the muddy old river. This water is all, even though it's a river, it's salt water because salt water comes up from the ocean. These rivers are strange right in this area here. They start on one side of Vietnam and run all the way through to the other side. It's not like a river that starts out from a little creek and runs out. Actually a great deal of the southern tip of South Vietnam is really an island. Anyhow the water is basically salt water in the river. We have to get this special soap that I never knew about before. We just got it yesterday—salt water soap. If you use plain soap it just doesn't work right with salt water, it just balls up and it doesn't take the dirt off or nothin'. Now we got this salt water soap and it works pretty good. So I got all cleaned up and shaved for a change, put on some clean clothes for a change, washed some clothes, and decided to finish up this tape and get some sleep if somebody doesn't decide we have some other kind of operation to go on.

Jack Burke hanging on to a line from the
boat while bathing in the river.

You'd be surprised if you were over here. You'd think it was a bunch of hippies over here for the long hair and mustaches and beards and everything that everybody grows. Its one of the privileges that a combat person will have over regular personnel. You'll probably never see it in person though because you're not allowed to leave Vietnam with a beard. You can have a mustache, but you can't have anything else; you can't have long sideburns or a beard or anything as far as I know. I know you can't go on R & R with them.
(Audio, January 1970)

The author sporting facial hair, love beads, dungaree shorts,
and a camouflage shirt with cut-off, ragged sleeves.

In July of 1970, Admiral Elmo Zumwalt, then the Commander
of Naval Forces in Vietnam, became the Chief of Naval Operations
and began issuing what he termed Z-grams. These orders included
the authorization of beards, sideburns, mustaches, and longer hair
if neatly groomed. He also wrote a Z-gram he first named "Mickey
Mouse, Elimination of" but renamed it "Demeaning and Abrasive
Regulations, Elimination of."[12] Every sailor I knew over there loved
Admiral Zumwalt because we (riverine sailors) were his special people,
and he allowed us a lot of freedoms that ran counter to normal Navy
regulations. With the regulations changed, I was able to return home
with a mustache, beard, and long sideburns.

---

12. *New York Times*

Well, they finished the big operation late this morning (January 24th). I believe it wound up with 27 VC killed and one VN wounded. Meanwhile there is another operation going on in Square Bay at the mouth of the Cua Lon. They have Chinese Mercenaries sweeping the beach down there. Tomorrow night is a USO show. We are supposed to be the VIP boat tomorrow, which means we'll probably take the USO people upstream a half mile or so and bring them back. Then they can say they rode a Swift Boat at Sea Float, Whoopie-do! We'll probably go to general quarters and load all our guns, so they'll think they're really doing something.

Two SEALs went out on a volunteer mission today from which they are not expected to return. I don't know exactly where they're going or what they're supposed to do, but I bet they make it back. These guys are like the people you see on TV or in the movies. You know—they always win no matter how badly outnumbered or anything. They're really great. And they're Navy too! They're just unbelievable. They go into the worst places. They're the smallest unit here. They kill the most VC and the VC have yet to kill or capture a SEAL here yet. Incidentally they are Navy special forces, but they're under the direct control of the CIA...

Well, that's all for now.
(Audio, January 24, 1970)

***

Tonight is, let's see, It's twelve midnight the 24th, well it's actually a few minutes after so it's the 25th. We were on standby for a SEAL unit that was running up a canal— ambush. This was about 30 minutes ago. We got a call, they got hit pretty bad and were taking on water, flooding. They called out helos; the helos were there in a couple minutes. We got under way. We were headed up that way and the SEAL boat was coming out already on its way back out, and the helos were in making a strike so we turned around and came back. Now they have a big gun ship here firing 3"/50s. They're big shells. They are firing into the area which was about maybe a mile up the river from here; a southern canal about a mile up the river from here.

Today is two days later, whatever day that is. Anyhow, the SEALs hit a claymore mine, a command detonated claymore mine. As soon as the mine went off, machine gun fire opened up on them. The minute that the SEALs started shootin' back, the VC stopped shootin' and probably climbed back into their holes or tunnels or bunkers whatever. They had a pretty good-sized hole in the boat and were flooding, but they made it back and got it patched up. No big problem. So there wasn't much to it. Nobody got hurt which was amazing. Really amazed, nobody on the boat got hurt at all which is par for the course for SEALs. Like I said before—they go through everything, do anything and never seem to get hurt.

They had Chinese mercenaries down at Square Bay on the west side of the tip of Vietnam, it's where the mouth of the Cua Lon comes out. They had 17 Chinese mercenaries down there making a sweep and two Swift Boats standing by. The mercenaries were attacked by two sampans with 14 VC in them carrying heavy weapons. There was a VN officer with them I guess, with the mercenaries. He got shot in the head and killed. From what I hear they killed 12 of the 14 that attacked them. They ran into so much trouble down there that they pulled them out. They're planning very shortly now to send the Montagnards down there and sweep the area.

Last night we had another ambush. We went out on ambush at 8 o'clock, well no I guess it was around 9. We stayed til 2 in the morning. The other boat that was out with us, they were about a thousand yards upriver from us, thought they heard people coming towards the boat. There was a lot of movement coming towards their boat from

the beach. They were beached and from the same beach they thought people were coming at them. They couldn't tell. They started their engines, backed off, and fired M-79 (rounds) *into the beach. They pulled away and we pulled out, came by the same area and opened up with all our guns on the same area which was - if there was anybody in there they were in a bunch of trouble, that's for sure. It could have been—most likely it was just somebody got a little nervous on the 56 boat and started hearing things because you hear all kind of noises, animals and everything in the jungle or woods, whatever you would call it. I don't know what you would call it down here. Parts of it you would call jungle, parts of it you would call woods. It looks more like a woods. So, anyhow more than likely he just got a little shook up.*
(Audio, January 27[?])

***

The only time we have milk here is when an LCM, which is a smaller type supply ship, comes in and resupplies us. We have milk for a couple days and once that's gone we don't have anymore because they can't keep it fresh long enough. We had an LCM in 2 days ago. I got some milk today and mixed up some onion dip...

If things work right so far they may just make it. We will be returning to An Thoi just before the Tet offensive, which would be nice to get out of this particular area during Tet. But I don't think we'll have a whole lot of problems unless they have something tremendous planned for this place. Intelligence does have it that Seafloat is the target of the Tet offensive down here, 'cause there's nothing else down here to attack. We're the only people here. But if you ever saw one of our general quarters practices, they give a red alert and we go to general quarters and we actually fire and everything. The VC would be in a lot of trouble if they tried to attack this place. They would be in a whole lot of trouble. If you can imagine 13 pontoons, the pontoons have machine guns, mortars, grenade launchers all the way around the pontoons. There's always boats at the buoys, and there's always boats tied up to Seafloat. When the red alert goes out they come over the radio and say "Sat Cong" which in Vietnamese means kill VC. They come over the radio and say, "All waterborne units, Sat Cong." The boats that are tied up to Seafloat take off and move out down river, beach, and prepare to fire the mortar. The boats that are tied to the buoys stay right where they are, go to general quarters and prepare to fire the mortar. With Seafloat firing machine guns, Mark 19s, and mortar and about 10 boats firing mortar and the other boats down here firing howitzers and the big gun boat they have sitting in the river firing the big 40mm rounds and the 3 inch 50 rounds and the helos firing, they (the VC) haven't got a chance here. They may throw a few mortar rounds in and mess things up a little, but as far as over running Seafloat, it will never happen. I'd venture to say they could send a thousand VC after this place and they'd never get it.

The people we [our ground forces] *captured the other day when they had the big sweep, where they killed 27 VC. The documents they captured told about the size of Swift Boats, the weapons it has, its fuel capacity, its ammo capacity, where the sleeping quarters are. They have charts with which points on a boat to hit with their rockets, what to aim at. They have diagrams of the bigger ships, er, boats rather. Everything that operates down here they have charts of and they're all about how we operate and how to get us, but the fact still stands that we are superior.*

There are different kinds of contact…*If you are out in the field and you say you made* contact *that means you've hit the VC or they've hit you and anyhow you are shooting it out; or you've seen them or they've seen you. Anyhow you say that you've made* contact *that way. That's one kind of* contact. *Radio* contact *means you can hear the other person and make communications with him on the radio.*

I don't know I must be getting blood thirsty or aggressive or something. I've been down here long enough nothing's happened to our boat. We've made no contact *at all. Anymore I am starting to wish maybe we'd make some* contact *instead of wishing we don't. When I first got down here, I didn't want to see nothin', I didn't want to run into no trouble at all, but the way things have been going lately everybody else has been gettin' to do something and we haven't been doing nothing. Well we've been doing things but our ambushes haven't panned out at all yet. I'd love some night to be sittin' on an ambush and see somebody, a boat full of VC trying to sneak across the river. But so far nothing's happened to us. I guess I ought to be thankful for that, which I am, but nothing's happened to us but we haven't made any* contact *at all yet.*
(Audio, January 25 and 26, 1970)

While listening to these tapes that I had sent home from Vietnam, various sounds appear in the background. At times, the sound of the diesel engines were heard. On a couple occasions, I recorded the test firing of our machine guns. Occasionally, there is the distinctive sound of my Zippo lighter as I click the lid open to light a cigarette and then flip it closed. In other portions, I left the tape recorder on next to our boat's radios to record ongoing communications between the boats, helicopters, ground troops, planes, and the base.

All units have their own unique call signs. All Swift Boats in a particular division had the same basic call sign followed by the boat's hull number. Thus all Swifts in Division 13, Cat Lo, used the call sign Elbow Gulf followed by the hull number; thus in Coastal Division 13 on PCF 63, our call sign was Elbow Gulf Six Three. In Coastal Division 11, An Thoi, all Swifts went by the call sign Abby November, making the 40 boats' call sign Abby November Four Zero. Given the low profile, the dark color of the pontoons of Seafloat, and its ability to pour out a firestorm of gunfire into the spooky looking surroundings of muddy banks and defoliated forests, Seafloat had the fully appropriate call sign of Munster, as in the ghoulish TV show of the mid-60s. The Navy Seawolf helicopters simply went by Seawolf with the helo's number. Spotter planes out of An Thoi were aptly called as Bird Dog.

View aft while transiting a small canal

On the morning of January 28, PCF 27 was carrying troops up a remote canal when an enemy mine went off about twenty-five feet behind the boat. There were no casualties, just some jangled nerves. That same evening, we got a call to go up the same canal for a medevac (medical evacuation). On our way along the canal, we heard a loud thud from the rear of our boat. It was not an explosion, and we were not sure what it was but later deduced that we had hit some hard object like a log submerged in the water which resulted in a telltale prop vibration at high speed. Our pickup location was about five miles up this canal. Once we reached the designated medevac location, we received a radio message that we had been given the wrong coordinates for the pickup. The medevac location was actually five miles inland from our location. I described this event on the tape as "a fool's errand up a dangerous canal." A helo went in and did the medevac pickup of the wounded.

Swift Boat approaching a bend in a small canal

Going into remote canals was always dangerous for a number of reasons. We always did so at general quarters with all guns loaded, manned, and ready for action. The main danger was how close we were to where the enemy could attack us. At such close range, the likelihood of the enemy's rounds finding their target were dramatically increased. On the river, we were sitting ducks; but in the canals, we were more like fish in a barrel, especially some of these canals that had high banks due to the extreme tide changes.

Low tide in a canal

The second reason that the danger was higher in the canals was mines. On the river, setting a mine was a real hit-or-miss proposition as to whether a Swift Boat would travel into the location where the mine was set. In a narrow canal, it is a sure thing that the boat will travel in the location of the mine.

This Swift Boat was not mined but destroyed by an explosive charge attached to it by a "sapper" swimmer.

The third reason for danger was the low water level and radical tide changes. Swift Boats had a draft of about five feet. If we went into a canal that had a depth of seven feet at high tide and stayed there while the tide went out, we could wind up sitting in four feet of water and be unable to get out of the canal until the next high tide. Operations in the canals required planning entry and exit times according to tide charts. This low-water issue also made our arrival and departure times fairly apparent to the enemy, meaning that if they wanted to transit a given area, they were fairly safe to do it at low tide, given that we did not have ground troops sitting in ambush.

Swift Boat lying in wait in a narrow canal

The last dangerous problem in the narrow canals was getting turned around to get out. A Swift Boat is fifty feet long and thirteen and a half feet wide. This means we could travel in a canal that was much more narrower than fifty feet but could not get turned around in such a canal to exit if need be. In really narrow canals, turning about was a tricky maneuver. The best way to communicate how that was accomplished is to give an analogy. Imagine you were driving on a country dirt road that was only wide enough for your car. The road had high banks on either side. In order to turn around you had to make a hard turn and ram the front of your vehicle into the dirt bank, attempting to get as high up the bank as you could go. Then you would cut your steering wheel all the way to the steering stop and back up until you hit the bank behind you. From there you would cut your steering wheel all the way in the opposite direction and drive forward, and if this did not allow you to make the complete about face, then once again you would drive as far up the bank in front of you as you could and continue this back and forth procedure until you were completely turned around.

The one advantage we had over a vehicle trying to make a tight about-face was the twin engines gave us the ability to do a "twist." The hydraulic "drive" or transmission of each engine allowed us to reverse the props. Therefore to "twist," we put one control forward and the other in reverse, which allowed the boat to twist in place. That is how we turned around in small canals, but if there was a strong current, sometimes the twist would not accomplish enough turn to get the boat fully turned around. So we would have to back up until the screws were churning up mud from the opposite bank and ram forward again onto the other bank and twist some more. This procedure was made more difficult if there was battle damage to the boat or wounded crew members.

We went out to the Krishna [ARL38 repair ship] to see why there was oil in our water [engine coolant]…While we were there I tried to get an injector pump for our Onan generator. I had a real hassle with these people trying to get parts…they wanted our old pump for supply reasons, bookkeeping reasons or something before they would give us a new one. So I had to go down and take off our old pump, take that up to them to get the new pump.

I was standing around and waiting and it happened to be lunchtime and nobody does anything at lunch time around the ship. So I was sittin' around waiting and some Warrant Officer came walking along and wanted to know what I wanted. We had occasion to run into each other and

158

speak before when I was having the engine put in and all. I told him I was waiting to get an injector pump, I was waiting for someone who had the keys to the supply to come back from lunch. He started telling me that he couldn't give me the pump because I didn't have my injectors, cause I had loaned my injectors to the 52 boat because their injectors went bad. [I figured] *As long as my engine wasn't running anyhow I could give 'em them until I got my parts. He told me that he couldn't give me a pump because I didn't have my injectors and he'd have to have the whole setup before he could do it and bla bla bla and started telling me that "you people don't understand that when we order parts we have to fill out this form and we have to make this number check out with that number and we're responsible for this and the other thing." I just turned around and told the guy that the Navy didn't seem to understand that we were fighting a war and didn't have time to fool around with filling out order forms and worrying about how it comes out on a computer and things like that and what Saigon, the headquarters in Saigon, wanted to know about this that and the other thing. We had boats to get underway; we had a war we were fightin', which I expected the way I told him to give me a reprimand or write me up or give me some kind of trouble, but believe it or not, he just stopped his harassment and went and got me the pump. He was very unhappy about the whole thing but he went and got the pump for me.*
(Audio, Jan 30, 1970)

***

We are presently tied up to an LST just outside the mouth of the river. (Actually about 5 miles out) We had to go back to the Krishna yesterday to have a new screw put on. We bent one going in a little nook off the river after an abandoned sampan. We hit a log or something. We will be

159

leaving for Seafloat soon. We came to the LST last night to get hot showers. The Krishna is having water problems, so we couldn't get them there.

I am enclosing a couple articles [only found one] *from a Navy newspaper. PCF-3 in the picture is being lifted to make repairs after being hit with B-40s in the Dam Doi River. The article makes the Tutuila's relationship with swifts sound much chummier than what it is.*

(Letter, January 30, 1970)

TUTUILA HOISTS 100TH SWIFT BOAT

Since her arrival in An Thoi, Republic of Vietnam, last June, USS Tutuila has lifted 100 PCF's (Swift Boats) with her heavy lift boom. Through hard work and long hours, individual accomplishments during these six months along with some meaningful statistics, serve to substantiate Tutuila's pride as "the PCF friend."

During the half year eighty major diesel engines have been overhauled, at an average of 300 man hours from the time the engines are disassembled to reinstallment. The crankshaft is miked, gears and other parts are inspected, repaired or replaced, and the block and heads are reworked.

Tutuila's Electric and Electronic repair shops makes repairs to ONAN generators, main engine starters, alternators and tachometers. A total of 60 starters, 40 alternators, 45 generators and 125 tachometers were repaired during the six month period. Seventy radar sets were fixed by six men, and at the same time they performed maintenance on 200 radios.

LCDR Bob Nolan, Tutuila's Repair Officer, saw to the repair of 249 pair of binoculars by the ship's Optical shop. The shop also took care of "PM" on 88 items such as compasses, telescopic alidades, spyglasses and ships telescopes.

Along side there is the Outside Repair shop. Located on pontoons moored alongside Tutuila, Navymen have repaired 125 propellors, 83 shafts, 67 rudders, 103 steering units and 91 reefers. "Battle Damage" repairs consist of 200 propellors, 150 mufflers and the complete renovation of six PCF hulls, and minor repairs to 30 more. In doing this, Tutuila men used 100 pounds of welding wire, 700 feet of rub rail material and numerous sheets of aluminum plate and "I" beam.

As Tutuila lifted her 100th PCF this month, she was ready for 101, and ready to keep the "Swifties" rolling along.

USS Tutuila lifts her 100th "Swift" onto pontoon moored alongside. PCF-3 sustained heavy damage and prepares to undergo complete hull renovation, engine, electric and electronic equipment overhaul. Supervising the lift are (L to R) Boatswain's Mate first class Larry Musick and LTJG Russ Naden of Tutuila's Deck Department.

Article from the Navy Newspaper *Jackstaff*

We left the Krishna early in the afternoon with two other boats and we were in the lead. Getting back into the mouth of the Cua Lon River is pretty tricky when you come into the bay. You have to go just in the right place or you run aground because the water is real shallow. We were going along about 20 knots. We were headed sorta for the beach and it kinda looked to me like the water looked different, much more still where we were headed for than it was where we were. Sure enough, the thought no more than went through my mind and "urump" and we were sittin' high and dry in the mud. It stalled our engines, filled our water suction inlets to cool the engines, filled them with mud, filled the strainers full of mud.

Cleaning the mud packed inlet strainers

We tried to back up but we were sittin' too low in the mud; we couldn't move. We were in about 6 inches of water. The other two boats almost piled up on top of us. The one behind us got stuck a little bit but they managed to work their way out. The one behind that didn't have any trouble at all. So we just had to sit there. We tried getting towed out. Hogan took all our tow lines and mooring lines and tied them altogether and waded his way out to the other boat. They tried to pull us off but we were stuck too bad. So we just sat around and cleaned guns, test fired guns, shot

Hogan walking our tow line out to connect
with another Swift Boat

the breeze, went to sleep for about an hour or so. The tide came in and we got a little more water and we tried again to work our way out. We managed to back up about 20 feet and get slightly turned around and headed about 20 feet and got stuck again—couldn't make it any further. So Jesse took the line out again, hooked it to the other boat and those two boats hooked together, tied lines between them started our engines and eventually worked our way. We were no more than about 5 minutes out of there and we lost our steering. I guess the mud being jammed against the rudders and pulling the boat against the rudders and stuff like that popped a piece of steering linkage out of place. So I had to fix that. By that time we were just about getting into the mouth of the river. We got about half way to Seafloat and we spotted a sampan on the bank. On the Cua Lon River except for where we have been redeveloping areas there's not supposed to be any people, sampans, or anything. In this place there wasn't supposed to be anything. So we went over and fired around the area to make sure the sampan wasn't booby-trapped, then went ahead and pulled it out and brought it back to Seafloat with us.

There's a new plan now for the ACTOV program. ACTOV is the Accelerated Turnover to the Vietnamese of the riverboats. I'm not sure if I filled you in on the situation so far. Coastal Division 15 in Quin Nhon was turned over in November to the Vietnamese. All Vietnamese manned Swift Boats there now have one American advisor aboard them. Da Nang is scheduled to be turned over in March and Cam Rahn Bay sometime around May. Da Nang is 12, Cam Rahn is 14. That leaves 13 and 11. 13 which is Cat Lo where I was from is scheduled to be turned over in June, which is a big surprise. They didn't have it scheduled to be turned over before. So by June of 1970 all divisions except for Coastal Division 11 will be turned over to the Vietnamese. Coastal Division 11 will have 33 American Swift Boats. All the excess personnel will be used for support personnel or be sent home, which means instead of the 4 to 6 months I expected to be here in An Thoi I guess I'll be spending the rest of my time here. Originally I believe An Thoi was scheduled to be turned over to the Vietnamese in June or July, but now that's been cancelled out and there's no time set for when An Thoi will be turned over.
(Audio, January 1970)

By now in the telling of my story, it should be clear that life in Coastal Division 11 was physically and mentally exhausting in addition to being dangerous. Therefore most men did a tour of several months there and were transferred to a safer division. Occasionally, someone would be removed from a crew for unknown reasons. In between the lines of the dialogue in the previous paragraph copied from an audio tape sent home is another message, I could be stuck there in hell for nine or ten months. Statistically, that made the odds good for getting killed or wounded. Even escaping that fate, just being in the living conditions for that long was hell. I spent six months in An Thoi before being transferred in June 1970 to be shuffled all over the Delta for the remainder of my time.

Some years after returning home, the local county organizations held a dinner to honor Vietnam veterans. During the dinner conversations, I overheard a conversation in which someone was talking about having to remove a naval officer from his command because of the stress he was experiencing of having to send men into combat and seeing the resulting casualties. He went on to say that due to the stress of duty in that area, combat personnel were only left there for four months and then rotated out. As he continued, I heard him say that he was the Personnel Officer for Coastal Squadron One in Vietnam and his previous statements were about Coastal Division 11 where I had spent six months. I concealed the scream of injustice that welled up inside me behind a front of macho man. My mind wanted to know: "Why? Why was I left there for six months if no one was supposed to spend more than four months there?" In a tone of contradiction, I informed this person that I had spent six months there. He had no explanation for how long I had been there. He was not serving in Vietnam during the months that I was in An Thoi. For years, I harbored anger over what seemed to be a grave injustice that caused me to endure more than I was supposed to have endured.

Approximately 3,500 men served on Swift Boats in Vietnam between 1965 and 1970. What are the odds that years later I would meet a former Personnel Officer from my squadron in Vietnam? More amazing is that he only lived a few miles from my home and later on would become my son's scoutmaster! Robert B. Spinner passed away on December 15, 2013.

I personally don't think the Vietnamese can handle the situation down here. They wouldn't last long down here considering that we're right in the middle of VC territory and there's nobody else here but us. The Vietnamese couldn't hold a place like this as we are. I don't believe they could. It's really a hard thing to believe, the situation that we're in right here. Actually if you were to count the VC that are in this territory and the American forces that are in this area, we're probably outnumbered maybe a hundred to one if you consider all the territory south of the Cua Lon River and the territory maybe 40 to 50 miles north of the Cua Lon River.

As I listened to this tape and my estimation of how badly we were outnumbered, I have to think I may have been exaggerating a bit.

They don't tell you about places like this in the newspapers when you hear your reports about the Vietnamese war. In the newspaper or on TV or radio they tell you the VC hit such and such a place so many miles north of Saigon or west of Saigon or south of Saigon or they might mention the delta, which would be the area we operate in from Cat Lo. They tell ya, everything seems to be relative to Saigon when they give you a news report. They just don't mention this territory down here. Actually it's a thorn in their side down here, something they'd rather not mention I guess. Nobody wants to tell the story, nobody much cares about it and it's totally VC. They just don't tell you about things like this. My luck I'd have to get stuck in a place like this. There's one thing for sure, this is where the action is. Not meaning that there's no action in other parts of Vietnam, there's plenty of action in other parts...

If you ever hear anything in a news report about the Ca Mau peninsula, which I think occasionally they mention, that is the territory south of us. (correction: Seafloat was in the Ca Mau Peninsula) *If you ever hear of the U Minh Forest that is the territory directly north of us; two of the strongest VC territories in Vietnam. I think occasionally they do mention these two places; the Ca Mau Peninsula and the U Minh Forest. We've got one on one side and the other on the other side of us. It just strikes me funny the whole time I was a civilian back in the states; in news reports and all I never heard much about this particular area and I don't imagine anybody else does.*

Today is the second of February. The 52 boat which is the one that Steve's on and the 12 boat were on their way out of the Cua Lon and on their way out somebody shot a B40 at them. Just one and that was all. They scrambled Seawolves and called a gunboat in and hosed the whole area down.

It's been a while since I put anything on this tape. Yesterday afternoon we had a tug to escort out of the Cua Lon. From the Cua Lon to the Bo DE and out to the South China Sea. This is normally just a milk run; we are just an armed escort in case anything happens which hardly ever happens. We took them out and on the way back in we were firin' what's called H and I that's harassment and interdiction, you just shoot any old place and if anybody happens to be in there it raises hell with them. We had just got off of the Bo De and were about a mile down the Cua Lon. We had stopped firing; we heard an explosion on one bank. We were leading and the 38 boat was behind us. We were far enough ahead that we couldn't hear exactly what it was, we thought maybe they were still test firing, but what it was, someone shot a B40 at them and small arms. So we turned around and went back and hosed the area down. Nobody well, they shoot once and that's it—they quit. They're lousy shots. They missed with the B40, missed with the small arms. Just like this morning they missed the 52 boat with a B40. They're bad shots. So we did basically what they did this morning. We mortared the area, shot .50 caliber all over the place and called Seawolves in. They shot rockets and mini-guns, the gunboat came in and hosed it down with the big guns. We put troops in and they swept the area to see if they could find anybody, but they didn't find *nothing. So for the cost of one B40 and a few small arms (rounds) from Charlie, he got us to expend about $10,000 worth of ammunition. It was fun though, doing all that shootin'!*

[The nickname or slang for the Viet Cong was Charlie which came from the use of the phonetic alphabet to communicate the letters *V* and *C* spoken as "Victor Charlie." "Charlie" was used for both the singular and plural, an *s* was not added to Charlie for the plural use of the name. I wish the nickname for the Viet Cong had become "Victor" rather than my name!]

I guess I'll have to write Mrs. Dey and explain this to her. She sent me an Aquarius coin, a lucky coin for Aquarians that's supposed to bring you good luck. It tells you your lucky days and all that good stuff. I had no more than received it and we went out on this mission and got shot at...I figured this coin was bringing me no good luck at that rate if I just got it and then got shot at...so I threw it over the side, which I don't think she will appreciate. But under the circumstances it wasn't bringing me any luck.

This isn't the first time this has happened to us. It happened to us at Binh Thuy, I didn't tell you about it at the time because I figured it would worry you too much to tell you stuff like that but you wrote that letter and told me that you didn't care what I told you. You realized I wasn't playing games over here so I'll tell you now. When we were in Cat Lo we were patrolling the Bassac we had the same thing happen. Somebody shot a B40 and small arms. They missed with the small arms and the B40 went somewhere between 3 to 5 foot over the top of the pilot house. That was kind of comical actually the way everything happened. They missed and we weren't even at general quarters. We didn't expect where we were for anybody to be shootin' at us. I was sittin' up on the bow with Steve shootin' the breeze and they shot this B40 at us, and I didn't know what it was at first because I never saw one before. He told me it was a

B40. Kind of casually, the whole thing was kind of casual you know, there was this big explosion. This thing went whistling through the air and I said,

"Steve, what was that?"
He says (calmly), "Well, (pause) that was a B40."

Immediately he turned his twin .30s to the bank to open fire and I ran back. We had troops on board and they were sleeping all over the deck and I went back and just walked all over them, you know, hands, faces, legs and things, stomped all over them, threw a belt in the gun and started shootin'. We ceased fire shortly after that, called in that we had been shot at and went back into the area on the opposite side of the river, beached and fired the mortar all over the area. After we finished with that, airplanes were there and they shot rockets and everything into the area. We went back and made a firing run on the beach on the other side where we got shot at from—made a firing run with .50 calibers and all of that stuff. We requested troops to be put in to sweep the area to see if we hit anything or what all was in there, but the Province Chief wouldn't allow his troops to go in there for some reason or another.

It's the same old thing if you get a B40 shot at you, usually, sometimes it's almost impossible to get the guy who shot at you, because he'll set it up on a bank where you can't see it and have wires running back to a bunker. He'll be maybe a hundred yards back or more in a bunker with two wires and all he has to do is wait for a boat to come along, touch the wires together and the rocket goes off and you can shoot everything you want, he's back in the bunker, you'll never hit him. But if you get small arms fire with it like we did yesterday, there's got to be someone in there shooting the small arms. Even so, they duck down in the hole and hold the gun overtop of their head; they don't even see what they're shootin' at. That's why they usually miss you. If they

169

ever hit you it would be bad, but they usually miss. It makes a terrible lot of work…I wish we had just ignored them yesterday and kept on going because you shoot up all this ammunition you've gotta clean all this empty brass off the boat. The boats just covered with brass and empty mortar tubes and everything. The guns are all dirty. You've gotta come back and clean all your guns, reload more mortar rounds, you know take 'em, bust them out of the box, strip them down, put them in the mortar box. You gotta haul more .50 caliber on and everything…

Last night they screwed us because we no more than came in from getting done with that… (the ambushed tug boat escort) *and they told us to reload and refuel and we were going out to foxtrot to be a standby for the Annex because the Annex has been hit a couple times. The Annex is a couple miles up the Cua Lon from here. That's where the civilians live and everything, where they repopulated and we got some people up there. We've been going up there the last couple of nights, shooting illumination and keeping the place lit up so they can see if anybody's around. After all this crap they told us to reload and refuel. We had to run right back out there again and standby and stay there all night.*

I've got my days mixed up, today must be the third, something's wrong, yea it was the 31st we got shot at with the B40. Yesterday we were cleaning guns and everything. That's right. So it was last night we went out on a Seal operation and they cancelled the operation and we came back and we stood by for Montagnards that are up this one canal here. We had to go get them this morning. We were standing by and we no more than got the radio call and the Kit Carson Scouts had seen somebody moving around by their camp on the north bank from Seafloat and all hell broke loose out there. They were shootin' up the whole place. I don't know whatever became of that. They didn't find anybody, but they had everybody shook up for a second.

170

So this morning we went and picked up the Montagnards. They didn't get nothin' last night, but another group, I don't know who, was out somewhere else last night and captured a whole bunch of VC. I don't know where they are or whatever became of that...No I'm wrong, it wasn't Montagnards that we went in and got this morning, that was Dewey Rifles, the Chinese mercenaries. That's who we went and got. This morning those guys left, they went back to Na Trang for Tet. Supposedly in a couple days we're supposed to get 3 companies of Montagnards down here which would be outstanding to make sweeps and all that. Without troops we kinda have our hands tied down here, because the boats can't go out in the bushes and look for people.

So we'll probably stay here for Tet, it should be interesting. There's gonna be a whole lot of dead VC around here if they try anything around Seafloat.

I've got a whole lot of letter writing to do; I don't know when I'm gonna get around to it. I've got a bunch of letters I haven't answered. There should be mail coming in again today. I don't know when I'm gonna get around to writing. I've been a long time getting around to doing this tape because I've been busy. There for a while we had a night operations for almost a week. Every night we were out. You can't sleep right in the day, you come in and you've got things to do. It gets to be a grind after a while - operation every night you're out. You get some sleep if it's an ambush you get a couple hours sleep. If it's a standby for the Annex you get a couple hours sleep, still it's not like getting a regular night's sleep. Things have changed since we first got here. When we first came here we were a new crew so they gave us a lot of slack. They gave us escorts and day operations; they didn't have a whole bunch for us to do, but now we're getting sick of everything.

The 52 boat's going out for repairs. They bent their screws up in the canal we were in today. We bent ours up

a little bit too. Theirs are bent up real bad. I can imagine them gettin' in a firefight with bent screws, 'cause they can only do a hundred rpms without shakin' the whole boat loose. Bet that boat was doing some shakin' when they got shot at and the people on the boat, ha ha. So they should be back tonight. I'll get to talk to Steve and find what all happened. Probably just one B40 that missed and that was it, no big thing. Those guys are bad bad shots. I'll tell ya they couldn't hit the broad side of a barn."
(Audio, February 1970)

***

Hi, today is the 3rd of February. I've got a pile of letters here from different people. I thought I would read through some of them that I got from you and comment on some of them. This one's from the 19th of January. In one section of the letter here you say: "It sounds like you are not too enthused about An Thoi or any of the operations," and you ask why is the U.S. still doing something down here when we (U.S. forces) *are pulling out.*

Well, I'm not too enthused about An Thoi. I'm not too enthused about this place, but somebody's got to do something down here. You can't just let 'em have free run of the area. If we were to just let them have this area without harassin' them here, interdicting them, ambushin' 'em, this would make it rough for the people further north of here. If they weren't doing their job, it would make it rough on the people further north of there. The whole thing works together.

What this place down here really needs is an Army division to help make sweeps and things like that to find their different supply places and things like that. True it will be turned over to the VNs someday but just because we're gonna be pulling out doesn't mean that we're just pullin' out

172

and dropping everything. We're trying to gradually pull out and turn things over.

You asked, "How do you fix a boat without parts?" That is slightly difficult but we always seem to find a way, one way or the other.

Going back to your previous question about why we are staying here: When you see people out fishing on the river, even though it's a couple miles of river where we restrict them to, and you see new hootches going up and more people moving into the area, you realize you are accomplishing something, somebody's got some faith in you that you are maintaining a certain amount of security for the area. At least when you can see some type of—something accomplished you don't feel like you're beatin' your head against the wall.

In this next letter you asked [referring to slides I had sent home], *"What are the little shacks built one by one with thatched roofs?" They are people's homes. That's what they live in.*

There's some good rumors going around now that Coastal Division 13 will be moved from Cat Lo to Sa Dec on the Co Chien River and Coastal Division 11 will be moved from An Thoi to Cat Lo. It sounds like kind of a screwy idea to me but this is what the rumor is, supposedly to happen in June. If everything goes as it's supposed to in June, there should be a good deal of Swift personnel in country and there is the slim, slim, slim possibility that I may possibly get sent home in June, but it's just a slim chance.

Hi, today is the fourth—my birthday. It's twenty of seven in the evening right now. I got some mail and I got a package that you sent me with underwear and all that stuff in it. You didn't get the lid closed tight on the powder and the powder was all over the place. The box wasn't crushed or nothing but the cookies were just a big pile of crumbs and little pieces.

From what I've heard they can't assign you to be an advisor on a Vietnamese crew. You have to volunteer for it and I would never volunteer for it. I wouldn't ride in the rivers or canal with- matter of fact I wouldn't ride on the Delaware River with a Vietnamese crew. I just don't trust them. You'd be takin' your life in your hands.

The last 24 hours things have been quiet around here. It's kinda' gettin' boring again. Yesterday we had a real good incident. Let's see, the day before yesterday we escorted two landing craft type boats from the LST in here with ammunition and escorted them back out again. We stayed out by the "T" overnight and then first thing in the morning we escorted the same two back in with more ammunition. On our way in we heard over the radio that two boats were under fire up in the Bo De. As it all turned out after we got all the stories straight, two Swifts were escorting a tug boat that was towing a barge, a sand barge, and the VC opened up and fired 7 B40s. As per usual their aim is pretty bad. They hit the tug with one and it didn't go off. They have poor ammunition too. If they're lucky enough to hit 'cha, then they have to count on the thing being good enough to go off.

Anyhow they hit the tug in the side with one and it didn't go off and they hit the barge in the side with one and it went off but it - you know, what are you going to do to a sand barge, you're not going to hurt nothing. They called in Black Ponies and Seawolves and they brought troops in. They captured—I didn't hear everything that they captured, but they captured 500 foot of copper wire, 14 rockets and all kinds of good stuff, but they did not capture anybody or get any KIAs. A half an hour later the B40 that went in the side of the tug went off, but it caused very little damage because it hit right around where the tug has rubber tires hanging over the side. Tugs have pretty thick wood—it just put a whole the size of a basketball in the side of it and that was all. Nobody was hurt or anything.

That was the fifth ambush they've had in the last 3 or 4 days. So you might say things are stepping up around here a little bit as far as them ambushing us. I guess it doesn't sound funny, but it seems funny, every time they shoot they miss. They just can't shoot straight. A tug boat, I can see them hitting a tug boat because that's fairly big, bigger than a Swift Boat and they can hit that. And then when they did hit it, it didn't go off anyhow.

Hi, today is the 6h of February, its twenty after nine at night. We're back at An Thoi. We left yesterday afternoon. We left Seafloat and came to An Thoi. The ride wasn't too bad; it was really nice out; it wasn't a very rough ride or anything like that. We got here around 7 o'clock. We stopped at the island and picked up beer. You could just feel the, I don't know what the word would be, you could feel the feeling in the crew that we'd been through a month of Seafloat and made it out, and you know, instead of being 7 people on a Swift Boat, you knew then that this was a crew—that it was a well functioning unit rather than just 7 people on a boat. It was just a funny feeling in all of us.

Plus we were happy to get back to some type of "civilization" if you can call two ships tied up off of the island of An Thoi "civilization."

We had big plans for all the repairs we were going to do on the boat, painting and getting it to look real pretty. Mechanically it's a real good boat but it doesn't look so good. So we got in and tied up, and Mr. Burke went up to the office to find out what the story was—what was going, what was planned for us and all that. He came back with some bad news that he was leaving the next day for Da Nang for 30 days temporary duty while they're having the turnover of boats to the Vietnamese. This at this particular time was a real bad note, after the feeling that was going through the crew that I just spoke of, then on top of it to lose an officer that you trust. I believe an officer that you trust is important over here, because he's the one who makes the decisions when you get shot at, where you go and what the boat does. You have to have somebody that you trust. The first month I was in Vietnam and he was my OinC, which stands for Officer in Charge, I didn't like the man at all. I really didn't like him. As I got used to him and his ways, I found, decided he was pretty good. Well he changed too. He came from all coastal patrols; he came from Quin Nhon where its all coastal patrols went to Cat Lo, where it's 95 percent river patrols. It's a much different thing coastal patrols from river patrols. Of course he changed in a month's time, too.

LTJG Jack Burke at the helm in the Swift Boat's pilot house

It's not always easy for enlisted men to get along with offi-cers, but it got to the point where I was really getting along well with him. He's not a very outgoing person, he doesn't get friendly real quick. He's not the kind that will just double up laughing over a joke or anything like that. He is an officer and he always let's you know that he is an officer. This was a real sour note to hear on top of everything else; we were losing him and getting an officer that was brand new in country. He just got here; we haven't got him yet.

Mr. Burke left this afternoon and we haven't got the new officer yet, but he said he was going to try to get this crew and this boat back when he came back from Da Nang. Just before he left he got word to us that they had okayed that he definitely would be coming back to this boat in 30 days. Of course knowing how the Navy does things, I wouldn't count on that a hundred percent. [LTJG Burke did return to Coastal Division 11, but not to our crew.]

We're going to be here for a couple days getting different repairs done on the boat and trying to get it in real good shape. I got the generator running today finally. Finally got all the parts I needed and everything and got them all together.

Before Mr. Burke left he said good-bye to all of us and said that he didn't want to leave the crew. He's been with Hogan since the two of them came into Vietnam. He's been with me for 3 months now. He feels that he has a real professional real organized crew and a real good boat and he just hated to leave it. Of course we'll probably be getting him back.

We'll probably be here 4 or 5 days and then we'll go on to Ha Tien. From Ha Tien they run this river [Giang Than River] *that starts in the Gulf of Siam, or the Gulf of Thailand, whatever you want to call it, and it runs up between Cambodia and Vietnam. The Swifts and PBRs and a couple other boats and some of those Vietnamese Junks patrol the whole area along there, between the two countries to stop the NVA from crossing from Cambodia into Vietnam.*

PBRs at Ha Tien

Vietnamese Navy Yabuda Junk called the Junk Force.

"Tet" their [the enemy's] *big offensive is supposed to be held on the 7th of February. I don't know exactly when Tet itself is but anyhow it looks like we're going to be here at the "Apple" during the Tet offensive,[13] which is real lucky.*

Hi, its 4:20 in the morning on the 9th of February. I've got the watch from 3:15 'til 5 o'clock, making sure none of the boats sink and nobody runs away with them or anything like that. It's kind of rough—they had storm warnings. This afternoon we all went in close to the beach and dropped anchor on the calm side of the island. It calmed down and we came back and tonight it got rough again. We're bouncin' and bobbin' around. I'm gettin' about sick of it right now.

---

13.   Tet is the is the Vietnamese celebration of the lunar New Year. In 1968 North Vietnamese Army and Viet Cong launched a major offensive into South Vietnam during Tet. Although the communist forces were repulsed and suffered a huge number of casualties, the American public was shocked by the news coverage which in turn further fueled the anti-war movement. Every year thereafter US forces were on guard for increased enemy activity during Tet.

Yesterday we had our boat up in the skids and painted the sides of the boat. They put new screws on our boat. They took it out of the skids this morning. We took it out for a test run. The port engine was pushing oil at full speed. We brought it back in and put straight pipes on, took the mufflers off and put straight exhaust on it and that cured that.

Charles Hunt, EN3; Jesse Church, RN3;
Tony "Ammo" Amoruso, GM3

We got our new officer today. He's much different than Mr. Burke. Just from talking to him for a little while. He's more—well—he doesn't play the officer role, up in the air quite as much as Mr. Burke does. He's more down to earth. Sounds like he's gung-ho for gettin' into the action which sometimes isn't too healthy to have an officer thinking like that. Sounds like he could be a lot of fun though.
(Tape, early February 1970)

***

I've got the boat watch here at the APL where we supposedly are based and live. That's a farce. A true swift sailor lives on his boat and steals what he needs from whoever [sic] he can. The "brown water Navy" is also known as the Hooligan Navy. Due to the problems we have procuring supplies, swift sailors have become Viet Nams most notorious "cumshaw" experts and down-right thieves, through necessity. "McHale's Navy" has got nothing on us. Anyhow I'm sitting here, making sure none of the boats sink or anything like that.

We got our new officer today. He's not as quiet as Mr. Burke. He seems like a real hell-raiser.

Its [sic] a little rough right now. The boats are bobbing around quite a bit. If it gets any rougher, we'll move all the boats into the beach.

We painted the hull of our boat yesterday.
(Letter, February 9, 1970)

CHAPTER 7

HA TIEN – DEADLY AMBUSHES

New Operation Area - New Officer - Deadly Ambushes

Today is the 11th of February, its 5 minutes after 1 in the afternoon, presently at Ha Tien. We came here yesterday afternoon and went out last night on an ambush and came back in today. Things seem a lot better here as far as action-wise than at Seafloat which would really be surprising. It should be the other way around considering this is right on the border of Cambodia and Vietnam. There's not that much action around here. For one thing there's so many boats around here that as you go up and down the river, there is just continual traffic of PBRs and Swift Boats and Monitors and Vietnamese Junks and all types of military river boats run up and down, there's so many of them out there. Just about every thousand yards up the river, there's a boat laying in ambush, every night, all night long. All day long boats patrol up and down. The place is pretty well under control.

In a few short days, I would learn that I was all wrong about the level of enemy action that would be encountered patrolling out of Ha Tien. Things would get hot and heavy!

They have a regular schedule here too, instead of like at Seafloat you never knew when you were going to go out. Whenever they gave you an operation to go on, you went out. Whereas here you have 4 night ambushes, 4 day patrols and then a day off. Then 4 night ambushes, 4 day patrols and a day off, a regular routine. The facilities here aren't much better than at Seafloat. You can take a shower here anytime you want though—that's one thing.

The generator that I've been working on, trying to keep running, gave out again. The engine is still running but the generator end of it just isn't putting any power out. I think I need a new armature for it. So all the food that we had to take with us that we had in our reefers, a reefer is a refrigerator or a freezer. The Navy terminology is reefer. All the food we had in our reefers, which we picked up before we came to Ha Tien, we had to give away because it was only going to go bad.

There's no supply facility here for us at all; at Seafloat they had some bare minimum of things. Here there's no supply facility for us at all, no repair facility or anything. This is mainly a PBR base.

On the ambushes out here they use sensors. Once you beach the boat for an ambush you go out about 40 yards on the beach and plant these sensors on the ground.

[I used the term *beach* for any land at the edge of the water whether it had sand or mud or vegetation or forest. In this area and Seafloat, it was not beach as we think of. There was no sand.]

You have a monitor that you listen to on the boat and if anybody, any motion that goes on near these sensors will sound off a beep on the monitor so you know something's moving out there. They're touchy and if you put them in the wrong place they keep beepin' all the time just from the wind blowin' and stuff. So you have to know how to use them just right.

We put them out last night and where we were beached in a swampy, marsh type area, all 4 of them continually just kept beepin' away because the water sloshing up against them kept activating them.

So with not much happening and a regular routine going on all the time, I guess there isn't going to be much out of the ordinary to write about or talk about while I'm here. We should be here for about, probably about a month. We're hopin' that at that time we will get Mr. Burke back.

Right where Ha Tien is, land wise it's a pretty location... it's right at the top of the Gulf of Siam. The river here, I don't know the name of the river, [Giang Thanh] parts of it are the border between Cambodia and Vietnam and most of it lays in Vietnam. Ha Tien sits right at the mouth of the river and right on the other side of the mouth of the river there are small hills on either side. Out in the bay there are little islands here and there. There's palm trees around. Then once you get past the mouth, it opens up into like a big bay or lake or whatever [Dong Ho Lake], which is real shallow except for one channel you have to go through. Once you get through that then you start up the river which is a real small river. It seems like every time I go to a new place the rivers and canals get smaller. When I was in Cat Lo, the Bassac River is a real big river. Somebody could shoot at you if you were in the middle of the river and they couldn't hit you because you were out of range. Every time I go somewhere the rivers seem to be smaller. This one's really small. You could almost consider it a canal. It's got a lot of bends in it; the thing is just one big curly cue.

Once you get past the bay the land just levels out to all marsh and swamp land. There's alligators out there and stuff like that. Anyhow, right at the mouth here it's real pretty, a real pretty scene. On the one little hill on the left hand side of the mouth, as you're looking up the river, is where they have the base here [command center, not the base] *for the Navy. Starting from there and running inland there is the town of Ha Tien, which I haven't been into yet. It looks like a fairly decent town for a Vietnamese town. I don't know what all they've got, supposedly they have one bar where you can get a beer and a girl. They have a tailor shop; I don't know what all they've got. I'll have to take a stroll in town one of these days. Supposedly the beer here is alright but the girls are a sure thing for VD, so everyone says. Well, at least they've got girls, that's more than Seafloat has or An Thoi.*

Storefronts on the riverbank at HaTien

They have VN troops on the right hand side of the mouth a little further in. They are what they call the Popular Forces. Vietnam has all different types of ground forces. They have PRUs, Popular Forces, and of course they hire the Montagnards and the Dewey Rifles [Chinese mercenaries], *and they have of course the ARVN, the Army of the Republic of Vietnam. Who else do they have? the Kit Carson Scouts which are ex-VC. There's all kinds of different units you run into around here, plus the other ones that are here,*

185

like the US is here, the Australians and the Koreans and so on. This is talking about all of Vietnam. As far as right here at Ha Tien, they just have the Popular Forces.

Patrol boats going out and coming in on the beginning portion of the Giang Thanh River before it narrows and begins to wind.

It's really something on the river when you go out for an ambush and when you come back in the morning. It's just like going to work—the rush hour going to work in the morning and the rush hour coming home. It's like the night shift and the day shift because everybody that's been on patrol all day long is coming in and everybody that's going out for a night ambush is going out. Everybody passed everybody, waves and the whole bit. Then in the morning everybody that's coming back from the night ambushes is coming in and everybody that's going out for the patrol for the day is going out. It's same thing all over again. I just couldn't believe the number of boats that they have out on this river. They said they've got it down to where it's almost impossible for the VC or the NVA to cross the river and I don't doubt it. They got so many boats out on this river.

Even so, I think if you knew what you were doing, I think you could still sneak across at night. You'd be taking a big chance, but I think you could do it.

So I think if anything, things are going to be boring around here with the routine of 4 night ambushes and 4 day patrols and the same old routine over and over again. The nice thing about it is at least you can plan your day and figure out what you're going to do and what time you're gonna' have off. It will probably be pretty boring. For instance last night we were on ambush for ten hours and we split up into two sections and half the guys sleep while half the guys are on watch. Then they switch, so you're up for five hours, just standin', watchin', tryin' to be quiet, which gets to be kind of boring.

It's funny the things that go through your head. You sit for five hours with very little movement. If you do talk to anyone, it's in a whisper. When we were at Seafloat our ambushes were much shorter, cause we didn't go out until maybe 9, 10 or 11 o'clock at night for the ambush and come in, in the morning. Whereas here you go out at 5:30 or 6 o'clock. 5:30 if you're going to pick up troops. If you are not going to pick up troops maybe you won't go out 'til 6:30 or 7 and you beach before it's even dark. It makes for a long night. From what I hear they run the day patrols the same way. You go out in two sections and half of you will be off and the other half will do the driving and manning the boat and then you switch.

Let's see today is the 11th, I've got 258 days left. That's not too bad. I've got 3 months out of the way. It seems like, it doesn't seem like a terrible long time to go yet. It seems like I'm making some headway with gettin' the days out of the way.

My blood must really be thin. I'm going to freeze to death when I get home. On these ambushes you really get cold. Actually the nights don't get any cooler here than maybe sixty degrees—that would be a real cold night. Like last night I had two long sleeve shirts on and I was still cold. During the day, it gets, I'd say like maybe today its 90 or 95 and that's like an average type day. You get used to it, I'm sweatin' a little bit. If you do any work you sweat, but you get used to it. At night you almost freeze to death. So when I get home it's gonna take me a couple weeks to adjust. I'll be bundled up like some kind of Eskimo or something the first couple weeks I guess. I can remember the first week or so I was in Vietnam. I could hardly sleep at night it was so hot. Just lay there and sweat and sweat and sweat. You wake up in the morning one big pool of sweat. Now at night you almost freeze to death.

This must be a fairly well-to-do territory, at least it's not a poverty territory. Most of the junks that sit right here at the mouth, that belong to the different people are painted. You don't see many junks that are painted in Vietnam, most of them never get painted. As you get farther up the river you don't see any painted. The poorer people live further up the river, but most of the ones right around here are painted all different colors.

You could just imagine a place like this would make— if you had some real type civilization—if this was a place that belonged to the Americans or the British or the French or the Germans or Australians or something like that, it would probably be a beautiful resort and recreation area, the way it's laid out and all. It's really nice territory here as far as geological things go. Of course this is only one little section covering maybe a quarter of a mile or a mile or so just at the mouth here. After that it turns into that big swamp area. At least this one little section here looks pretty decent.

My assessment of Ha Tien's potential for development and tourism was accurate seeming somewhat prophetic. Today multiple websites list it as a popular tourist site thanks to its beautiful beaches and landscapes.

In the textbook *Changing Environments*,[14] author Susan Bermingham states,

> *The Viet Namese government have devised a 15-year plan for tourism development 1995 to 2010…Vietnam is rich in historical interest and cultural architecture, and tourism is seen as a means of enhancing the economy. The government has identified tourist development "hotspots"… Specific locations are…The Ha Tien–Phu Quoc (Kien Gang) area, an area with potential for the devleopment of eco-tourism.*

In a legal document[15] dated February 3, 2009, the prime minister of Vietnam, Nguyen Tan Dung decided,

> *Article 1. To approve the master plan on Socio-economic development of Vietnam's sea and coastal areas in the Gulf of Thailand up to 2020.*

The twenty-one-page document lists specific goals. For Ha Tien it says,

> *To build Ha Tien into a major regional tourist and service center and concurrently a modern border-gate city in the country's southwestern border area.*

***

> *It's really funny. Everywhere you go there's supposedly a big Tet offensive—the VC are planning on taking this area, the VC are planning on mortaring this, the VC are planning on taking that over. There are so very few places that it ever turns out. When we were on the Mekong river, when I was*

---

14. *Changing Environments* published in 2000 by Heineman pp. 198–199
15. Decision No. 18/2009/QD-TTg printed in Vietnam's *Official Gazette*

stationed at Cat Lo, supposedly there was a regiment of NVA waiting across the Cambodian border that were going to take over Chau Duc during Tet. That hasn't happened yet. Some places have been hit, but all the ones you hear about don't get hit. Seafloat was supposed to come under tremendous mortar attack and just about be blown out of the water and that never happened—3 mortar rounds that missed. Ha Tien, there was supposedly 3 regiments of NVA on the other side of the border, that were gonna' overrun Ha Tien. That never happened. You just hear all these wild stories about what's going to happen for Tet and they never happen. Well they do a little bit, but they never turn out to be what they're supposed to be. That's why you never worry about anything over here until you come upon it.

Just like when I was stationed at Cat Lo, guys would say,

"Ah man, you don't want to go to An Thoi, that's the worst place in the world to be. You know, people are gettin' killed there every day."

Anybody that had been to An Thoi came back to Cat Lo. They were supposed to be the roughest people around. They had really seen the war and all this. Guys got orders to be transferred to An Thoi. They were chewin' their finger-nails off and stuff like that. I didn't really worry that much because people build things up to be more than what they really are, in some cases. In some cases they don't tell you enough. Things are nowhere near as bad here as people make them out to be. That is, the people that are here in Vietnam make them out to be. The people in the States make them out to be another story again.

Jesse's got about 18 or 20 more days until he goes on "R & R" He's going to Hawaii to see his wife. He's the only married person on the crew. That's all he thinks about— getting to Hawaii to see his wife, which I can't blame him. Matter of fact, that's all he thinks about is his wife.

We brought a NIS agent with us from An Thoi to Ha Tien. NIS is Navy Investigation Service. We were talking

to him on the way here and his particular specialty is investigation of narcotics charges. We were talking to him and
asked just how serious the drug problem was over here. He
said it is very serious. I asked him if it was any more serious
in the riverine force end of the Navy. In other words, the
Brown Water Navy, than it was in the regular Navy and
he said, "Yes, for the most part it was worse in the Brown
water Navy than it was in the regular Navy." Which
amazed me 'cuz most of the places where you are, where
I've been anyhow, you can't even get half the necessities of
life, how you gonna' get pot? I guess it depends on where
you are. I haven't run into anybody yet that has had it with
them or used it here in Vietnam as far Brown water Navy
goes. I don't know. That surprised me.

We also yesterday had a couple Army guys we brought
up here: a special agent and a couple Commanders. It's
really funny to see these people because the majority of
them, well a couple of the Army guys, were brand new in
Vietnam, must have just got here. The other guys have desk
jobs and things like that. It was really funny to see these
people compared to us. Like we're completely browned and
tan from being out in the sun all the time and these people
were all, like, you know, like looking American civilians, all nice and white and pink. We look like a bunch
of animals, you know, beards and the heavy tan and all.
When we got underway it was rough for the first hour or
so, which I guess I'm gettin' a little bit accustomed to occasionally and the rest of the crew is fairly well accustomed to.
We were bouncing around a little bit and these guys, it was
funny, they wouldn't say anything, like these are officers
and special people and all this. They wouldn't say anything
but you could see the look on their face that they weren't
feelin' too well. After about an hour or so it smoothed out.
It wasn't ridin' too bad.

Its two o'clock in the afternoon now. I guess I'll finish this up and try to find a place to mail it from and maybe catch a couple hours sleep before we take off tonight.
    So I'll say good-bye, take it easy.
(Audio, early February 1970)

Up to this point in telling the story of my experience in Vietnam, the letters and cassette tapes sent home have given nearly a day by day rundown of what was going on. Suddenly there are no more tapes for months until July of 1970 and the next letter is dated February 18, a week since the date stated on the last tape and over a week since my last letter. The reason for this gap in communication will become clear as I relate from memory the event that occurred during the lapse in communication.

As the tape indicates we arrived in Ha Tien on February 10 with our brand-new OIC, LTJG William B. Kean III, who in the months to come would come to be known as Wild Bill Kean. Lieutenant Kean was brand new in Vietnam and not yet broken in. We, as a crew, were brand new to the geography and operation area of the Giang Thanh River and Vinh Te Canal. Rather than assign us to day patrols first so we could get accustomed to the area, we were first assigned to night ambushes. Our fourth night ambush was on the evening of February 13. We were assigned a location about a mile into the Vinh Te Canal.

According to numerous sources, ownership of the land where the Vinh Te Canal was built had long been contested between the dynasties of Cambodia and Vietnam. Establishing a border between the two countries was one of the several reasons for building the canal. The canal has a history of violence and death which peaked in its five years of construction from 1819 to 1824. The American participation in the canal's violence was only a few short years. Death and violence continued even after the United States' withdrawal from the war and beyond the end of the war.

After the American war ended in 1975, violent incidents soon erupted again on the Vinh Te Canal. The

Kmher Rouge forces, in 1977, massacred over 3000 ethnic Vietnamese villagers at Ba Chuc living several kilometers from the canal.[16]

Getting to our assigned location required an approximately twenty-mile ride up the narrow winding Giang Thanh River to a point where the river heads off in a northerly direction into Cambodia. The Vinh Te Canal is entered by heading in an easterly direction. At that intersection of river and canal, there was a very small South Vietnamese outpost.

On the left is the VN outpost, the Swift Boat on the right is actually sitting right on the borderline.

Beached right next to the outpost was a "monitor" from the disbanded River Assault Group (RAGS) part of the Mobile Riverine Force (MRF). This monitor stayed on station 24/7 to provide protection for the Vietnamese outpost.

---

16. Springer Science & Business Media. *Environmental Change and Agricultural Sustainability in the Mekong Delta* edited by Mart A. Stewart, Peter A. Codanis

The monitor was one of those boats configured and armed for the knockdown—slug-it-out operations a few years back when the Navy first moved into the rivers and ran large scale sweeps and battles in VC held portions of the rivers and canals closer to Saigon using units from the US Army's Ninth Infantry. The Navy-reconfigured LCMs (landing craft mechanized) used for landing troops in WWII adding plate and bar armor for protection from enemy rockets. Rockets would hit the iron bars that were spaced out from the hull and detonate without penetrating the hull. Kapok-type material was added between the iron bars and hull on some boats to absorb shrapnel from the exploded rocket. In addition to machine guns and cannons, this monitor was mounted with a 105 mm howitzer.

Monitor picture courtesy of the MRFA.org

We made our turn to the right in front of the outpost and proceeded to our assigned location about a mile up into the canal. The current in the canal was too strong for us to maintain our position against the bank, so a line was tied to a tree on the canal bank with us positioned nose into the canal bank.

As usual, we broke into two watch sections with a man in the gun tub up top, a man on the aft 50 mount, and a man at the helm listening to the radios and sensors. The other half of the crew would attempt to get some sleep. I never slept inside the boat in dangerous areas because when a rocket hits, not only does it release its own metal fragments, it also makes shrapnel of the metal surrounding the impact and explosion spot. All this shrapnel blows inward, so being inside the boat is a bad place to be when in an area where an attack might occur.

I do not recall that we put sensors out that night. If we did put them out, I know we did not retrieve them. Sometime during the evening, it rained, so we donned ponchos. Lieutenant Kean preferred that we use the sound powered headphones so the three men on watch could communicate anything they heard with each other in a whisper without having to leave their mounts. The down side of this seemingly good practice was that we could not hear the night noises very well with headphones on our ears, and those noises not heard could be an approaching enemy.

Sometime past midnight, I was at the aft mount wearing jungle greens, flak gear, a poncho, a sound-powered phone with a long cord, and the larger-style helmet that accommodates the wearing of the headphone. Suddenly, there was a loud explosion and a bright flash. The next thing I realized was that I was lying on the fantail tangled up in poncho and phone cord, and that our twin .50 caliber machine guns up top were blazing away. I remember struggling and fighting to get untangled so that I could get up. It was like someone had tied me up. Once on my feet, I could not fire from the aft mount as turning the mount toward the direction of the attack would have me pointing the weapon directly at the main cabin of the boat. Not knowing what had hit us but realizing that it was low on the boat, I mistakenly assumed we had been mined. I could hear the engines straining and feel the boat pulling hard, but we were not going anywhere. The bowline tied to the tree would not let go. Bill Hogan left the pilot house and attempted to go forward on the bow to untie the line holding us from breaking free to get away, but the nonstop muzzle blasts from the twin .50s were directly over top of him. Each time he tried to reach the stanchion that the line was secured to at the very peak of the bow, the muzzle blasts pierced his ear drums causing severe pain. Jesse Church was in the gun tub on the twin .50s with R & R in Hawaii at the forefront of his mind. Determined to keep the enemy from being able to fire at us again, he never let up on the .50s as the heavy steel barrels of the guns began to glow a reddish orange in the night. Finally, one gun jammed and he continued firing with just the one .50. Eventually, Hogan managed to get to the line and free us from the bank of the canal. Back in the pilot house he jammed the throttles backward to remove us from the bank, and the boat rammed into the canal bank behind us nearly throwing me to the deck again.

Finally, we were turned and starting to pull away, and I was able to open fire with the .50 on the aft mount. Once we had cleared the kill zone, I ceased fire and looked forward to assess our situation. Tony Amoruso came staggering out of the pilot house in his underwear and asked in his New York accent, "Charlie, what happened?"

I don't remember the exact wording of my reply other than I indicated that we had been hit. My answer did not matter much as Tony was deaf from the blast of the rocket. Later he discovered a tiny piece of shrapnel in the end of his nose. He was extremely lucky as the rocket entered the boat only about five or six feet from where he had been sleeping in the tiny forward berthing compartment. No one lives if they are five or six feet from a B40 rocket when it goes off. The rack Tony was sleeping on was constructed from a body-length sheet of quarter inch aluminum. On top of the sheet of aluminum was a thick heavy mat about three inches thick. Most of the shrapnel from the rocket blasting through the hull of the boat was absorbed by the aluminum plate. Any pieces that managed to pierce the sheet of aluminum were absorbed by the thick mattress, except for the tiny piece that found its way into the point of Tony's nose. The greater damage was done to his hearing, but thank God, the total loss of hearing was only temporary for about a day. The partial loss has lasted. When a rocket explodes, it creates a tremendous shock wave or pressure, so much so that the boats which were hit low on the bow usually had the main cabin windows blown out. I was standing on the fantail of our fifty-foot boat when the rocket hit and the concussion knocked me off my feet. Tony was in the confined space of the forward berthing compartment when this rocket blast went off. It still is a miracle that he sustained no serious injury and can still hear at all.

I saw smoke coming from the forward compartment that Tony had come out of. There was a small fire, mostly just some of our clothes and papers burning. One of us grabbed a fire extinguisher and put the fire out, I don't remember who, maybe me, maybe another crew member. At that point, there was just a state of confusion and chaos, and I was just moving from one thing to the next. The weeks of training for this type of situation were kicking in and carrying us through the necessary motions to survive without having to think too much.

Our Vietnamese trainee had a small shrapnel wound in his midsection and seemed to be okay, but I had seen them be deadly before. I broke out a battle dressing and tied it on him or handed it to someone else to do it, I don't remember clearly. While I was doing this, I could hear more machinegun fire coming from the ambush site we had just left. As I ran back out to the fantail of our boat, I could see that some of our boats from farther up the canal had moved in and taken the area under fire.

Suddenly, I became aware of a very heavy feeling. After you live on a boat for three months, it is almost as if you and the boat are one. As the Engineman, I was always keenly aware of the sound of the engines and the feel of how the boat moved. We were feeling heavy and low. I looked over the side, which confirmed my feeling; we were sinking. A check of the bilges showed we had taken on about a foot of water. The rocket had penetrated our hull below the water line because the bow had been rammed up onto the bank, exposing part of the hull that was normally underwater. The motion of the boat moving forward in the water was forcing water through a hole that was nearly the size of a volleyball. I informed Lieutenant Kean that we were sinking ourselves as we made our way out of the canal. We needed to stop and get our bow up above the water line to make an emergency repair. It seemed like the safest place to make emergency repairs was right in front of the Vietnamese outpost at the junction of the Vinh Te Canal and the Giang Thanh River. As we proceeded to the outpost, I got our bilge pumps going to start pumping us out, but the small pumps were no match for the rate that we were taking on water.

We beached immediately in front of the outpost, and Lieutenant Kean ordered other crew members to put up illumination flares. We had both handheld pop flares and illumination rounds for the 81 mm mortar. Both types have small parachutes that unfold once the round explodes in the air. The parachute allows the burning illumination to hover in the air and provide a prolonged period of bright light. The larger 81 mm rounds light the night up like daytime for a while. The flares gave us light to see what we were doing as we made our repairs. Our cover boat and two PBRs joined us to give us cover.

One of the unique capabilities of the PBR (Patrol Boat River), the thirty-one-foot fiberglass patrol boat that the movie *Apocalypse Now* made famous, was the boat's water jet drive pump made by Jacuzzi. Not that the jet pump drive is so unique but the option to use it to pump out a sinking boat was a lifesaver. The jet pump had a cap that could be removed to attach a long, large, flexible hose to the pump and insert the suction end of the hose into a sinking boat. This maneuver required the PBR's drive control to be engaged and the engine rpms raised. This action caused the PBR to want to drive forward so it had to be tied to the sinking vessel or both boats had to be up against the bank. Once begun, this setup could pump out a sinking vessel extremely fast.

While one of the PBR's started pumping us out, I moved on to place a temporary patch on our hull as I was trained at NIOTC. Our damage control bag was simply a sea bag filled with various materials to make emergency repairs with. It included an assortment of cone-shaped wooden plugs, lengths of rubber hose, clamps, sections of rubber matting, and a steel *T* for applying what was termed a T-patch on the hull of the boat.

The *T* was a threaded rod secured perpendicularly to about an eighteen-inch piece of steel. The *T* was to be held on one side of the damaged area while any piece of flat material with a hole in the middle was held on the other side of the hull with any material attainable to be packed in between the hull and the flat patch. Finally, the threaded rod of the T was fed through the hole in the flat material and a nut was run down on the threaded rod to pull the patch up tight to the hull.

The trainers at NIOTC had told us that if we did not have or could not find a flat board of some sort to use for a patch to rip a cabinet door off one of the cabinets in the main cabin. It being no time to worry about the decor of the main cabin, I proceeded with great gusto to rip a cabinet door off and hand it to Tony along with a .38 caliber police special and instructions to jump over the side and shoot a hole in the middle of the door. Tony, still dazed and somewhat confused, obeyed and jumped over the side. He laid the door down and took aim, pulled the trigger several times, and only got a *click, click, click.* He then turned and looked up to me and said, "Charlie, give me a bullet." (I had handed him an unloaded pistol.)

Once the hole was blasted through the door we applied the "T-patch" and Tony was hoisted back up from the muddy, grass spot he had been working in. Meanwhile a radio call had been sent to medevac our wounded trainee. When the PBRs jet drive pump had most of the water pumped out of our bilges, we began our slow journey down an unfamiliar river back to Ha Tien—unfamiliar because we had never before navigated the winding river in the dark. Every one thousand yards of river we passed another boat was laying in ambush which gave a feeling of some degree of security. An LZ (landing zone) was decided on and we met the medevac chopper to get our trainee to medical assistance.

Our patch was far less than water tight, and water forced its way past the patch whenever we were underway, forcing us to stop several times and enlist the assistance of another PBR to pump out our bilges again. The trip back to the base at Ha Tien took more than twice the usual time due to the need to go slow and stop to get pumped out. It was around 5:00 AM when we got back and rammed the bow of our boat up on the beach next to the floating base.

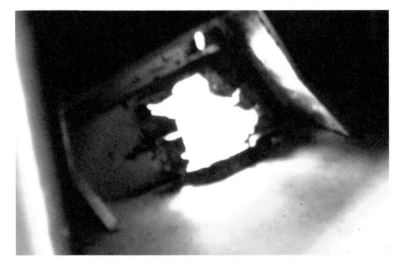

Hole in PCF 40 viewed from inside

After getting some food, we spent the morning cleaning up the boat and assessing the damage. Repairmen from an LST just off the coast came and applied a temporary fiberglass patch to the damaged hull.

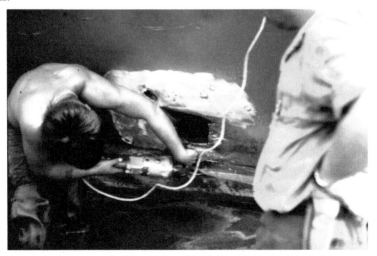

Preparing the damaged hull for fiberglass patch
(Note the repairman running an electric grinder
while standing knee deep in water—even with the
rubber boots it was a dangerous maneuver.)

I attempted to apply a bit of humor to a serious situation by painting *OUCH* above the damage. It was funny until later in the day when a sailor was killed in another ambush on the river. Then the higher-ups wanted to know who had painted the *ouch*, but no one ratted me out.

Shrapnel holes in the raised portion of the pilot
house deck and empty .50 caliber brass

PCF 40 with temporary patch on hull and temporary wood where main cabin windows had been blown out from the rocket blast

As soon as the patch was complete, we were ordered to make the two-hour transit back to An Thoi for repairs. Once we arrived at the repair ship, we were ordered to inventory everything on our boat, then inventory everything on PCF 9, transfer anything we needed, rearm, and get back to Ha Tien for another night ambush. Unreal, just unreal! After the night we had just been through and no sleep and the transit back to An Thoi, we had to go back and be out on ambush again right away? Some of us on the crew had been in wet clothes since the night before and had nothing to change into because the fire in the forward compartment had burned our clothing stored there along with damage to other of our personal items.

Wet, tired, and with nerves jangling, we dutifully followed our orders and were back on the river again that night. This is how it is in a combat zone. Personal discomfort is not a factor; the job of guarding the river and canal from enemy transit was the mission and priority. Like it or not.

I elected not to tell my parents about this incident, believing that it would be a little too stressful for them to hear about. In retrospect, forty-some years later, as I read the letters that I had sent home to them, I don't think I should have told them as much of the enemy action that was going on as I had told them.

The first time that I got the opportunity to lie down in a rack and try to sleep, I kept being awakened by a bright light being flashed in my eyes, or so I thought. On the first night that it happened, I thought that one of my crewmates was playing games and shining a flashlight in my eyes when I tried to get to sleep. After the third or fourth time that night I got up and told the guys to knock it off. Eventually, I discovered that no one was flashing a light in my eyes. Somehow my subconscious was repeating the bright flash of the exploding rocket in the middle of the darkness. The flashes went away after a few nights.

The next time we passed by the Vietnamese outpost and looked closely at the spot where we had beached to make emergency repairs, we made a scary discovery about the outpost's defenses. The riverbank in front of the outpost was covered with land mines to prevent any attempt by the enemy to get to the outpost from the river. We had literally beached in a mine field, and Tony had jumped right into the middle of it. To make things even more dangerous, he had fired a round through the cabinet door into the ground there, possibly setting off a mine.

Soon after the attack on February 13, night ambushes had the name and tactics changed for the boats operating out of Ha Tien. Ambushes were more accurately called water-borne guard posts. Instead of staying completely quiet, we were issued a half case of M79 grenades to fire throughout the night to discourage anyone trying to sneak up on a boat as had happened to us. If any of the sensors indicated movement, we were to fire grenades in that direction. I think this strategy caused a fair amount of creature casualties as innocent critters passed by the sensors.

Decades later, some of the details of the ambush on February 13 are no doubt a little blurred in my memory and the Navy's version is somewhat exaggerated. With these concerns in mind, I contacted two of my old crew mates, Tony Amoruso and Jesse Church. I requested that they write up their memories of that night. The following are the accounts that Tony and Jesse sent me. There are some minor discrepancies between our stories but essentially our stories are the same.

February 13, 1970

PCF 40 was sent to Ha Tien on the Gieng Thanh River, which is on the Cambodian border. It was our first time in this area and we would be here for 30 days. We were the new kids in the neighborhood, not new to combat, just new to Ha Tien. Jesse and I were into our tour for 8 months and had seen plenty of combat, not only in the rivers but also along the coast, Jesse had already been wounded once, by now we were seasoned vets. We met up with Charlie and Hogan when we got down south. Lt Kean joined us later. I remember talking to the other Swift sailors about Ha Tien. They said it had been real quiet for a few months, not any real combat happening. Our mission on the night of February 12, 1970 was to set up post on the Vinh Te canal along the Cambodian border. As we left the base our Vietnamese sailor asked where we were going. When we told him the Vinh Te Canal, he went into the cabin and came out wearing two flak jackets. I remember somebody saying "what does he know that we don't". It did make me feel uneasy. I went to my station to ready the twin 50's, Hogan and Lt. Kean were in the pilot house, Charlie and the VN on the fantail and Jesse on the bow.

I'm not sure how many boats were involved but I do know there were PBRs and Swifts. We got to our position and beached the boat and tied her up for the night. Lt Kean, Tony and the VN took the first watch, Charlie, Jesse and Hogan took the midnight watch. We did not put the sensors out because of the rain. I kept a can of oil in the gun tub and brushed it on the guns as the rain kept washing it off. All was quiet. Midnight came and Jesse took my place, Hogan took the pilot house and Charlie was on the fantail. Normally on a night ambush we never slept inside the boat, it was safer outside, but the rain made it hard to sleep, and we were told it had been real quiet for months, so Tony and the VN went inside. I think Lt. Kean did also. I went to the bow and thought about getting into Jesse's rack but something said don't, so I climbed into mine. I don't know what time it was when the rocket hit and I think we got hit with more than one. The noise was deafening and I remember I was sitting up saying, "What the f@#k was that." (They say that just before you die your life passes before your eyes. I did experience this and saw all my family and friends crystal clear, and it stopped at the third grade. At this time I had a vision of my child hood friend telling me to get out of the cabin. It all seemed so surreal and I never told anyone about this for years, thinking people would say I was crazy. That child hood friend is now my wife.) I could not find my glasses or my boots but I did have a t-shirt and pants on. It was dark and the cabin was filling with smoke, something was burning. I got out through the hatch above me which put me on the bow. I think I was dazed and disoriented because I just stood there looking around trying to figure out what happened. I then went down the port side to the rear of the boat. Jesse was firing the .50s nonstop. I noticed all the windows were gone and smoke was coming out. When I got to the fantail you were trying to get up and were all tangled with wire and poncho. I think Hogan was trying to untie the boat and Lt. Kean was in the pilot house. Hogan finally got the boat untied and started to pull away. The Vinh Te Canal is not very wide and as he was about to hit the opposite bank you yelled and I took over the aft controls, turned the boat and put the engines in forward. I think while I was doing this either Hogan or Lt Kean took the fire extinguisher and put the fire out. After Hogan took control of the boat, I walked over to you and was just about to ask you what happened and you opened fire. I remember my head pounding and all sounds were muted I guess I got really pissed, picked up the m-60 and with great words of profanity starting fire at the river bank. I put down the 60 and went back to the bow, still in a dazed state. Lt Kean waved me forward, as I got close to him he told me to grab his legs as he laid down and hung over the side to insert a DC plug into the hole to slow the water down. I hooked my feet inside what used to be windows and held his legs. None of this worked because the hole was larger than the DC plug and it floated right through. At that time Lt. Kean decided to beach the boat as we were clear of the fire zone and sinking fast. Our boat was low in the water. We beached PCF 40 close to a small ARVN Army base. At this time I went back into the cabin to check on the VN. He was sitting on the bunk in the main cabin also dazed, pointing to his wounds. I noticed that he was not even bleeding and told him help is on the way. I then went up to the gun tub to check on Jesse. He was surprised to see me and asked if I was ok. He thought I was either dead or seriously wounded. The 50's were so hot they were cooking off. I pulled a round out of each belt, which left about 4 or 5 rounds left on each gun and told him to fire them off and clear the weapon. This being done we headed down to the main cabin which was knee deep with water. All the radios were out I think, but soon a PBR came along side and pushed a large tube through what used to be a window and sucked most of the water out with their Jacuzzi engines. We were then able to access the damage. We had been hit above and below the water line right on the stabilizer and the hole was large and ragged. At this point Charlie came into the cabin with a .38 pistol and said, "I got to do this." We looked at him and jokingly said, "What? Are you going to storm the beach like John Wayne"? He then ripped a cabinet door off and we followed him out to the fantail. He instructed me to take it and the .38 on to the river bank and shoot a hole into it. This was so we could patch the hole using the door and a T-bar. So there I was on the river bank ready to shoot a hole into a cabinet door and all I heard was click, click, click. Still dazed and confused I asked him if he had any bullets as I had been handed an empty gun. We then proceeded to patch the hole as best we could. This was not easy because we had been hit on the stabilizer and it was hard to get the patch secure. I remember stuffing whatever material we had around the cabinet door so when we got under way it would slow the water down. At this time we got under way to go further down the river to meet a Medivac Chopper at an LZ to get the VN medical attention. This was not easy because we kept taking on water, but not as bad as having no patch. I do remember seeing a p250 pump to help with the water. Where it came from or how we got it is a blur. Charlie had all he could do to keep the bilge pumps going and making sure the engines were working and of course the p250 wasn't working too well. At this point all I remember is going down the river very slow, still taking on water, and scared we would get hit again because of our slow speed. I don't remember how long this took but when we did get to the base the sun was starting to rise. We beached the boat and started checking all the damage. The boat was a mess large hole in the bow, burnt stuff in the bow berthing, water damage everywhere, no windows and lots of small holes on starboard side. Everyone was taking pictures and amazed that no one was killed. The repair ship sent in a crew to do some repairs so we could get out to the ship. They also gave us another p250 pump just in case. We went to the chow hall to get some food and there was the VN on a stretcher all bandaged up and resting, he was going to be ok. After breakfast we headed out to the repair ship thinking we would get some time off while they repaired the boat but were met by a crew who stripped our boat and loaded us onto PCF9 and sent us right back to Ha Tien and we ended back up the Vinh Te canal that night.

This is my recollection of Friday February 13, 1970. Although some of it is blurry we seem to agree on most of it.

With all the confusion and chaos I feel we all did a great job of holding it together and helping each other. It was our night from hell and the best is we survived. This was one of many a fire fight and what's good is we lived through 365 days of Hell and are alive to tell about it. Welcome Home brother glad we all made it home.

(Tony Amoruso's account of February 13, 1970)

***

Vinh Te Canal February 13, 1970

What I remember about the day is the damn rain. It seemed to be raining every day now for a month, with little let ups here and there. It started out like a normal patrol, but the Vinh Te canal has been known to be a hot zone, for a long time, but it had been quiet lately. So the day started out with two PCFs and two PBRs, entering the Giang thanh river, which takes us to the Vinh te canal. The patrol went down like usual, we setup for the evening ambush and watch. The first watch went with Tony, (Ammo) and VN, (I think his name was Tran), and LT. Kean. No sensors were set up, because of all the rain. The sensors would pickup the rain drops so there would be no way we could hear the noise of anyone coming into our location, so no sensors. The first watch went down without any trouble. Now around midnight my watch came up, with Hogan in the pilot house, Charlie on the aft 50 and 81 mm mortar, me on the twin .50s on top. I felt uneasy when Ammo woke me up, because you really never get any real sleep when on patrol, just cat naps. I know it was raining because I could hear it all night long. So my watch began, wet! As soon as I got up on the twin .50s I had this feeling about a tree off to my left. I keep watching it. It was the only tree in that area and it seemed out of place. So as the night went down I would look at that tree quite often. It so happened to be

208

on our left side of the boat and that is where we were hit. We never saw the B40 rocket coming in. I have no idea where it was before we got hit. Never saw it come in, but it knocked me off my feet down into the twin .50s turret. All I could think of was to cover everything I could see with the twin .50s. Starting with that damn tree. Both .50s operated flawlessly and the cover went down from side to side with no let up. I had no idea where they were so I laid down a complete cover in case someone was still out there. At this time I could not see any in coming rounds. All I did hear was what was happening on the boat. First the engines started up but not going anywhere. We were moving forward and back like we were stuck in the mud on the river bank. I keep firing the twin .50s over and over. If someone was out there he is DEAD. Finally the boat broke loose and we hit the opposite side of the canal. Which at that time was not that far. It so happens these canals are small, some so small that you have to back out in reverse. At that point I could see the bank on the canal and it gave me the opportunity to open the twin .50s so I could clear whatever was there and then some. Next thing I remember we are headed down the canal out of the fire zone hot spot. I hear next that we are taking on water, lots of water and we have to find a beach to run up on to assess the damage. It so happens that the RV village was up the river a short distance. I now can see the other Swift Boat and PBRs open fire on the hot zone we just left. Charlie is handing Ammo a board and the 38 revolver. I hear click, click, click and Ammo yelling for bullets for the .38. I guess he is going to shoot a hole in the board for damage control! Right now my twin .50s are so hot the right barrel is glowing orange and it's pointed into the village. The right barrel goes off, (cook-off) the barrel is too hot and the rounds are going off by themselves. Lt. Kean said to point it into Cambodia. All I can think about right now is anyone dead or hurt. I know Ammo was in the cabin along with the VN and I had not seen Hogan. Ammo jumps up to help with the twin .50s and the cook-offs. The first thing I said was damn you're all right! How is everyone? Ammo said he was deaf and could not hear but was all right. Everyone else is OK. We are now joined by the PBRs so they can help take out some of the water we had taken on. This does not take that long before we are under way again in a short time. I climb down from the twin 50s and we were trying to keep up with the water still coming in. So I remember the buckets of water, hand over hand from the cabin, trying to keep up with the water. The PBRs were alongside tied together and pumping water out. It took hours before we made it to the river base. At that time we ran the boat, PCF40, on the beach so we can assess all of what has happen in the past 12 hours. I'm still feeling the adrenalin and shaking all over, and being soaking wet all night long. We looked at the damage and cannot believe someone was not dead. Someone was watching over us for damn sure!

February 13, 1970 yes we remember and so should everyone else that fought over there, hell is right here on EARTH!

(Jesse Church's account of February 13, 1970)

***

Just a short note to let you know I'm okay. The routine of being out from before dusk to after dawn, doesn't leave much free time. While we're off we have to get the boat ready to go out again, eat, clean up and get some sleep if possible. This doesn't leave much time to write. We haven't had a day patrol yet—due to circumstances. Tomorrow is our day off, maybe I'll get a chance to write more then. Maybe on days I can write more.

Things haven't been as calm here as people said they are. Several days ago 2 MSRs (Mine Sweeper River) were ambushed and 6 guys were wounded. You might have heard that on the news. It was on the Am. military radio station here. Also in the news, a PBR in Chau Doc, (on the Mekong R.) went into Cambodia by mistake and the crew is being held by the Cambodians.

Well, that's all I've got time for now.

(Letter, February 18, 1970)

In Ralph Christopher's book *River Rats*, he attributes the capture of an American PBR and its crew in early 1970 to too many beers and a tide change that turned the beer barge around while they imbibed there. He further states that it took several weeks of US-Cambodian negotiations to secure their release. After a shipload of farm machinery and heavy earth moving equipment were delivered to Phnom Penh, the sailors were released and flown to Saigon for court martial and never returned to that patrol area. The PBR was never returned.[17]

I should have got drafted. I joined the Navy to stay out of the rice paddies and jungles and keep from getting shot at. I accomplished nothing. I've been shot at as you know and nowadays I'm occasionally tramping through the jungle with an M16, just like the Army and Marine guys do. When we beach the boat here for a night ambush, we have to go out and put out sensors, which beep through a speaker back on the boat when somebody gets near them. This keeps anybody from sneaking up on the boat. We go out 2 at a time and take turns each night. There's very little dry ground here, so we usually wind up wet and muddy. Some fun, huh! The mosquitos bite you from head to toe. They bite right through your clothes and pay very little attention to insect repellent.

I'm glad we're going on days as night ambushes get rough on the nerves.

[17.] Ralph Christopher, *River Rats. p. 57.* Author House Publishing 2013

I went into town other day and ordered 2 sets of tailor made jungle greens. The town is now off limits, so I don't know when or if I'll be able to get them.

Ha Tien is a small town but is fairly modern for its size and location. It stinks like all Vietnamese towns.

The crew is having difficulty getting along with our new officer. He's got a lot to learn, but he'll learn or get killed. He's coming along.

(Second letter, February 18, 1970)

When I wrote in the second letter of February 18 that Ha Tien "stinks like all Vietnamese towns," I was not being derogatory about the towns, I literally meant the towns stink. The stench comes from several sources: open-air drying of fish, the making of fish sauce, and in some places unsanitary conditions. It was normal to see fish laid out on the side of the street drying in the sun.

There are many types of fish sauce with various ingredients. The most common name we used in Vietnam was *Nuoc Mau* and there is also *Nuoc Mam,* but the basic ingredient is the juice obtained by alternately layering dead fish and salt in a closed container and collecting the "juice" as the fish rotted. It doesn't take too much imagination to think of the odor that the process sets off. The odor kept me from ever wanting to find out how it tasted. Many crews would not allow their Vietnamese trainees to bring the pungent, odiferous sauce onto the boat.

One day in the latter part of February of 1970, we were heading up the Giang Thanh, I believe it was early afternoon. As we turned a bend in the river, we sighted two PBRs headed in our direction. When the approaching boats were about five hundred yards from us, they were attacked. Multiple rockets came zooming out from the growth on the east side of the river. Several of the rockets found their target. We were watching all this unfold right in front of us. The first PBR took several hits, was set ablaze, went out of control, and then went crashing into the river bank just short of the ambush site. I saw a body fly off the boat when it impacted the bank. The second PBR was returning fire into the ambush site. I do not recall if the second PBR was hit or not, but in all, five rockets had been fired.

As the second PBR barely cleared the kill zone, our two Swift Boats took up the fight and took the ambush site under heavy machinegun fire providing cover for the two PBR crews to take care of their wounded and begin pumping out the flooding PBR. Our two Swifts did not receive any return fire. On the part of the four boats involved, they performed as if the whole event had been choreographed and rehearsed, lending credit to the training we all had received. It was only in a matter of a few minutes that the fire on the damaged boat was put out, the crewman that had landed on the bank was retrieved, first aid was administered to the wounded, the two boats were tied together, the jet pump rig was pumping out the flooding of the damaged boat, and they were underway back to the base. We moved out of the immediate kill zone and commenced mortar fire into the ambush site. I do not remember if there was a sweep of the area afterwards or if any enemy was found as we continued on to our assigned area when we completed our mortaring of the site.

Remember how I wrote before and said that in spite of everything, we had a lot of fun. Well, since Mr. Burke left, things have changed. Mr. Kean is much different and has a lot to learn. Things have been drudgery with him. We've been on days yesterday and today. They are much easier and it gives you a chance to relax a little. I sure hope we get Mr. Burke back.
(Letter, February 21, 1970)

***

Just a note to say hi! Today is our last day of day patrol. Then 1 day off and back on nights again. I'd rather stay on days. I don't like nights.

Just think, if, if I get out of Vietnam in June, that means I only have about 100 days left right now. I doubt it, though.
(Letter, February 23, 1970)

***

I received 2 letters from you yesterday. One of them had some newspaper articles in it. It sounds like we really socked it to the NVA in Laos. I hope we don't get to [sic] tied up over there too. But, if we have to—I guess we will.

Wow! A boat just arrived from An Thoi. I didn't get any mail, but I got 3 packages from you, 1 from VFW and 1 from the Rodgers. I don't know where to put all the stuff. I went all through the stuff and stowed it away... The bottle of shampoo broke and was all over everything. Nothing was ruined but I had to wash a lot of stuff off...

That's all for now. I want to get some rest, before we go out tonight.
(Letter, February 26, 1970)

It was about this time, about a week and a half, since we were ambushed in the Vinh Te Canal and made the long, slow journey back to our base, that I received a message from my mother that would one day become a contributing factor to a complete change to my life. Mom told me that Reverend Robert Murphy, the pastor at my home church in Titusville, had awakened on the night of February 13 (actually early minutes of the 14th) and had the feeling that I was in grave danger. He stayed awake praying for me for four hours until he felt that I was safe. The timing of the pastor's prayer and our first real close call coincided, except for the time zone difference half way around the world. Nonetheless, the exact date and time match made it seem as if God had His eye on me and wanted me to know it. In some ways, it was almost eerie. It was more than I could process and figure out at the time.

I received your tape yesterday. It was good to hear everybody's voices. It just hasn't been convenient to make one here like it was at SeaFloat.

We're really making a hole in the packages already.
Those Hunt's snack packs are great. You know the little
cans of fruit and pudding.
(Letter, March 1, 1970)

One of the most frustrating things about the enemy contact, as it usually occurred, was that we never saw who was shooting at us. Rockets and bullets came flying at us and we returned fire, but we never saw our targets. Often rockets were set up in tubes concealed in the brush and launched remotely from a hole or bunker. The enemy would hold his rifle over his head while down in a hole and fire without exposing himself and disappear through a tunnel.

At 1300 hours (1:00 PM) on March 6th that changed. PCF 96 was in the lead and our crew on PCF 9 was following. From my location on the fantail of the trailing boat, I did not see the enemy on the west bank as they took aim at PCF 96. This was not one of those times that I had written about so often when they couldn't hit the broad side of a barn. These guys were right on and of course as close as they were, how could they miss?

I heard multiple rockets make a short trip before the sound of them exploding into PCF 96. Immediately the 96 boat's machine guns were returning fire followed right up by Tony's twin .50s up in our gun tub taking deadly aim on the enemy from his elevated position. I no more smashed down the trigger on the aft .50 and we were hit in the starboard bow. The scene was like slow motion in my brain. The power that the enemy rockets pack is amazing. A loaded Swift Boat weighs in at about twenty tons. This twenty tons of boat and weapons was traveling at perhaps fifteen knots or more. When the rocket hit, I could feel the boat lift and the boat's forward motion delayed for just a split second. I was standing approximately thirty feet from the blast and yet I could feel the pressure from the blast pushing on my face like a wave of air flattening out my flesh. Sitting on the starboard side of the fantail off to my left was Klaus Loquasto. Klaus was the only member of my class at NIOTC that I was ever on a crew with. He had taken Jesse's place while Jesse was on R & R. One of Klaus's unique character traits was his perfect posture

215

at all times. In a classroom, he sat straight up as if at attention. He never slouched. At meals, he sat at a table straight up. Lying on his bunk, he lay straight out on his back. Sleeping—no fetal position, no contortions.

Most men fire an M60 machine gun sitting with the weapon resting on a pivot on the railing or they lie down and stabilize the weapon on its forward tripod. When we were attacked, rather than crouch down or flatten out, Klaus stood straight up, placed the M60 to his shoulder, and opened fire. I had seen men fire an M60 from the hip like John Wayne, but I had never seen it fired from the shoulder. He gained a whole new level of respect from me.

The 96 boat was hit twice low on the starboard side of the bow. The two rockets hit within several inches of each other in an over and under pattern. A third rocket hit high on the rearmost part of the main cabin, just below where the life raft was located. A broken piece of the life raft flew up into the forward gun tub. I don't know if it was the life raft hitting him or the blast, but the forward gunner wound up lying in the bottom of the gun tub. His sound powered head phone or part of the life raft was jammed in the trigger bar of the twin .50s and they were firing wildly in no particular direction without being aimed. The gunner pulled himself up and got his guns under control.

The 96 boat cleared the kill zone and beached down river on the opposite bank to begin damage control and first aid. I could see blood on every crew member. In just the short distance from the ambush to where they beached, they had already started taking on a lot of water. We stood guard between the 96 boat and the ambush site until a nearby pair of PBRs came to our aid to provide assistance. We (the 9 boat) returned with the PBRs to the riverbank where we had been attacked.

While Lieutenant Kean and several crewmen from the PBRs went ashore to see what they could find, I checked on our damage. The rocket had entered high on the starboard side of the hull, just below, and a little ahead of the starboard door to the pilot house. Exactly at its point of entry on the inside of the hole was where the boat's main wiring harness ran. The harness was blown apart and we lost the use of a lot of our electrical equipment. From its point of entry, parts of the rocket traveled transversely through the boat, making it through the forward berthing compartment, the main cabin, the bulkhead between the main cabin and the engine room, and pierced a cooling tube for the port engine, allowing water sucked in from the river for cooling to flood into the bilges of the engine room. I managed to make a temporary repair to the coolant tube by wrapping it with tape, wrapping a hunk of rubber hose around the taped area, and securing the rubber with worm gear clamps.

The impromptu search team retrieved one rocket launcher, four B40 rockets, and one dead enemy body. They also reported blood trails heading back towards Cambodia.

Lieutenant Kean on PBR with captured weapons laid on deck

Meanwhile, a P250 portable emergency pump had been brought out to PCF 96 and temporary patches were attempted. Nonetheless it had to travel slowly and was sitting way low in the water, nearly sunk, by the time it reached Ha Tien.

A Swift Boat was tied onto either side of PCF 96 to ram it up on the beach to pump it out.

Pumping out flooding Swift Boat

PCF 9 stayed on station with PCF 22 until properly relieved. Back at Ha Tien, the crew took turns examining and posing with the captured weapon.

**Posing with captured rocket propelled
grenade launcher and rocket**

After temporary patches were put on the PCF 9 and PCF 96, we returned to the repair ship at An Thoi for repairs.

Chapter 7 of *Swift Boats at War in Vietnam* begins with an account of the March 6 ambush and credits PCF 9 and PCF 96 with eliminating a North Vietnamese "hit team."

PCF 96 in the skids and PCF 9 being lifted

Damage to rear of main cabin of PCF 96 cut away

Fan from berthing compartment damaged by rocket explosion

My guitar—body cracked by rocket blast

Once we were back at An Thoi, there were no other boats to send us back out in so we got about five days off to recuperate while we waited for our boat to be repaired. Like the hit we took on the 40 boat back in February, I decided not to relate the most recent event to my parents as I felt it would be too worrisome for them.

> *We are back in An Thoi for about a week I guess and then I think we're going back to Sea Float. Right now I guess Jesse is in Hawaii with his wife. Its really good a guy can get away to see his wife like that. He couldn't wait to get there.*
> *I dropped my tape player and busted it up, so I won't be able to make or listen to any more tapes until I get another one. I should be able to get one here.*
> (Letter, March 9, 1970)

***

After being on two boats that were hit with rockets and the grind of so many night ambushes, my nerves were shot and I felt like a I needed some time off from riding the Swifts. I had a shaky feeling inside that wouldn't stop and just felt awful all the time. I went to Lieutenant Kean to request some time off. We stood on the deck of the repair ship as I made my request as I didn't want the rest of the crew to hear my plea for some time off. Lieutenant Kean told me there was no way that I could get off the crew because every boat had to have an Engineman and there was a shortage of enginemen right now. In addition, every boat and crew were needed to fulfill the operation orders for the op areas. With regard to how bad I was feeling, he gave me advice that I hated at the time. He told me that the sooner I resolved in my mind that I had to stay on the crew, the sooner I would start to feel better. I walked away disappointed and angry, but as time went on, I found that he was right. Much to my surprise, once I accepted that I had no choice, I did feel better. That was the up side. The down side was that something inside went kind of dead. I suspect it is some type of subconscious self-defense, I don't know. I think it was the beginning of the development of the "thousand-yard stare," that sort of stare that is looking but not seeing because some part of the mind is defending itself by staying locked up. I really don't know how to explain it, but there was a change.

> *We are the duty crew today, so all we do is sit around and give people rides here and there when they need them. It's kind of nice to be off the front line (as you might say) for awhile. Just think 7 1/2 months to go. 4 1/2 months out of the way.*
>
> *The guy that we called "Poopsey" in NIOTC is at Sea Float I hear. Gradually as the divisions get turned over, we'll all be together again I guess. I heard a rumor that Ajax* [from class at NIOTC] *was being sent back to the states because he couldn't ride the boats because of his hearing.*
> (Letter, March 12, 1970)

Hearing loss is a common problem among veterans. It comes from the high decibel level noise experienced while firing machine guns and being near explosions. *A dangerous sound is anything that is 86 dB (sound pressure level - SPL) or higher.[18] A soldier near an M60 machine gun is exposed to 150 decibels and within 50 feet of an exploding grenade, 160 decibels.[19]*

I can testify from my personal experience of firing thousands of rounds of .50 caliber and having thousands of M60 rounds fired near me, that the decibel level of the .50 cal. is higher than 160 dB from the M60.

When loading 81 mm mortar rounds in the drop fire method, the round is inserted tail first into the muzzle while holding the forward part of the round with both hands. As soon as the round is dropped into the mortar barrel, the loader has to turn his body back away from the blast coming out of the muzzle. The blast is not just sound, it is also phenomenal pressure. *Blast pressure also damages hearing. Eardrums can rupture at pressure as low as 5 pounds per square inch, a fraction of what it takes to damage internal organs.[20]* I got a little sloppy on one firing mission when I was loading round after round in rapid drop fire mode. I did not get myself turned away far enough from the muzzle, and the pain in my right ear felt like someone had stabbed me in the ear with a knife. Thankfully, no permanent damage was done.

David Ajax had done a tour in Vietnam on PBRs before reenlisting and volunteering for Swift Boat duty, so he already had a year of machinegun fire pounding away at his ears before this tour. In addition, he carried the scars in his lap area from his twin .50s blowing up on him while firing them on his first tour. He did not leave Vietnam at the time of my March letter as the rumor suggested. He was transferred to Coastal Division 13's gunnery staff where I would eventually catch up with him. As of this writing, David and his wife Peggy are living in Panama and serving as missionaries.

---

18. *"The different types of hearing loss."* dangerousdecibels.org
19. backhome.news21.com/article/hearing/
20. Ibid.

CHAPTER 8

DEEPER INTO ENEMY TERRITORY

You gotta go out and face it...you gotta learn to conquer your fears...and get back out on the sea...a wise sailor learns to respect the sea...
—LTJG Richard C. Wallace, 1968

Well we came to Sea Float on the 16th. The land base they are building here is coming along. Things are pretty inactive here lately.

Mr. Kean is coming along pretty well and it's no big problem getting along with him anymore.

I got some 10 cent stamps finally. Still no tape recorder. I could use a laundry bag if you could get me one. Also, ice tea mix, all you can send.

Jesse should be back any day from R&R. Hogan goes on R&R at the end of this month. I haven't been sending any money home, because I've been letting it build up on the books, so I'll have money saved for R&R.

Hope all is well with you.
(Letter, March 19, 1970)

***

The Navy gives us tropical greens,, but the camouflaged [sic] tiger greens like are in the picture you have to buy yourself.

The mosquitos [sic] *are bad, but we get all the insect repellent and spray we need.*

It was good to see the kids [my niece and nephews] *in the pictures. I'm glad I'm not married and have a wife and kids at home.*

I borrowed a tape player to listen to your tape. [The last page of this letter is missing.]
(Letter, March 21, 1970)

***

Yesterday when I wrote, we were at sea. We anchored, acting as a radio relay for ground forces sweeping the peninsula [the very southern tip of the peninsula]. *They found all kinds of stuff. It sure is annoying sitting there bouncing around for 24–30 hours. We almost sunk on the way out. A salt water pipe broke and half flooded the engine room. It ruined the generator, so we're without a cooker and refrigerator again. Those 2 items sure can make life nicer. I don't know when we'll get it fixed as the boat is still operation without it, so they don't worry about getting parts for it or anything.*

We're going on an operation tonight at 2 a.m.
(Letter, March 22, 1970)

The swells during the time we were anchored just off the southern tip of the peninsula ranged from three to five feet. Using a stern anchor allows the swells to contact the flat section at the stern and keeps the boat from rolling side to side which makes sitting there a little less stressful. At one point, we received a radio request for fire support. The 81 mm mortar has a range of 3,940 yards, which is a little more than two miles.

Being accurate is deadly important when it comes to delivering "indirect" fire. Indirect because we can't see what we are shooting at from two miles away. Since this requires accurate calculation of our location and the target location, the propellant charge and mortar elevation are selected from a chart. In addition, the heading of the boat has to be considered to figure out how many degrees the mortar needs to be rotated relative to the boat's heading. With all that figured out, the obvious problem on this particular day with the boat bobbing about in rough water is how to have the correct elevation of the mortar. Initially this seems impossible and granted even the solution seems a little sketchy, but evidently works fairly well from my experience.

To create the opportunity to fire the mortar when the deck of the boat is level requires setting two anchors, one fore and one aft. That in itself is a bit of work and depending on what type material is on the bottom it can be difficult to get the second anchor to set. Here's the sketchy part—the anchors are set so that the seas are hitting the boat broadside causing the boat to roll side to side. The final step is to fire on the upswing when the deck is level with the horizon. That was my job. Evidently, I "got the hang of it," as the report came back that we were on target with requests for more rounds. Now if you have ever been on a boat that is rocking and rolling, you know that keeping your footing and performing any task is complicated by the motion of the boat. Imagine handling multiple high-explosive rounds that don't take well to being dropped on a hard surface!

> *I applied for a cut out [early out] of the Navy. So that when I leave Vietnam I'll be out of the Navy. Pretty good huh. I should get it. Usually all you have to do is put in for it when they announce that early outs are available and you get it.*
>
> *Operations have stepped up here at Sea Float. We are using the canals to probe deeper and deeper into the VC's territory. We've been finding all kind of things. POW camps, training camps, villages, supplies, etc. Last night we mortared a party where they had music and everything. If we only had more ground troops here, we could do a much better job. But Saigon is only worried about its main cities an doesn't want to be bothered with Cau Mau Peninsula.*
> (Letter, March 27, 1970)

I remember the night we were called on to mortar the "party." We had taken up an ambush position in the ever-dangerous Dam Doi River a short distance from its junction with the Cua Lon and Bo De Rivers and northern canal. Our cover boat was one that had been turned over to the Vietnamese. It was a short distance away in the Bo De. There was a ground force, I think a Seal team, a good way up the canal. In the middle of the night the ground force broke radio silence and requested fire support. It seemed they were on west side of the canal and had watched as people started arriving at a location on the east side of the canal. Shortly after a number of persons arrived, the gathering turned into something of a party complete with singing. I guess they thought no Americans would be up the canal late at night. The ground force elected not to risk getting caught by the enemy in midstream and called for fire support.

One of our crew listened to the ensuing radio communications as Munster (the call sign for Seafloat's command center) explained that the PG with the three-inch gun was on the other side of the Peninsula on a firing mission and no Seawolf helicopters or Black Ponies were available; everybody was busy elsewhere. Finally, a call came to us from Seafloat:

"Abbey November Niner, this is Munster, over."

"Munster, this is Abbey November Niner, over."

"Niner, request you provide fire support for Tradewinds, over."

"Munster, we are in a nice spot and would like to stay in place, over."

"Niner, need you to break away and support Tradewinds, over."

"Munster, the prizes in our magic box are low on energy, don't know if they can make the trip, over."

"Abbey November Niner, your orders are to make communication with Tradewinds and provide support, over."

"Munster, this is Abbey November Niner, understand your last and will join the party, but be advised it will take a little time to properly prepare our prizes to make the trip, over."

"Niner, keep me advised, out."

What we were trying to tell the operations officer at Seafloat, without coming right out and saying it, was that we were low on mortar rounds and we had the propellant charge bags on most of the mortar rounds stripped down for short range to use during close combat. In order to reach the target location, we needed to steal charge bags off some rounds and add them to others. This would give us some rounds with enough charge to reach the target and leave us with some rounds with no bag charges.

Our 81 mm mortar rounds had a charge two built into them. An additional seven bags of charge were attached around the narrow tail section of the round by means of a button hole-type attachment. Relying solely on my memory I estimate the bags were about two and a half inches long and three-fourths-inch wide with little button holes slit at each end. Around the tail section of the mortar round are little ear-shaped tangs to attach the bags to by slipping the slit in the bag over the tang, one on each end of the bag.

Begrudgingly, we pulled away from our ambush site trying to make as little noise as possible, but two twelve-cylinder diesel engines aren't very quiet! The tedious task of carefully transferring charge bags from one round to another was done with one man removing bags, one man putting bags on, and a third man holding a flashlight fitted with a red lens to lessen the enemy's ability to see the light at night. Meanwhile, radio contact was made with the troops, coordinates were received, and mortar positioning was computed. The boat heading had to be held constant in one place in order for the mortar rotation to stay correct. This was possible due to the twin screws and controls that provided forward and aft application of power as needed to stay in place. At this point our location was fairly well compromised if there were any enemy near us.

As per normal procedure, our first two rounds fired would be "Willy Peter" (white phosphorus), which burns bright when detonated. The bright explosion and fire allows the spotter to determine what corrections, if any, are needed to hit the target. When all was ready Lieutenant Kean gave the order:

"Commence firing, two rounds—Willy Peter."

The proper response would be something, like

"Aye, aye, sir, commencing fire, two rounds—Willy Peter."

I don't recall if we followed all that protocol that night or not, and I don't recall if any corrections were necessary to be on target. What I do recall is that we followed up with a number of high-explosive rounds, and the SEALs radioed that we were right on target and they could hear people screaming and running.

On another day in March, we were returning down a canal that was immediately north of Seafloat. We were coming around a bend in the canal and getting near the area were the Montagnards or Chinese mercenaries had their camp. There were some small arms fired, not a lot, and it was difficult with the noise of the engines to determine where the shots had come from. Lieutenant Kean stepped out of the pilot house and ordered us to open fire. Given our proximity to the camp and the direction we were headed, I thought it possible that it was simply our ground force doing some testing of their weapons. It did not sound like an attack. I was concerned that we would be firing on the camp and, furthermore, I did not perceive that we were in any immediate danger. I did not fire. Lieutenant Kean viewed it as a refusal to follow orders and threatened something or another. So I took aim in a direction that I felt would not endanger anyone in the camp. That was one of those tough decisions when I had to choose whether to follow orders and risk needlessly harming friendlies[21] or to not follow orders and risk penalty. I think I found a way around the dilemma. No one was injured at the camp, and there was no confirmation of an attack.

Note stakes for fish traps on right side of canal

[21.] Friendlies, military slang for friendly troops, in some cases it may mean civilians.

On yet another day in March our boat PCF 9 and Vietnamese-manned PCF 691 were returning from a night ambush in the Cai Ngay Canal with Montagnards aboard. Two rockets were fired over the fantail of PCF 691. Both boats returned fire, cleared the kill zone, and mortared the ambush site. Then we moved back in and inserted the Montagnards. Their search turned up a homemade twin rocket launcher.

As I said in my letter on March 27, we were probing deeper and deeper into VC territory by means of the narrow canals. I do not remember or have recorded the date or which of the many canals, but I remember one day going deep up one of the northern canals a long way from Seafloat. There wasn't much depth to the canal and the banks were high. I was feeling a little more scared than normal. As we went deeper and deeper, there were warnings for us. Punji sticks could be seen on every square foot of canal bank that wasn't covered with vegetation. Punji sticks are sticks about one or two feet long that are sharpened on one end and forced into the ground, sharp end up, in groups. Anyone who steps or falls on the sticks is impaled. Often they were dipped in human waste to cause infection. There were also signs in Vietnamese that said, "Death to those who enter." These signs were there to scare us—they worked!

I was about as scared as I have ever been in my life. We were really, really in the enemy's territory. I would say I was near panic at times. I calmed myself by looking out the corner of my eye at the American flag that flew on the back of the main cabin and repeating in my head, *For God and my country, for God and my country, for God and my country.* I am not sure how many people would agree as whether what I was doing was for God or not, but I was doing it for my country.

Years later when my Army Ranger cousin Joe was headed for Operation Desert Storm in Iraq, he called me for advice. He was concerned, as many soldiers and sailors are before combat, as to how he would perform when the "shit hit the fan." I told him a couple things. First, his training would kick in and take over; second, all of you will be looking out for each other; lastly, I told him about my terror in that canal that day and how I had just kept repeating to myself, *For God and my country, for God and my country*. Years later, he thanked me for the advice and words that I had given him.

Finally, we came to a wire cable stretched across the canal in front of us. This cable would have been put there for several reasons: First it could simply be to warn them that we were coming. Second, it could have been there in hopes of us coming upon it fast and some of the crew being knocked off or injured by the cable. But the most likely and scariest reason to put that cable there was to have it connected to a mine hidden in the water below the boat, with the mine fixed to be detonated if the cable was disturbed. Now comes the really scary part. Lieutenant Kean ordered one of the crew to cut the cable. Our damage-control bag carried a large pair of bolt cutters just for such an occasion in addition to damage control work. So we stopped in the water and cut a cable that could blow us out of the water. This was a true moment of fear that was approaching panic! My body was fighting itself. My lungs were trying to expand far enough to get more oxygen to feed all the muscles in my body while every muscle was tensed including the ones holding my lungs from getting enough air in.

The cable was cut, and there was that anxious moment while I held my breath, braced, anticipating, waiting. Would there be a delayed explosion? Would the boat lift in the air from the blast? Would we be sinking with a hole in the bottom of the hull that we could not patch? Were the VC watching and waiting to attack us after the explosion? If we were blown off the boat, would we have to choose between climbing onto the punji stick covered canal bank or staying in the water like fish in a barrel? Would our cover boat that was following us be able to pick us up if any of this happened? How long before helos or help could get to us way up here? All these thoughts, conscious and subconscious, went through my mind in seconds that seemed like hours.

There was no explosion and no attack—yet. I exhaled. Now we had truly entered the enemy's backyard; this was "Injun country." As we progressed farther, we came upon sampans and hootches, all of which we destroyed in true style of the old "Sealords Raids" done a year or so earlier when the Navy first entered the Ca Mau. We were creating explosions, fire, and smoke that let all the Viet Cong or NVA for miles know exactly where we were and no doubt pissing them off a bit.

Eventually, it was time to turn around and "get out of Dodge!" as the tide was going out. Even way up these small canals there could be a drastic change in water level, leaving us a big target sitting in the mud with just a couple feet of water around us. Once again, the bringing of the boat about-face was accomplished by ramming the bow onto the canal bank and doing a twist with one control forward and the other reversed. Of course by now, any enemy who had not been prepared for our unwelcomed excursion into their domain had had time to collect themselves and their weapons to give us a "warm farewell." About halfway back out of the canal, a few rockets were fired at a safe distance over us. We returned fire but continued our exit, wanting to get out of the canal before the water level went down any farther.

Fear

Fear comes in any level of intensity and length of duration. When trying to communicate fear, it would be clearer to the reader or listener if one could put fear on a scale with an x and y axis. The horizontal or x axis being for time, and the vertical or y axis being intensity. In fact, there should be several different words in the English language that would more accurately communicate the type of fear a person is experiencing or has experienced. But I guess that is why we have adverbs and adjectives.

Fear can come instantaneously at an extreme level of intensity, or it can build slowly or it can just stay at a given level over a prolonged period. Fear can be a good thing, and it can be a bad thing. Then again maybe fear is neither good nor bad. Fear is an emotion, and I am told that emotions are neither good nor bad. More accurately, it is what we do with each type of fear that determines whether fear is either good or bad.

I have experienced all sorts of fear. I prefer the quick ones that I can do something about right away no matter what the intensity level may be. An example would be being shot at and returning fire.

For me the worst kind of fear is the long-duration fear. An example of long-duration fear would be the monsoon storm we had ridden through back in November. The intensity level is not as awful as the duration. Fear that lasts for hours and days, which you seem to be unable to do anything about, is the worst kind of fear. It is debilitating. It sucks the life out of you. Over a prolonged time, a person becomes zombielike.

There is fear that is right up front that is all encompassing of your senses. There is fear that lingers in the back of your mind or subconscious but influences your decisions, words, and actions. Days and days of combat missions makes a person an expert on fear.

This discussion of fear could go on and on like Bubba describing to Forrest Gump the endless ways to have shrimp. Not long into my time in Vietnam, I resolved that I would rather go into any river or canal against any enemy force than ride through another monsoon storm. "And that's all I've got to say about that."

One day while escorting a tug and barge into Seafloat on the Cua Lon River, we were the lead boat, and our cover boat was bringing up the rear behind the tug and barge. One rocket was fired at the trailing Swift Boat. That boat moved up to cover the tug. We turned around and beached opposite the ambush site and commenced mortar fire on the location the rocket had come from. I don't remember much more about that.

Thanks for the newspaper clippings and jokes. We returned to An Thoi yesterday. The trip wasn't too bad. Jesse is on staff now. Toni and Jesse each received a medal and citation for a firefight they were in, while in Da Nang. Medals sure are pretty, but they aren't worth it.

Well if Cambodia and Laos and Vietnam all get organized and get together, maybe in time we can crush the NVA.

I haven't put my R&R request in yet. I wanted to put off R&R as long as I could resist, so that when I returned from R&R, I would have very little time left in V.N. But my willpower is failing and I think I'll go sometime in July.
(Letter, April 5, 1970)

When a person got close to DEROS (date eligible for return from overseas), he was labeled as being "short," meaning he had a short time before he would go home. Hence he was called a short-timer. "Short-timers" would boast about how short they were with lines, like

"I'm so short I can sit on a dime and my feet don't touch the ground."

or

"I'm so short I have to play handball against the curb."

or

"I'm so short I don't have time for long conversations."

Almost everyone had a short-timers' calendar on which were a lot of small blocks with numbers in each block. The calendar was used to keep track of and visually see the countdown of how many days a person had left to go home. Every day the person would block out another day's number. Most of the calendars had the numbered boxes inside the form of some object like a "fill in the block" painting.

A number of times in my letters and tapes sent home, I talk about the turnover of boats and divisions to the Vietnamese Navy and how it might shorten my year in Vietnam. Excepting some special forces personnel, the normal tour of duty was one year. I once heard that the most important morale booster in Vietnam was the knowledge that you were going home after one year. It was important to have that date to look forward to with the hope of making it to that date. It is obvious in my letters from the number of times that I wrote about the possibility of shortening my tour of duty—that getting an early date home was extremely important to me. In the end, I did get out of Vietnam twenty days early.

CHAPTER 9

BACK TO HA TIEN

After we finished our second deployment at Seafloat, we got some time off back at An Thoi. All our Swift Boats recently had radio "scramblers" installed to prevent the enemy from listening in on our radio communications. The scrambler code changed every day and had to be programmed by means of little toggle switches on a removable circuit board. Both the transmitting radio and the receiving radio had to have a scrambler with the correct daily code in order to communicate with each other. Now, with the scramblers installed, for security reasons, no boat could be left unmanned in any location. Even when our boat was in skids, on a barge, next to the repair ship in the Gulf of Siam, someone had to be on board and awake on watch to make sure the scrambler was not compromised. It was boring and seemed almost pointless, given where we were, to have to guard the scrambler.

I remember sitting in the pilot house in the middle of the night all alone one night and having the strangest feeling. It seemed like life at home was so far away that it was not even real anymore. It was as if being on a boat in Vietnam was the only life I knew and that it was the only thing I would ever do; I would never go home again. Maybe it was in the back of my head that I would die there in Vietnam. Maybe that made it easier not to let myself think about how badly I wanted to be home. Maybe if I divorced myself from the possibility of getting back home, it couldn't bother me anymore. Just like in the previous month when I accepted that I could not get off the boats for a while to collect myself, I started to feel better. I probably felt better because I was a little more numb inside. Anyhow, it was a strange feeling, also probably strange for a reader to comprehend.

There isn't a lot to do when your division headquarters is a barracks barge and a repair ship anchored in the Gulf of Siam. So it was a real treat when we were able to see a USO show. It was a live Australian band doing '60s rock-and-roll music with female dancers. They performed on one of the barges next to the APL and repair ship. I really enjoyed it. Two songs that got played a lot in Vietnam were "Leaving on a Jet Plane" by John Denver and "We've Gotta Get Out of This Place" by the Animals. They performed both of them. The only other song I specifically recall them doing was a Beatles song, "Octopus's Garden."

> *Well, we arrived in Ha Tien yesterday. We saw a U.S.O. show on the 12th and then we brought them to Ha Tien with us yesterday. 4 girls and 3 guys. All Australian. Wow—real live Caucasian girls in the flesh. Mostly in the flesh, too.*
>
> *Someone stole my camera while we were in An Thoi. $77.00 down the drain. Well, I've got the tapes and a recorder now—all I have to do is take time and make a tape.*
>
> *Guess what—199 days to go. I'm getting there.*
>
> *Hogan is back from R&R in Hawaii. One week away from it all, seems to do a lot for a guy.*
> (Letter, April 14, 1970)

***

> *I got a package from the VFW the other day. Please thank them for me.*
>
> *I broke my glasses in two while cleaning them, so I've been wearing one of the pairs the Navy made me while*

I was at NIOTC. I think I've finally bent them around to fitting half decent. I don't like them at all. I wear my sunglasses most of the time, during the day now.

I heard today that thousands of Vietnamese troops were sweeping through Cambodia. Sounds like good news.
(Letter, April 23, 1970)

As evidenced by the date on the above letter, I heard about the "Cambodian Incursion" days before President Nixon announced it to the American people in his address of April 30, 1970.

April 28, 1970 Nixon authorized U.S. combat troops to cross the border from South Vietnam into Cambodia. On April 30,1970, in a 2700 word televised address to the nation, Nixon sought to justify his decision as a required response to North Vietnam's aggression. His speech triggered a fresh wave of antiwar demonstrations, which led to the killing of four Kent State University students when Ohio National Guard troops fired on protestors.[22]

What became known as the Cambodian Incursion actually began in early April when Republic of South Vietnamese forces…mounted multi battalion raids against Communist bases in the "Parrot's Beak…"[23]

ARVN [Army of the Republic of Vietnam] *opera-tions across the border which were launched on April 1 through April 16 to the distance of 8 kilometers inside Cambodia. On April 20, South Vietnamese armored squadrons and ranger battalions conducted an operation in the "Parrot's Beak" area then penetrated a NVA base area in Cambodia opposite the province of Chau Doc. A major incursion of Cambodia was launched during the night of*

[22.] Politico

[23.] *The Encyclopedia of the Vietnam War: A Political, Social, and Military History* edited by Spencer C. Tucker p. 157

April 28, 1970, by South Vietnamese forces against the "Parrot's Beak" area.[24]

Eventually the Cambodian Incursion involved 50,000 ARVN and 30,000 U.S. troops, the largest operation of the war. The operation provided a year of respite to the Vietnamese as the Americans withdrew.[25]

***

Well, I'm half way done. Another 6 months and it will all be stories of the past. I think Steve has about 15 days left.

It's been raining a lot lately. It's sure a pain in the neck. And when it's not raining, its unbelievably hot.

We've got another new crew member, but Tony will be leaving soon as he only has about a month left to go. That will be the last of the original crew we had when we first came to An Thoi. I'm gonna hate to see him go. We got along almost like brothers. (Arguments and all—like brothers.)

There sure is a lot happening in Southeast Asia these days. Who knows what will become of it all. Who knows— the NVA may even be crushed. But that's too good to be hoped for. Who knows—maybe they'll start sending "Swifts" up the rivers into Cambodia. That would be exciting to say the least.

I just heard about Nixon sending Marines into Cambodia. Wouldn't it be great if we made the right moves to end the NVA once and for all.

(Letter, May 1, 1970)

---

24. *The Vietnam Peace Negotiations: Saigon's Side of the Story* by Nguyen Phu Duc, Special Assistant for Foreign Affairs to the President of the Republic of Viet-Nam, page 245

25. Weymouth D. Symmes. *War on the Rivers.* Pictorial Histories Publishing Company Inc. 2004

***

The allied push into Cambodia during the spring of 1970 brought the SEALORDS forces into a unique operational environment. At 0730 local time on 9 May, 10 days after ground troops crossed the border, a combined Vietnamese-American naval task force steamed up the Mekong River to wrest control of that key waterway from North Vietnamese and Viet Cong forces. The flotilla, led by a Vietnamese naval officer, was composed of American PCFs, ASPBs, PBRs, HAL-3 and VAL-4 aircraft, Benewah, Askari, Hunterdon County, YRBM 16, YRBM 21 and 10 strike assault boats (STAB) of Strike Assault Boat Squadron 20, a fast-reaction unit created by Admiral Zumwalt in 1969. The Vietnamese contingent included riverine assault craft of many types, PCFs, PBRs, and Marine battalions. Naval Advisory Group personnel sailed with each Vietnamese vessel. By the end of the first day, Vietnamese naval units reached the Cambodian capital of Phnom Penh, while to the south the combined force stormed enemy-held Neak Luong, a strategic ferry crossing point on the river. For political reasons, no U.S. personnel were allowed past Neak Luong, midway to Phnom Penh. Although the American component pulled out of Cambodia by 29 June, the Vietnamese continued to guard the Mekong and evacuate to South Vietnam over 82,000 ethnic Vietnamese jeopardized by the conflict.[26]

***

[26.] Naval History and Heritage Command, The Navy Department Library. *By Sea, Air, and Land. Chapter 4: "Winding Down the War," 1968–1973*

Two days ago I received a letter from Dan and a package from his parents. I also received a package from you.

I was really shocked to hear Dan is getting married. I really am sorry to miss that wedding. He's marrying Pam Richmond. She was a year behind us in H.S. He used to go out with her in high school. Back in the days of my red and white '54 Dodge that had gone through the whole family. And the days of my Blue 57 Plymouth. Ah - those were the days. Carefree youth - experimenting with life and love - our biggest problems being gas money and nagging teachers. Vaguely aware of some sort of messed up war in some never-before heard of country on the other side of the world. And look at me - I've read two books in the last 3 weeks and I'm trying to write like some kind of author already.

Well now from the past to the future—my request for separation from the Navy upon return to the United States has been approved. That means that in 172 days (plus a couple days in the States for paperwork) I'll be out. Isn't that great! It may even be less than that.

We've got a new guy on the crew named Mike something or other-ski. He's from Long Island. What an accent. He's a full-blown hot-rod nut, so we have a lot to talk about. (and argue about)

Guess what just hit me between the eyes like a ton of bricks—today is Mother's Day. HAPPY MOTHER'S DAY!

How do you let a mother know that you think she did one hell of a good job? Do you give her a commendation medal? Do you promote her to E-5? Do you give her a weekend pass? Do you award her a citation? No! All she needs to hear is—I love ya, Mom.

All the activity in Cambodia has not made things too much different here. "BUT" There are rumors going around about 20 or 30 boats going into Cambodia soon. Who knows?!?

We are due to leave here soon, but I hope we're here to go into Cambodia if they do it. That may sound crazy and I definitely would be scared, but it's the idea of being one of the first boats into Cambodia (although we wouldn't be the first because 100 boats already went up the Mekong River into Cambodia). It just sounds so adventurous to me, as if I'm starved for adventure! It really wouldn't be that dangerous considering the places they send 2 boats—20 or 30 boats could take care of thereselves [sic] almost anywhere. With our mobility, speed, and heavy firepower we're definitely hard to handle. The only advantages the enemy has is the element of surprise and the fact that he can be dug in and we're out in the open.

I can see it in the Hopewell Valley News now: "Charles W. Hunt, EN3, was aboard one of the riverine craft to move up the Gianh Thanh River into Cambodia. After crushing slight enemy resistance they…and so on." Wouldn't that be neat? Yeah, I know—you think your son has turned into a bloodthirsty, war monger. Nope—I'm still a devout coward, but going into Cambodia intrigues me to no end.
(Letter, May 11, 1970)

For readers not familiar with the logistics of the Vietnam War, Cambodia was (or tried to be) a neutral country, but they could do nothing to stop or deter the North Vietnamese from using Cambodia to transport troops and supplies and establish bases and staging areas. Until 1970, the United States respected Cambodia's desire to be neutral, but the buildup of troops along the border made it necessary to strike inside Cambodia before the Communists launched a major offensive.

The operation was a great military success as it destroyed numerous enemy bases and supplies. This setback to the enemy bought more time for an orderly turnover of the war to the South

Vietnamese forces. At home in the United States, the incursion further ignited the antiwar sentiment and protests.[27]

Well, the big question in your minds I know is how is the Cambodian drive affecting Swift Boats. So far—here it isn't affecting them at all. I imagine that by the time you receive this letter you will have heard on the news that an ARVN unit is making a sweep here. So far we have no special orders or operations and were told to go about our normal patrolling. I've heard very little about how it's going so far. Just that they've found supply caches and a couple ARVNS have been killed and about 14 wounded. I think that moving into Cambodia is the best thing that the U.S. has ever done here. Every rocket and mortar round and bullet that they capture is one less that will have the chance of being shot at me or any other American. I am disgusted with the U.S. peoples response to the decision our President made. Everybody thinks they're such a damned good authority on this war. I can't express to you how strongly I feel about all this and the war itself. What really perturbs me is that so many of the guys over here don't believe in what we're trying to do here. Well enough of this—if I kept going I could write a book on it all.

What can you do? Believe in your country and your President. But that's not enough. Tell the people you talk to. Reassure them that it's a just cause, that we're doing what we sincerely believe is right. Everyone that disbelieves speaks out but the others are always silent.

I may go on R&R the same time as Bill Metcalf from Pennington. I don't know yet. If so, I think it will be in August.

(Letter, May 18, 1970)

---

[27] University Press of Kansas, review of John M. Shaw. *The Cambodian Campaign, The 1970 Offensive and America's Vietnam War.*

In response to my last letter, my parents submitted part of my letter of May 18 to the *Hopewell Valley News*, and it was printed:

PEWELL VALLEY NE

Letters

TO THE EDITOR:

EXCERPT FROM VIET NAM:

The following is an excerpt from a letter written by Charles W. Hunt, En 3, U.S. Naval Reserve, to his parents. The Hunts and the Hopewell Valley News feel that the people of this area would be interested in what their son has to say. . . . The letter is dated May 18.

"Hi! . . .

"Well, the big question in your minds, I know, is . . . how is the Cambodian drive affecting swift boats. So far, here, it isn't affecting them at all. I imagine that by the time you receive this letter, you will have heard on the news that an ARVN unit is making a sweep here. So far we have no special orders or operations and were told to go about our normal patrolling. I've heard very little about how it's going so far. Just that they've found supply caches and a couple of ARVNs have been killed and about 14 wounded.

"I thing that moving into Cambodia is the best thing that the U.S. has ever done here. Every rocket and mortar round and bullet that they capture is one less that will have the chance of being shot at me or any other American, I am disgusted with the U.S. people's response to the decision our President has made. Everybody thinks they're such a damned good authority on this war.

"I can't express to you how strongly I feel about all this and the war itself. What really perturbed me is that so many of the guys over here don't believe in what we're trying to do here.

"Well, enough of this . . . if I keep going I could write a book on it all.

"What can you do? Believe in your country and your President. But that's not enough. Tell the people you talk to. Reassure them that it's a just ..use, that we're doing what we sincerely believe is right. Everyone that disbelieves speaks out, but the others are always silent.

"I may go on R & R the same time as Bill Metcalf from Pennington. . . ."

"Charles"

About this time in Ha Tien, we got news that PCF 50 had been sunk in the Dam Doi River when it was hit by a large recoilless rifle round. Once the area was somewhat secured, they were given orders from Coastal Squadron One headquarters to "scuttle" the boat. Shortly after those orders were carried out, stripping off guns, radios, and critical gear and smashing lots of things on the boat, a second call came not to scuttle the boat. Too late!

PCF 50 was one of the boats that seemed to get right into the thick of it a number of times and take a lot of damage and casualties in the process. I have copied three of those occasions from the Swift Boat crew directory at Swift Boats.net where there are firsthand accounts.

As the last report below states, on May 18, miles away from the forces invading Cambodia, PCF 50 was in the notorious Dam Do River when it was hit by a 125 mm launch bomb. The story, as I heard it, was that the boat sunk right on the spot. I did not see the boat until a later date when I was back at Cat Lo when it was in a repair shed there.

On the morning of 3 November 1968, PCF 36, PCF 43 and PCF 50, along with VNN Coastal Group 41 units, with a Regional Force embarked, carried out a raid up the Ong Doc river, 65 miles south of Rach Gia on the Gulf of Thailand. While PCF 36 remained a few miles from the river mouth to support a Regional Force sweep to the south, PCF 43 and PCF *50 proceeded to a point 10 miles up river to take suspected enemy positions under fire. Sniper fire was received killing the after mount operator of PCF 50. PCF 50 spotted the sniper and killed him as he attempted to escape.* During the operation, *USS DuPont DD 941* and *USCGC Ingram WHEC 35* provided 5 inch naval gunfire support.

At 1300H on 4 December 1969, US PCFs 50, 56, VNN PCF 3805, an LSSL with Seawolves providing air cover, were conducting a psyops patrol on the Song Dam Doi about 25 kilometers northwest of Sea Float, when they were ambushed by an unknown number of VC with B-40, AK-47 and M-16 fire. *The lead boat, PCF 50, took a B-40 hit head-on, in the pilot house, killing the bow gunner, RD3 Martin S. Doherty, and wounding the OinC, LTJG Robert S. White and helmsman, QM3 Thomas R. Terfehr. A second B-40 hit close aboard to port, wounding two (2) additional crewmen, EN2 John R. Phillips and BM3 Roy D. White, on the fantail.* The VNN PCF 3805, took a B-40 hit low on the port bow and another on the port side of the pilot house, killing the USN advisor, BM1 Don E. Stevenson, and seriously wounding the VNN OinC and XO. PCF 56 received a B-40 near miss that wounded the OinC, LTJG Patrick L. Evans. The Seawolves and LSSL responded with saturation fire into the area and silenced the enemy fire. A VNN reaction team was inserted and a ground sweep resulted in the capture of two twin B-40 rocket launchers, two entrenching tools, wire, and batteries. Two members of the VNN reaction team also received minor wounds.

On 16 May 1970, PCFs 50, 64 and 692 were proceeding east on the Song Dam Doi, when all units were taken under heavy automatic weapons fire and rocket attack. *PCF 50 was hit port amidships, by a 125 mm launch bomb, and suffered a 5'x6' hole.* PCF 64, astern, was hit by a B-40 rocket on the fantail, killing two (2) US Navy personnel and wounding three (3) other US Navy personnel as well as four (4) *Kit Carson Scouts.* All units returned fire and spotted for SEAWOLF helicopters and BLACK PONY aircraft as they launched numerous strikes. PCF 50 was stripped of all her weaponry and most of its other gear, then left in the river, because of the extensive amount of damage she had suffered.

PCF 50 was recovered the next day, 17 May 1970, by various SEAFLOAT assets and the help of heavy air cover. It was then transported to NSA Cat Lo by barge for repair.

PCF 50 was returned to full operational status on 12 November 1970.

CHAPTER 10

LAST MONTH IN AN THOI?

Proud Miserable Vagabonds

Depending on how we viewed our lives in this Brown Water Navy, we could feel like miserable vagabonds or proud warriors and at times a bit of both. We were sent from one forward base to another, never staying anywhere long enough to feel like we belonged there. We operated day or night, depending on the operations area and what was needed at the time. Sometimes we were on station for days at a time. Eating and sleeping took a backseat to accomplishing the mission. Sometimes we might come in from being out all night, eat, get a couple hours of sleep, and then be sent right back out again. If the boat's generator was operating (it was a finicky piece of machinery that often let us down), we had cold water and real food in our small reefers (Navy's term for refrigerator and freezer). When the generator was down, we had warm water and C-rations or LRRPs.

As we were on the water, the mosquitoes fed on us nightly. No matter how thoroughly I applied insect repellant, the mosquitoes found a place to bite such as the corner of my eyes, the edge of the mouth, or in the ear. During monsoon season, it rained on and off all night long. While it was raining, the mosquitoes left me alone, but the rain washed off most of the repellant so that the minute the rain stopped, they were back before I could get repellant back on again.

The heat was offensive but made much worse due to the clothing worn at night to keep the mosquitoes from our skin. The helmet and flak jacket added to the heat. Rashes, crotch rot, and athlete's foot were difficult to stay ahead of given the heat, humidity, and random ability to get a shower.

Life had hours of boredom dotted with instantaneous bursts of excitement and adrenaline.

Underneath of all the annoyances of this crazy existence lay the knowledge that any day on the river could be our last day, or worse, we could be severely wounded or captured. All this slowly took its toll on me and I suppose many others.

On the other side of the coin, there were parts of this life that we loved mostly for reasons of feeling special or macho. Being part of the activity at Seafloat and Ha Tien was exciting. We were where it was all happening. We were on the A team now. We were gettin' it done. We were some tough dudes. We delivered that awesome firepower. We didn't have to put up with the usual spit and polish bullshit that the regular Navy dealt out. There was a lot of macho talk that fueled our pride in who and what we were.

Then there was the camaraderie like nothing I ever experienced before or since—living together, eating and sleeping together, sharing twenty-four hours a day together, learning and knowing that your buddy would always cover your back. We functioned in combat as a single unit—boat and men. For a relatively brief period, we were a brotherhood living a unique experience unlike any other. Yet in time, all the circumstances and experiences wore us down, and feelings and emotions became more and more calloused. We were no doubt transformed and took on that blank serious look that I had seen on the crew from Coastal Division 11 several months back when PCF 63 was on border patrol out of Coastal Division 13. It took time to change us to what we had become, and back home in the States, it would take time to get back somewhere near normal again. Whether any of us are entirely "normal" is questionable. I guess it depends on the definition of normal.

My last month (5 weeks) attached to Coastal Division 11 in An Thoi were spent zigzagging back and forth between CosDiv11's base and both of the forward support bases at Ha Tien and Seafloat as described in the following letters. We operated out of both forward bases for a while before returning to An Thoi each time. Finally, the orders came for PCF 9 and our crew to report back to Coastal Squadron One headquarters in Cat Lo. The transit from An Thoi included one last trip through the Ca Mau Peninsula, affording the enemy one last chance to get me. From CosRon1,[28] we were soon reassigned to Coastal Division 13 that was now newly headquartered in the town of Sa Dec located in the middle of the Mekong Delta.

We returned to An Thoi 2 days ago. We are having repairs done and when they're finished we'll be off again. Maybe patrolling Cambodian coast or back to Ha Tien or down at Sea Float. As you've probably heard already and can read in the enclosed article, our division and the VN division are patrolling the Cambodian coast now in addition to our other areas. We are really short on boats. Instead of having 5 or 6 here at a time for repairs, they have 1 or 2 at a time. Things are hot and heavy at Sea Float as you can see by the other article enclosed. Please don't be alarmed by the article. That is the first U.S. fatality at Sea Float since December. And in the same amount of time the operations at Sea Float have netted us about 200 enemy dead. So no one can complain about the ratio. The man that was killed was on the 64 boat. It had a rocket burst in the air. The 50 boat was hit by a 122 millimeter launcher bomb. It put a 6' x 4' hole in the side of the boat causing $35,000 worth of damage but remarkably no one was seriously hurt.

---

28. CosRonOne is the Navy's shortening of Coastal Squadron One. Commander of CosRonOne was ComCosRonOne

PCF 35
PcF 50
PCF 64
_____

Sea Float

Enemy gunners attacked a U.S. Navy patrol boat with rifles and rocket propelled grenades Friday afternoon 172 miles southwest of Saigon, according to American officials. They said the Navy crew lost one man dead and four wounded, and that another three former enemy troops serving as scouts were also wounded. Enemy casualties were unknown.

newspaper article from Navy Times? or Star and Stripes newspaper?

I don't remember if I told you or not, but we've got a new officer. Mr. Kean is now on PCF 691. Mr. Klinedinst (our new OinC) seems to be pretty good. He's much easier to get along with than Mr. Kean. But I think they'll never be another Mr. Burke. He was really good.
(Letter, May 21, 1970)

***

Well by the time you get this letter I'll only have 5 months to go. It doesn't quite seem like forever anymore.
(Letter, May 24, 1970)

***

Well, we're back in Ha Tien. Now, I'm the only one left of the original crew. I also have more months of patrolling in Cos Div 11 than most everybody else in the division. Which means that if they ever get an abundance of enginemen in this division (which they've never had) I'll have a good chance of going to a staff job. I spoke to the Commander last week about being put in Ha Tien as a staff Engineman

255

as they have none here. He said he'd like to, but can't spare any enginemen.

Today at Ha Tien the base is moving from a complex of barges to a newly built land base. It's something to see a whole base disappear before your eyes in a couple hours. I guess the whore house will have to relocate soon also.

I don't know if we'll have a barracks at the new base or live on the boats as always.

I guess you flew the flag yesterday more proudly than ever. [Memorial Day]

Ha Tien will be turned over to the VNs late in June. I hope so, that would give the division a lot less to do and make it easier on everyone. All we would have then is Sea Float and a couple coastal patrols.

Last night one of the VN Swifts patrolling the coast of Cambodia captured a large junk filled with oodles of B-50 rockets and AK 47 rifles.

Another little tidbit of info. Remember the article I sent you about the boats that were ambushed at Sea Float. It said that enemy casualties were unknown. Well, they are now. They killed 11 of the VC that ambushed them and they were in bunkers, too. Just goes to show you, it doesn't pay to mess with a swift boat, but every now and then they (VC) have to be reminded.

On July 1st our boat is supposed to go to Cat Lo for a complete overhaul, so that it will be ready to be turned over around Sept. 1st. I don't know if we'll stay there with the boat or not. If so, maybe I'll get to go see Tim Housel[29] as he is near Cat Lo now.

I had a funny dream last night. It was about all the kids from the Washington Crossing area that I went to school with. Vinnie, Dennis K., Bob Mickel, Gail Turner,

---

[29.] Tim Housel was a high school classmate and his father was my employer when I worked at Housel Brothers. Years later I learned that Tim's job with the Army was the preparation of Psychological Warfare materials.

Sally Astbury, etc. It was a short one with very little to it, but I remember all the faces. It's funny the things your subconscious digs up.

My $12.95 Timex gave up the ghost last month so I bought a new watch. Its a Seiko, waterproof, shock resistant, stainless, self winding, automatic doo-hoozer that tells you the day of the month and a built-in alarm system and 17 jewels and a luminous dial. What do you think it cost me? $32.95 Not bad, eh!
(Letter, May 31, 1970)

As the beginning of my letter of May 31 states, I was now the last man left from the original crew that was formed when I arrived at An Thoi back at the end of December 1969. At this point I had five months experience operating in Coastal Division 11. Regardless of rank, I was the most senior man on the crew as far as experience. This meant I was often the one they turned to know how to handle things that came up. It also seemed that I no longer formed strong bonds with my fellow crewmates. I am sorry, but I don't even remember the names of some of the men I served with beyond that point. Perhaps I no longer wanted to get close with anyone. Maybe I didn't trust "green" sailors? Maybe I was just burnt out? Probably just a combination of all three possibilities.

Tony and Jesse leave for Saigon tomorrow and 2 days later fly for home.

Since our Onan (small auxiliary generator for cooker, fans and refrigerator and freezer) is working real good now, we've been doing a lot of cooking. So I need a box of aluminum foil and a spatula. Also a plastic ice tea pitcher. Some assorted plastic containers to keep food in would be good to have also. (Letter, June 1, 1970)

Cooker on top of counter with reefers below. Tiny sink with hand pump for water is not visible between cooker and bulkhead. Note fan in top left corner.

Back when Bill Hogan was on the crew, he would occasionally prepare a complete meal with meat, potatoes, and a vegetable. That was quite a feat with our little electric cooker, which was not much more than a glorified hot plate, and it was much appreciated. Once he was gone, we rarely ate a regular meal. Often we would eat just one type of food like just meat or just potatoes. Our favorite practice at Ha Tien was to go get a 50 lb. bag of potatoes, a number 10 can of shortening, and a big can of ketchup. Then we would eat nothing but french fries for days. We took turns peeling potatoes, cutting them into fries, and dropping them in the hot oil in the small deep fryer section at the back of the multipurpose electric cooker.

Neil eating on the mortar round storage box

Steve sitting on a small crate the mortar rounds came packed in and using a .50 cal. ammunition can for a table.

As mentioned before, when the generator was inoperable, we had no cooker, frig or freezer, and meals sucked. Then we had either C-rations or "LURPS." C-rations came in a plain brown box and included a main meal in a small can, some variety of fruit in a small can, and crackers in a small can. Depending on which box you got, it may have pecan roll, fruit cake, or pound cake in a can. My favorites were pound cake and any of the fruit varieties. Also included were either peanut butter or cheese spread.

We could put the drab green-colored meal cans of C-rations on the engine if we were underway, and the heat of the engine would heat the food inside if we were patient and waited long enough. C-rations are a little short on flavor. C-rations was what we called them, but actually, C-rations were discontinued years earlier. C-rations were replaced in 1958 by MCRs, meals combat ready. They came in eight varieties: meat and spaghetti in tomato sauce; chopped ham, egg, and potato; meat and noodles; pork and rice; frankfurters and beans; pork and beans; ham and lima beans; and chicken and vegetables.

LRRP pronounced "lurp," stood for long-range reconnaissance patrol food packet. It was freeze-dried, dehydrated food in a tinfoil packet. We had to add hot water and mix it for what seemed forever to get it to soften and plump up to be edible. The lurps also came in eight varieties: beef hash, beef and rice, beef stew, chicken and rice, chicken stew, chili con carne, pork and scalloped potatoes, and spaghetti with meat sauce.

Both C-rations and LRRPs came with an accessory packet, which varied a little from each other but basically included small packets of instant coffee, cream substitute, sugar, and salt. Also two pieces of gum, a couple sheets of toilet paper, matches, and four cigarettes. When we were at Sea Float, we were each allotted two cans of beer a night. A lot of trading went on between beer drinkers, smokers, gum lovers, and persons favoring some particular item in the C-rations; this was done in order to get more of what a person liked in exchange for what they did not like.

The Head or Bathroom

The naval term for the bathroom is the *head*. The term originated from the location where it was placed back in the days of sailing ships.

The place for sailors to relieve themselves was all the way forward on either side of the bow. The figurehead was situated just below the bow; hence one would go to the "head." There were two reasons for the bathroom to be located forward on the bow. The first had to do with wind direction. Sailing ships normally traveled with the wind coming from the general direction of the stern to fill the sails. This location assisted in the removal of foul odors from the head. Second the design of the facility allowed for water splashing over the bow to clean the head.

When the Navy set out to provide boats suitable for close-in coastal patrol, there was no time to design and build enough boats. They decided to purchase boats already in production, which were being used to transit back and forth to oil rigs in the Gulf of Mexico. Modifications were made to adapt the boats for use in combat. Originally, there was a toilet located in the forward berthing (sleeping) compartment. It was typical of marine type design, which had a pump handle alongside by which a system of valves and a pump were activated to remove the waste. The sleeping compartment was very small and crowded, so the toilet was sandwiched between the two lower-level berths. This design had no means of removing foul odors that the sailing ships had incorporated. Imagine someone taking a dump about two feet from your head! Pee-eww! Further, imagine someone urinating while the boat is in rough water or making a hard turn, then instead of being pee-eww, it would be pee on you! Therefore, all toilets had been removed from Swift Boats.

If we needed to urinate, we just did so over the side of the boat. Of course, if we were traveling at high speed, that would be a little tricky, and there might be a little more spray than just sea spray.

We had a metal bucket with a line (a rope in land-lovers' terminology) tied to the bail (handle) to use for defecation. First, we would drop the bucket over the side and fill it about halfway. Then we found a spot on the fantail to sit on the bucket. When finished, we simply dumped the waste over the side and then dropped the bucket in for a good rinse. The bucket filling and rinsing was tricky when we were underway. Many a bucket was lost by a new crew member the first time he attempted getting water into the bucket if he was not severely warned by a seasoned "bucketeer" as to the power of the water. For some reason, new guys never understood how powerful the water force would be when the bucket entered the water while underway. Too bad no one ever got a picture of the look of surprise mixed with puzzlement when the line was ripped from a new guy's hands as the bucket was whisked away. That look was soon followed by a look of chagrin when he realized the predicament he was now in. The look of chagrin then gave way to one of concern of his impending discomfort. To make things worse, he now had the whole rest of the crew pissed off at him for losing the bucket, which was an important part of daily life. Now he would have to learn an even trickier and somewhat dangerous alternative method of relieving himself. Nature's demands forced him to attempt to get this lesson learned.

At the rearmost part of the fantail there was about a thirty-inch gap in the low railing. Now keep in mind this procedure was being done while traveling at twenty to twenty-five knots, which is about 23 to 29 mph. The boat is on step which means the bow is up, the deck has a tilt to the rear, and the boat has lifted a little higher in the water. Depending on weather and water conditions, the boat may be bouncing or leaning, which could result in a man overboard.

Getting into position was tricky and best done with your pants off for several reasons:

1. Dropping drawers was awkward once the "launch" position was reached, which demanded holding on to the rail.
2. The possibility that some portion of one's discharge might land on one's pants.
3. The likelihood of the boat's rooster tail wake soaking your pants.
4. The individual might get dragged into the water if the pants get caught and pulled away during the cleansing maneuver.

The first move was to get around or over the mortar box. Then turn and face forward, get a good grip on the railings at either side of the opening, and plant your feet firmly on the edge of the deck. The next move is to sit back, hanging butt over the water, but not too far back. Once the main part of this mission of relief was accomplished, clean-up could be done without the need for paper by simply squatting much lower and allowing the boat's rooster tail to perform the most powerful deuce ever experienced by mankind. Of course, if the boat were traveling slow, the trick then was to use toilet paper while holding on to the rail with only one hand.

If nature called while we were in a populated area, we did attempt to hold off until we moved around a bend in the river or got farther away. Crude as we were, there was some degree of modesty, and besides, it might be poor for public relations with the locals to be riding by displaying our junk or delivering a nasty moon.

Well, guess where I am now? We had to go back to An Thoi from Ha Tien because I had to have an engine replaced. From there they sent us to Sea Float. Right at the moment, things are pretty slow around here. On the 10th of this month Cos Div 11 is turning 7 boats over to the VNs ... when this takes place they'll keep 4 U.S. Swifts here at a time instead of 8 to 10. This means that once I get out of Sea Float this time, there's a good chance I'll never have to come back here. Looks like the turnover of Swifts may eventually benefit me.

Well I finally made up my mind on an R&R date. August 4th and if there's no flight available then it will be August 11th.
(Letter June 5, 1970)

***

RAIN + MOSQUITOS + RAIN + MOSQUITOS + RAIN + MOSQUITOS + RAIN + mosquitos and rain + mosquitos + rain + mosquitos + rain + mosquitos and more rain and more mosquitos. [sic]

I never saw so many mosquitos [sic] *in my life as Sea Float has now. And there* [sic] *vicious too, they eat insect repellent for breakfast and us the rest of the time. We've got net all over the boat but can't keep them out. I don't know if I'll be here when it gets here, but rush 2 cans of bug killer, they're all out here.*

Mr. Burke is a full Lieutenant now and works in the operations office here.

Enclosed is captured VC propaganda—Save it.

(Letter June 7, 1970)

ĐỒNG BÀO THUỘC GIA ĐÌNH BINH SĨ NGỤY
VÀ ANH EM BINH SĨ NGỤY HUYỆN TÂN CHÂU
A N   P H Ú

Càng thất bại, Mỹ - Thiệu - Kỳ - Khiêm tăng cố xô đẩy binh sĩ ngụy đi càn quét gây tội ác với đồng bào hòng kéo dài ngày tàn của chúng .

Đồng bào thuộc gia đình binh sĩ ngụy nên kêu chồng, con, em mình hãy bắn vào đầu Mỹ và bọn ác ôn lập công trở về với Mặt trận hoặc bỏ súng về nhà làm ăn .

Anh em binh sĩ ngụy kể cả anh em phòng vệ dân sự hãy đề cao tinh thần dân tộc, cương quyết phản chiến khởi nghĩa hoặc làm binh biến hay rời bỏ hàng ngũ ngụy quân trở về với nhân dân để góp phần chống Mỹ cứu nước .

Lập công thì tùy theo công mà được đãi ngộ thích đáng .

Đồng bào và anh em binh sĩ ngụy nên khẩn trương kẻo muộn .

ỦY BAN MẶT TRẬN HUYỆN
TÂN CHÂU AN PHÚ

This document was authored by either a Viet Cong or NVA soldier. I am told that it is poorly written, indicating a lack of formal education. The document urges wives and mothers to call upon their husbands and sons to shoot Americans or desert from the Army. It also offers a reward. The following is the translation that I received.

Civilians Belong to Infidel Soldiers in Tan Chau District, An Phu

Suffering more defeats, Americans, Thieu, Ky, Khiem[30] always try to push infidel soldiers to patrol, creating much more crimes to prolong their days.

Families belong to infidel soldiers should call up on yours husbands, son to shoot to the heads of the Americans and those evils or to abandon their weapons to come back to Frontline or to come home to work.

All infidel soldiers and civilian officers must up hold the nationalism of your people, must anti war and abandon your organization to come back to civilian to fight Americans to save our country.

Your works will be rewarded depend on it integrity. Frontline, Tan Chau, An Phu

**

Things are so-so at Sea Float, not too busy, not too much extra free time, lots of mosquitos and rain.

I have made no headway at all of deciding what to do with myself when I get home. I know college or a technical school would mean a better job and more money in the future and I'll never have a better opportunity to go to school what with the Veteran's benefits plus the money I've saved.

But on the other hand I could go back to Coleman's [the Oldsmobile dealership that I worked at before going on active duty] *I know what it's like there and for the most part I like it. They really want me back too. That doesn't put any extra money in my pocket but it's a good feeling to be wanted and know you're doing a good job. I'll never get rich there or even into the higher echelon, but I'll*

---

30. Thieu was the President of South Vietnam, Ky was the Vice President and Khiem was the Prime Minister

never starve either. I could work on diesels and make much better money but I like cars better.

The decision all lies on this fact. I can go back to something I know all about that doesn't have much of a financial future or I can spend a pile of money and 2–4 years of my life to learn to do something that pays much better, but that I don't know if I'll like.

There is another factor that enters in here that I shouldn't let influence me too heavily but it does. If I go back to school, it will mean another 2-4 years of skimping and will probably take all the money I have saved. But if I go back to Coleman's, I'll have enough money to buy a new or fairly new car and motorcycle and generally live pretty well while I'm single. If I did this I may be sacrificing the future's financial happiness for the present's financial happiness.

So I have a decision between money and doing what I like doing.

One of our new crew members, Mike, who is what they call a materialist, believes in what you call the almighty dollar regardless of whether one is happy in his work or not. He doesn't believe in God. He has never loved anyone other than his parents and feels females are only for sex.

Lately, because of him, I have become more aware of the precious non-monetary gifts my parents have given me and realize that they are much more important than money. My parents didn't have a brand new house for me to live in but they showed me how any house can be warm to the heart and comfortable to live in with a little work. More important they gave me a home to live in - not a house.

Rather than drill into my head how much better I'd make out in life if I made lots of money they showed by their example in their own lifes [sic] how well one can make out in life if he has faith in God.

Rather than show me how happy one can be with the things money can buy, they showed me how happy one can be with the one he loves. Truly loves - another thing they helped me understand.

Rather than showing me how happy one can be by traveling in the proper social circles they showed me how happy one can be spending a little time with his family.

Love and understanding are the gifts my parents gave me and I'm glad they gave me them for no amount of money can buy that.

I just hope Mike opens his eyes some day because he's not a bad guy and I'd like to see him get a chance to enjoy what really are the better things in life.

In conclusion, you can see that all this compounds the difficulty of my decision. Also what I have written may seem sort of unaprapo (spelling?) to be writing to my parents, but if one puts it off and puts it off, one day he will find he no longer has the chance to tell his parents how he feels.

Guess what I all of a sudden (a couple days ago) decided to buy if I don't go to school? A Corvette! I always liked them, but decided they were too expensive and impractible [sic]. *But I think I may buy one and just keep it for about a year or so. Maybe that will finally get the hot rod stuff out of my blood. Maybe I'll never get it out of my system.*

I think what I'll probably do when I get out is loaf around for about a month and then go back to Coleman's with the understanding that I may decide to quit and return to school. That will give me a chance to adjust to civilization again and get back into the swing of things before I make up my mind.

I wish I could talk to you about all this, it would probably all be clearer to you then, even though I'm sure you understand.

Well, take it easy,

P.S. 141 days to go

(Letter, June 10, 1970)

Graveyard Ambush

Graveyard in canal - defoliated land

Last night was a real spine-tingler of an operation. We had a night ambush in a canal that had a graveyard and scattered graves in it. The area has at one time been defoliated or bombed with napalm as there are no greens growing there, just dead trees, mud and gravestones. During the night we heard a small engine like a sampan motor but it never came our way. We also heard several gunshots and saw what looked like a signal light in the distance. All this is common in Vietnam but the area it all came from is not supposed to have anyone in it. No civilians or friendly bases or anything. So you know who it was. It must have rained a dozen times and every time it stopped raining the mosquitos[sic] returned with reinforcements. In the middle of the night, the dead tree we were tied to fell over scaring everyone out of their wits. All these things combined made quite an eerie night. I could tell you dozens of stories but we'll save them for when I get home. I only wrote of this for lack of anything better to write about.

Our new officer, Mr. Klinedinst, is a real slob. He keeps his person clean, but he just leaves his clothes and things laying all over. He saves all kinds of junk and he doesn't care whether we ever clean the boat up at all. With 6 guys on a 50' boat this makes difficulties. The place generally looks like a pig pen. This slob didn't even want to wash his own dishes. (We straightened him out on that though.) I'd like to see his house, its either a pig sty or his poor wife has to pick up after him continually. Other than being a slob and somewhat lacsidasical (spelling) and always mooching cigarettes, he's a pretty good guy. He's a real switch though after Kean who was a stickler for keeping the boat neat and clean. By the way, Kean hates Klinedinst with a passion. They are 2 opposites that don't attract.
(Letter, June 12, 1970)

On June 13, 1970, while traveling on the Bo De River with PCF 3 as our cover boat, three rockets were fired at us. None of them hit either boat. We returned fire, cleared the kill zone, then beached and commenced mortar fire on the ambush location.

In our training at NIOTC, we were taught to return fire when attacked and make high-speed firing runs back and forth through the kill zone until the enemy fire was suppressed, unless we received severe damage or casualties. Making repeated firing runs was not always practical and in some cases exposed a crew to unnecessary danger. Therefore our rules of engagement were changed. The new tactic was to clear the kill zone, beach several hundred yards upstream from the initial attack, and commence mortar fire while calling for air support.

One thing that you should never do in warfare is use the same tactic over and over again. The enemy then knows what you are going to do and can plan how to counter your maneuver. Eventually, the enemy caught on to our new tactic and set up double ambushes.

Knowing that we always went to the opposite bank after clearing the kill zone to deliver mortar fire, the VC positioned a second group of attackers upstream and on the opposite side of the river. On at least one occasion, a Swift Boat started to beach exactly at the location of the second ambush and received a direct hit in the pilot house, causing multiple casualties. Therefore the Officer in Charge (OinC) was allowed to make the determination whether to make one, two, or no firing runs through the kill zone or to clear the kill zone and beach at a safe distance out of enemy range, either upstream or downstream from the initial attack and commence mortar fire. This flexibility to choose how to counter an attack, depending on the circumstances at hand, seemed to work well and keep the enemy off guard.

On June 15, we were assigned a mission to once again probe one of the notorious northern canals. Shortly before the mission was to commence, one of the Swift Boats that had been turned over to the Vietnamese arrived with a full VN crew. The newly arrived Swift was assigned the mission we were supposed to go on, and we were ordered back to An Thoi. Later in the day we got word that the Vietnamese Swift had found a 500 lb. bomb in the canal, but it did not go off. I don't know how accurate that story was. How did a 500 lb. bomb get there, unless it was one that the United States had dropped and it did not go off? Anyhow, they found some type of explosive that was meant for us, and I quickly became a strong fan of the turnover process. Who knows, maybe we may have approached whatever type explosive it was and had it explode on us?

> *We returned to An Thoi from Sea Float yesterday. I got a whole bundle of mail and 2 packages...I enjoyed the clippings from home. Things and people sure are going to be different when I get home. Of course, I will be different also I guess...*
>
> *That's about all—will keep you informed of my whereabouts.*

(Letter, June 16, 1970)

***

We're in Ha Tien now…

I haven't got the copy of the Hopewell Valley News that you put my letter in. I forget what I said and curious what all they printed. Mrs. Dey mentioned it in a letter and Paul VanNoy [Vietnam veteran] wrote me a letter to say he agreed and congratulated me for speaking out. I imagine there's a lot of people that were glad to see it. As my officer says, I'm a real patriot. Any American who isn't should spend 24 hours as a prisoner of war as I did in survival training. As I think I told you when I was home, when they raised the American flag at the end of the 24 hours, most of us were in tears at its sight. Whatever it meant to any of us before was felt 1000 times as strongly then. I've got an old torn and tattered flag we took off of our boat and I intend to hang it in my room. Because while standing only about 10 ft away from that flag, I've killed for it and almost been killed for it. I hope stating those facts doesn't shock you too much, but like you said, you know I'm not at a picnic over here. (Not actually that particular flag but what it stands for.) Do you think I can possibly stomach today's unpatriotic demonstrators after that? No way in hell, they'd best stay clear of me when I get home. I've close to the same hatred for them as the people that shoot at me.
(Letter, June 17, 1970)

***

Hi Dad,

I just found out that yesterday was Father's Day. So Happy Father's Day! I'm trying to think of something nice to say but can't, as in one of my letters a while back I said how I feel and I don't believe in continually repeating these things.

I hope you had a nice Father's Day.
(Letter, June 21, 1970)

***

The new base here at Ha Tien will really be nice when it's all finished. The rooms are really spacious. It's a shame so many Americans have had to live under rotten conditions in this country and now that we're turning over our assets to the Vietnamese we build brand new bases for them[sic]. *It really makes us mad sometimes. We still live on the boat, they haven't finished the barracks for "swift" people yet. The new chow hall serves the same lousy food the old chow hall did, but now we have to wear shirts in the chow hall.*
(Second letter, June 21, 1970)

Somewhere between June 22 and June 24, we were ordered back to An Thoi with orders to proceed from there to Cat Lo to prepare our boat for turnover. The route from An Thoi to Cat Lo took us back down to the Ca Mau Peninsula to use the Cua Lon and Bo De Rivers to cut through the peninsula from the Gulf of Siam to the South China Sea. This route was a shortcut rather than go all the way around the southern tip of the peninsula by sea. The shortcut also allowed us to do a layover at Sea Float. This was my final journey through the dangerous rivers of Ca Mau. Just this one last trip, and I should be relatively safe for the remainder of my time before I go home. Just this one last chance for the enemy to get me, and then it's all downhill from here. This was the day I was waiting for, for so long.

On the trip from An Thoi to the mouth of the Cua Lon River, PCF 3, which was making the voyage with us, blew an engine. With only one engine functioning, our travel speed was greatly reduced. PCF 3 radioed in to Sea Float that our ETA would be delayed due to engine failure. Evidently PCF 3's radio transmission was "in the open." "In the open" means they did not encode the message to keep the enemy from knowing they were an easier target, since they were unable to reach high speed on only one engine. It was surprising to realize that even in this Godforsaken, nowhere land, the enemy had the capability to tune in to our radio communications and was listening. In addition to that, he had the resources to put together an ambush with very short notice. More than once, boats had been ambushed after they had radioed in to the base that they were in any way less than fully functional.

I guess they were listening in this day, or maybe we were just unlucky this day. After we were well into the river, rockets suddenly were exploding as they hit the water around our boat, causing momentary geyser-like spout-capped explosions. Okay, I've seen the rockets before and heard the zing of the bullets. All our guns were blazing away on the location the rockets had come from, but I saw something that I had not seen before. I saw a rapid succession of telltale spouts of water leaping up from the river water between me and the riverbank. The trail of water spouts were automatic weapons rounds walking their way out to me! My mind was saying, "Hey, this ain't right! I'm leaving this place, this is my last time through!"

It was my habit in a firefight to crouch down behind my weapon in the attempt to have the gun mount afford me some small amount of protection. This time around, I was as low as I could get and still able to see over the machine gun. The fifteen- to twenty-round bursts we had been taught to use as we spotted in our field of fire on to a target were totally abandoned. My thumbs were locked onto the butterfly trigger and not letting up until we cleared the kill zone. The word was passed that we were going back for a firing run. I had fired almost all the four hundred rounds in my "super shooter" and needed to throw another can of ammunition onto the mount and feed the new belt of ammo into my gun.

There are a number of things about machine guns that you don't see in the movies and probably only those trained on machine guns know. Furthermore, unless one has used (or misused) a machine gun a lot, they may never experience these dangerous malfunctions. One is a "cook off," another is a "runaway gun," and the last is a "burned-out barrel." These oddities are caused by an extremely hot gun—hot because it had done a lot of rapid firing.

In the excitement of the moment, I did not think about how badly I had overheated my weapon. In one motion, I strode to the side railing of the fantail and bent over to lift a fresh can of ammunition. At that precise instant, just before I lifted the heavy four-hundred-round "super shooter," my weapon "cooked off" one round.

Had it happened a split second before or after I had bent over, the .50 caliber round would have exploded my skull like a ripe coconut.

There was no time to reflect on my nearly accomplishing for the enemy what they had been trying to accomplish for so many months. I opened the top of my .50, threw the last few hot rounds left on the previous belt of ammo over the side, slapped the new belt of ammo into place, slammed down the top plate, and double-cocked a fresh round into the chamber, ready to go back and teach these jerks not to shoot at me when I'm getting outta here.

As we reentered the ambush site and opened fire, I was having trouble seeing where my rounds were going. Quickly I figured out where they were going. They were going everywhere! When I fired, I could see some rounds chopping leaves off the trees, other rounds kicking up mud on the bank, and still other rounds splashing in the water. I had burned the riflings out of the barrel of my machine gun because of not letting up on the trigger back when I saw those rounds walking right out to me. With the riflings damaged from the excessive heat, rounds I fired now were coming out of the barrel in an ever widening swirling pattern, giving me no accuracy at all. Thankfully, we received no return fire from the enemy on our extra firing run.

We stayed in the area while troops were brought out to make a sweep of the area. The troops recovered a dual rocket launcher that had been carefully set up in the brush; its green color making it difficult to detect. We never would have seen it at the distance we were from the riverbank. It was the kind that was set up and aimed at a particular point on the opposite riverbank. The enemy would be some distance behind in a hole or bunker with a small battery and two wires that led up to the rockets. When a boat approached and was nearly in between the tubes and that chosen point on the opposite river bank, the wires were touched to the battery and the rockets were launched.

We had been instructed in the past never to discard old batteries where they could be retrieved by the enemy and to destroy any type tube that the enemy could fabricate a launcher from. Now we knew exactly why.

Hidden rocket launching tubes—note: one round was not fired

Neither boat suffered any casualties to the crews, and the only damage found to our boat was a bullet hole in one rung of the ladder on the side of the main cabin. Had our boat been going a bit faster or the enemy pulled the trigger a split second later—that round would have gotten me. Death in a firefight is only a matter of a tiny fraction of measurement away. A bit more speed, a split second sooner or later, a micron of weapon aim—up, down, left, or right—can make the difference between life and death. We each would like to think we survived because we were good at what we did, but can we be so bold? Can we say, "Our number just didn't come up that day"? Or do we give credit to God for watching over us? But how can any of us know? Unfortunately, this type of questioning can be the seeds of what is known as survivor's guilt. Sadly, some veterans live with guilt that they survived when others did not.

We proceeded on to Sea Float and began the cleanup of empty brass, the cleaning of our guns, and swapped stories of what had just happened as each of us had seen it. While cleaning up, my crewmate that was on the M-60 machine gun aft with me confessed to us that he turned his back to the ambush and fired on the opposite bank because for some crazy reason, he had thought that if he didn't look, then it couldn't hurt him. Go figure.

The picture above shows the littered deck in the aftermath of the June 26 ambush. Positioned on the right side of the aft mount is a full four-hundred-round "Super Shooter." Draped over the left side of the gun mount is my flak gear. On the right side of the picture, to the rear of the boat, is the empty "Super Shooter" tossed to the deck in the heat of battle. Forward of the empty can is the damage control bag. In front of the DC bag are two empty mortar round packing tubes. On the bottom of the picture, dead center, is the lid of a 7.62 mm ammo can, and strewn all over the deck is .50 caliber brass.

I was not aware of it at the time, but this would be the last time I fired a .50 caliber machine gun. The rest of my time in Vietnam would be easy duty in safe places. The final weeks would be spent preparing and transporting boats for turnover to the Vietnamese.

Same scene as above showing more empty mortar tubes and another ammo can on the left

Adrenaline

Adrenaline is a wonderful God-given thing. It gives us the strength and energy to do Herculean things when necessary. It automatically flows when needed. It is a magnificent drug. But like any powerful drug, it can become addictive.

Months of searching for an elusive enemy were dotted with adrenaline highs when we found him or more often when he found us. These highs and lows were overlaid onto the long-duration, low-level fears to create a new creature that I had never been before. A creature that craved adventure, excitement, and action while at the same time scared and wanting out of it. I suppose it's much like the drug addict that craves the next high but realizes that getting that high might cause his death. Like the drug addict, I was bored and restless when I had not had a high for a while, but at the same time I wanted to be done with something that could end my life.

I can remember sometimes after a firefight walking about the brass-littered fantail of the boat with excitement running so high I felt like I would burst. Often we (the crew) would relate highlights of what had just transpired like a group of high school football players in the locker room after winning the big game. If there were US or friendly casualties, there was just as much adrenaline flow but without the celebratory mood.

During my last two months in country, I was transferred to patrol in a very safe area. It seemed to be the squadron's pattern to start off our time in Vietnam in a semiactive combat location to get our feet wet, no pun intended, and then transfer us to a hot spot like Coastal Division 11. Toward the end of our tour, we would get transferred to a relatively safe area or duty. These last two months were extremely boring with no action at all. It was like a drug addict going cold turkey. I was bored and missed the adventure and excitement that provided the highs, but I was relieved that the worst of the war was over for me.

Suddenly, as I write, I wonder if my past adrenaline addiction has to some degree been responsible for my intense interest in watching my two grandsons wrestle. Perhaps it is a vicarious experience. Maybe the release of adrenaline experienced through the excitement of watching them in combat on the wrestling mat feeds a bit of that old addiction.

CHAPTER 11

TURN OVER TO VIETNAMESE

We're in Cat Lo. We left Sea Float at 4:30am on the 27th.
PCF 3 came with us and they blew an engine on the way
so we didn't get here until about 10:00 that night.

It's nice to get back to something that somewhat resem-
bles civilization.

They're doing a lot of repairs on our boat and so are we.

Mike got himself in a real mess last night. He got in a
fight in a bar in Vung Tau and broke the place all up.

Swifts are being painted black now instead of grey. It's
about time. They stick out like a sore thumb in a river or
canal when they're grey...

There's hardly any mosquitos here at all.
(Letter, July 1, 1970)

The "fight" mentioned in the preceding letter is a story worth telling. Mike had gone into Vung Tau on the evening of June 29 seeking female "companionship." He negotiated for a full night of "companionship," often promised by the ladies of the evening, like "I love you long time." That evening, after spending a "short time" with Mike, the young lady left when Mike fell asleep. Hours later, when he awakened and found her gone, he realized she had not upheld her end of the deal.

280

The next day, Mike complained all day at the base and announced his plan to go back and get part of his money back. He did some drinking before we got to town and was fired up when we got to the bar where the young lady was. I do not remember why the other Mike from our crew and I waited outside a short distance away, but for whatever reason, it was determined that this was the first Mike's grievance and we were staying out of it.

While we were waiting, we started to hear some shouting and then the sound of breaking glass that sounded like the proverbial "bull in a china shop." It seemed that when Mike threatened violence, the bar tender had broken a bottle on the bar to use as a weapon, and then bottles and glasses started flying at Mike from all directions. All the young ladies in the bar joined together in the assault on Mike. From outside, the next thing we saw was Mike headed for the door with a half-dozen hookers hanging on his back. Whether it was the drinking that Mike had been doing or the load he was carrying, his approach to the front door was slightly off. When he crashed into the doorpost, the whole front of the building shook. He took a few steps back like a ram preparing to butt heads with his opponent and charged forward again, this time making it through the doorway. He began to peel the hookers from his back as they screamed and punched and kicked him. The last girl closed the door behind her, to which Mike kicked the door glass in, shattering it to pieces amidst his verbal tirade.

As Mike approached us with a trickle of blood down his head, the second Mike asked in his New York accent, "Are you entirely through now?" as if he had kept us waiting too long over a trivial matter.

We turned to head for a different bar, but the sirens were already going off. Mike took off running, and the other Mike and I proceeded as if nothing had happened. The Vietnamese Army military police were called Quan Canh and for short, QC. Those and the US MPs were there in minutes. We played stupid, but Mike was caught shortly thereafter.

My letter of July 6 states that he did not get in any trouble, but as I recall, he had to pay for all the damages he did to the bar.

With our regular hours on the base and our evenings free, the trips into Vung Tau became a regular event. Base rules were that we had to be back on base by 8:00 or 9:00 p.m. when the gates closed. The gates reopened in the morning shortly after muster was held for the Swift Boat crews. We were allegedly not allowed to stay overnight in Vung Tau, but on occasion, we were otherwise occupied and stayed in town overnight. Besides that, the Lambretta ride back through some sketchy, rural areas in the dark at night was not particularly safe. There were teenage gangs in Vietnam called cowboys. There had been incidents when lone servicemen had been attacked by the "cowboys." On one such evening, when I had made that ride alone, the Lambretta driver started slowing way down in one of those remote areas. Fearing that he was setting me up, I leaned forward and spoke in his ear,

"You di di mau now or I 'crocodile' you!"

That jumbled bit of English, Vietnamese and Vietnamese metaphor translates to:

"You go fast now or I will kill you!"

To my relief, the threat spurred an immediate burst of acceleration.

> *Not much to write about. We're still in Cat Lo… We've been working a normal 8am til 4pm routine on the boat. 8 til 11 or 11:30 - 1 til 3:30 or 4:30 - Sundays off. In our free time we've been catching up on a lot of drinking we've missed in Cos Div 11.*
>
> *Vung Tau which is a 15 minute ride away is making a fortune off of our crew (when its not repairing damages). Mike didn't get in any trouble for busting up that bar.*
>
> *It sure would be nice to get some mail, so I could know what's going on at home.*

We've been having a lot of fun. We're going to hate to return to Cos Div 11. It sounds as if that's where we'll be headed.
(Letter, July 6, 1970)

I wish my stories about how I spent my time off in Vietnam were not filled with bars, drinking, prostitutes, and fights. I am not proud of these parts of my story, and there has been the temptation to omit the telling of these things but that would be deceitful to the truth. Telling the whole story demonstrates the "devil may care" foolishness of youth when it is coupled with the stresses of war.

One night, I returned alone to the base at Cat Lo from an uneventful evening in the bars at Vung Tau. The biggest event that evening thus far had been being slapped in the face by a prostitute that I had managed to insult. My nose was still smarting from the slap that had jammed my glasses into the side of my nose. I was in that relaxed, unworried, taking-nothing-serious mood that an evening of drinking can induce, but extremely hungry.

As I made the walk from the main gate and headed for the barracks, two other Swift Boat sailors approached me in a state of great agitation, reporting about some Army dudes were in the enlisted men's club looking for a fight. I don't recall the reason for a fight; in fact, at the time, I didn't much care about a fight or a reason for it. I was hungry and one of these harbingers of potential conflict in the club had a hoagie (called a submarine sandwich or grinder, depending on where you hail from). In order to mooch part of the hoagie, I went along with the plan to confront the Army guys. In my past experience, most of these disputes did not result in an actual fight. Usually, a lot of hostile words were exchanged, everyone "rattled their saber," so to speak, and then parted ways.

Now with the hoagie firmly in my possession, the three or us entered the club and stood face-to-face with the agitators. I was enjoying the hoagie as hostile words were exchanged by the others when suddenly, my "lights" were out. Everything was black momentarily, and then I had the realization that my head was bouncing back and forth as I lay on the floor. I reached out and tied up with my arms the attacker that had just "blindsided" me. Gradually, my vision returned from the momentary blackout as the guy locked in my bear hug struggled to break loose. To my shock, the faces of the other two guys that were with me were covered with blood. Clearly, we got the bad end of this engagement with the Army. One of our assailants yelled out, *"Do you guys want some more?"*

My quick visual assessment of the condition of my other two Swift sailors combined with the fog in my own brain after a sound battering led me to concede that we had enough. My fellow sailors readily agreed, and we backed out with our "tails between our legs" as our assailants hurled insults regarding the Navy's lack of manliness. Left behind was the remainder of the hoagie that had gotten me into all this. As the Kenny Rogers song goes, *"You gotta know when to hold 'em, know when to fold 'em."* This clearly had been a night to fold 'em.

Back at the boat, a check of my head revealed several lumps and a small tear between the top of my ear and my head. I was in much better shape than the other two that had led me into their dispute.

Guess what! Just guess what? It's too good to believe! Our entire boat and crew has been transferred to Coastal Division 13. Tomorrow morning we get underway for Sa Dec and from there I think we're going on to patrol at Chau Doc. If you remember, I've been there before and there's nothing to it. You just anchor in the middle of the river about 1000 or 2000 yards from the Cambodian border and goof off all day. I'm really glad we're not going back to Cos Div 11, it was a real hellhole.
(Letter, July 12, 1970)

***

Well, on the 13th we went to Sa Dec, which is the [new] headquarters for Cos Div 13 and we got checked into the division. We stopped in the Gunner's Mate shack to get some parts and guess who the staff Gunners Mate is - Ajax. On the 15th we came to Chau Duc and today we are on patrol. We patrol 3 days and have 1 day off. All we do is ride up river to about 100 yards from the border, shut off our engines and drift down river about a mile and then drive back up to the border again. We do this 24 hours a day, and allready [sic] *its boring, but I'm not complaining—nobody's shooting at me—so I refuse to complain. It is considered a pacified area here. Hardly anything ever happens here. We don't even uncover our guns and we only have one guy on watch at a time. It's certainly a change from Cos Div 11 far more went on there than I ever told you about. For example, I may be getting a Navy Commendation Medal or Bronze Star but I don't know, so don't go telling the world about it.*

So my life has changed from one of long hours, combat and poor living conditions to one of fresh milk and ice cream, scads of free time and no worry of the enemy. I'm sure you'll be glad to hear that.

Things are really looking good what with 3 weeks to R&R, 105 days to go and being transferred to Cos Div 13. As Woody said, "The war is over for us." I hope so!

I lost my Christian fellowship cross that Rev. Murphy gave me. I've worn it since the day he gave it to me and I was really mad that I lost it. I'd really appreciate it if you'd get me another one with a chain for it and send it to me.
(Letter, July 16, 1970)

***

I received 2 letters from Anna saying that Geo. had broken B.A.'s nose…I wish I knew exactly what happened. My first reaction was that of any normal brother I guess. I vowed that Geo. Wells would be lucky if all he had was a broken nose 98 days from now. But upon thinking it all over, I realized that 3 months from now that really couldn't accomplish anything except make more trouble. Depending on the situation, I still may mutilate him. It's hard to let anybody break your sister's nose and get away Scott free no matter how big he is...Let's just hope it's all smoothed over by the time I get home.

Things are pretty quiet and dull around here. Just like a vacation - swimming, sun bathing, reading and exercising to keep from gaining too much weight.
(Letter, July 23, 1970)

Within a day or two after being separated from active duty, back home I confronted my brother-in-law about his breaking my sister's nose. His apology seemed a little glib to me to which I detailed for him the means by which I would retaliate if he ever were to harm my sister again. Whether he was truly sorry or deterred by my threat of retaliation, she was never physically abused again to my knowledge.

Hi, today is the 25th of July, Saturday, it's about 12:30 in the afternoon. We, re sitting on the Mekong River about a quarter mile from Cambodia. It's a real nice day, it's sunny and there's a cool breeze. You just wouldn't believe what the difference is between being here and being in An Thoi. Everybody kids, this is like an R&R spot sit around and watch the border and keep track of anything that comes across here, such as a civilian tug or something like that, which is just one a day or something like that. There are Vietnamese river boats that go up now and then. All we do is make sure nothing tries to come into Vietnam that we don't want coming in and make sure no U.S. people go into Cambodia by mistake. That's the extent of all we have to do here.

During the day we go right up to the border just about and stop, shut off our engines and just drift down the river with the current about 3 miles. That takes about 45 minutes or an hour. We start up again and run back up there again and start drifting again. At night we just patrol back and forth for about 3 miles on the river. We just keep going up and down. It only takes one guy at a time because there's really nothing to do. The river is wide enough, it's so wide here that if anybody shot at you they couldn't hit you anyhow. So you don't have to worry. It's nothing like the other division, the other division, everywhere you went the rivers were small and it was pretty well barren country. Anywhere you went you had to be in flak jackets and helmets and guns loaded and the whole bit. Whereas here there is so much population, there are so many other boats, there is so much of everything that as most of the people you talk to around here will say; 'The war is over here in this section.' It's considered by Saigon and the U.S. to be a paci-fied area more or less, as pacified as it can be in a war zone.

We got mail this morning... and some more ice tea. You just couldn't believe how much ice tea we go through. Anna keeps sending ice tea [powdered mix] and we just drink ice tea by the gallons, you wouldn't believe it. We sure do appreciate her sending it all the time. Everybody looks forward, when we run out, to when the next package is coming. Everybody knows what it is when they see it, before it's even open they see the grey envelope, they know we got ice tea again.

As I move around Vietnam, I haven't been all over Vietnam, but as far as the delta area goes, I've covered a good deal of the delta. I find that people sometimes have a hard time describing what this war is like and have all different outlooks on this war. I think I know what that reason is now, because everywhere you go is a different situ-ation; a different logistical setup, a different way of fighting the war, every place I've been so far is different from the other place. The logistics were different, what our job was, was different, everything was different. People's outlook were different and I think this is one of the big reasons why you can talk to one guy that was in Vietnam and he'll say it was hell, he was gettin' shot at all the time and another guy will tell you he never got shot at once. Another guy will say the NVA are a big threat and another guy will say the

287

VC are a big threat and I think this is what the story is, it's just that everywhere you go it's different and it effects people's outlook on this war differently. If you spent all your time in Vietnam down at Sea Float, you would say this is the most backwoods, worthless, hunk of land. There's just VC running all over and it's really a bad place. If you spent all your time in Ha Tien, being right on the Cambodian border, you'd have a different sort of outlook. If you spent all your time here in Chau Duc where it's almost entirely peaceful, you 'd have another outlook. You would say this war is won. You go to Cat Lo where there's Australian bases and Korean bases and U.S. bases and Vietnamese bases and all kinds of bases, just military power all over, you'd say it's so populated and so many troops all around that the VC can't do much of anything anyhow, just make a little harassment every now and then. So anywhere you go it's different. The people look different in some ways. That's why everybody has a different outlook on this war I think.

But, if people were to see this territory right here that I'm in now, as it is now and if they could see what it was like or talk to somebody that was here 2 or 3 years ago, in this area I'm in right now, they'd say that we've done an outstanding job here. This river I'm on now, maybe not in this exact spot, but these rivers of the delta, 3 years ago, 2 years ago, was where real heavy fighting went on. A lot of men from the U.S Ninth Infantry died here. A lot of sailors died here. You can't tell me it was a waste here.

The atmosphere here is so much more relaxed compared to Cos Div 11. It's got more military, what would you call it? - Bull shit, because you find that when you're in a situation where you have military forces that haven't got a real hard job to do, there is a lot people concerned about how clean things are and how nice things look. When you're in a situation where you've got a hard job to do and poor resources, people tend to overlook a little dirt here or this not looking so good there or something like that. But as far

*as a lot of things here, they are much more casual about
things up here.*

See ya in 90 some days
(Tape, July 25, 1970)

At this point in my tour of duty, it was time to get to Saigon by whatever means possible for my flight to Australia for R & R (rest and relaxation). After six months "in country," every serviceman was eligible for a week of R & R. We had to apply for our choice of destination well in advance, and our name was put on a waiting list. The approved locations were Bangkok, Hong Kong, Japan, Hawaii, Taiwan, and Australia. Each serviceman had to have accrued enough cash on his pay records to be allowed to go to the destination he chose. Hawaii was the most expensive place to go and required about $550. Most married men chose Hawaii because their wives could meet them there, and they could spend the week together. Australia was the next most expensive, requiring about $450. I do not remember the exact dollar amounts. The guys who went to Hong Kong usually bought tailor-made suits dirt cheap. Taiwan and Bangkok were the least expensive, around $200 as I recall.

*Well, I'm in Sa Dec right now. I flew down here yesterday
on a Medivac helo. I've always wanted to get a ride in a
helicopter but have been leery of it over here considering
they've shot down 3 thousand some odd helos over here
[5,086 of the 11,827 sent to Vietnam were destroyed].[31]
It was fun though and the view of the countryside is really
something from a helicopter. To the crew of the helicopter
it's like driving down to the corner store. They were eating
box lunches and listening to the Armed Forces radio station
just as casual as could be. There were a couple guys in the
back with minor wounds and traces of blood and mud here
and there from past medivacs.*

[31.] Vietnam Helicopter Pilots Association website

I leave here on the 6th. I have to go to NHa Be to get paid. Nha Be is 15 or 20 miles from Saigon. Then I go to Saigon and wait around until the 9th for my flight to Australia.

I can't help but keep thinking that it won't be long now and I'll be home. Any of the guys you talk to who have been away from home (meaning overseas) for a year or more always say that things and people really change while you're gone and it's very hard sometimes to fit back in. A guy also gets different outlooks on things after being over here and has difficulty getting along with his old friends. I'm really not worried about it though.

I got a letter from Tony. He's home in New York. His girl is going with a hippie and all his friends are on drugs. His brothers are bums, so he's going to move to California and go to school.

That's about all.

(Letter, August 4, 1970)

***

I received my "Combat Action Ribbon" today, although I actually earned it back in Dec. The Navy is a little slow with its paperwork. It's no big thing, if you get shot at and you shoot back you are eligible for the Combat Action Ribbon.

(Letter, August 5, 1970)

***

Right now I'm in Camp Alpha next to the Ton Son Nhut Air Base. I got here this morning. Boy, you wouldn't believe the hassle I've been through getting paid. Camp Alpha is where they get you ready for R&R, all the final red tape and they tell you all the do's and don'ts for going on R&R. I've only got one more thing to take care of and I'll be all ready for my flight tomorrow evening.

(Letter, August 8, 1970)

Sydney, Australia

Unfortunately, I did not write home anything about Australia. Maybe I was having too much fun to write? I had written to Bill Metcalf, who had drilled with me at the Reserve Center in Trenton, and we arranged to go on R & R at the same time and meet up in Australia. I don't remember anything about the flight to or from Australia or much about my week there but will relate the bits and pieces that I do remember.

Once we arrived in Australia, we got a motel room and settled in. The Australians were very hospitable to American serviceman. There were families in the countryside that would take us in for the week if we wanted to do that. The first or second night we went on an evening cruise. Besides food and drinks, the boat was full of girls. "Round-eyed" girls! Bill met up with a girl and got together with her the next day. That was the last I saw of him. All this preparation to meet in Australia and do R & R together—*whoosh*—gone. Oh well, I couldn't blame him. I was probably just jealous. So I was left alone for the remainder of the week.

I vaguely remember going somewhere to see the Australian wildlife, I do mean animals, not the bar scene—that would come. I remember also buying a boomerang and getting some brief instructions on how to throw it so that it would come back to me. I spent some time in a park near the motel practicing and got pretty good at throwing a boomerang. Sometime during the week, I took a daytime boat ride to an island where, whomever it was that provided the trip, barbecued steaks for us.

In Australia, they had "pubs." A pub was basically a bar for men only. I discovered that to meet girls, I had to go to a "club." Australia had been an R & R location for several years already, so the clubs were big and business was booming. I quickly met a girl that I spent the remainder of the week with. Now I no longer could hold a grudge against Bill. She showed me around Australia and helped me shop to pick out gifts to send home. We went to see the brand-new movie *M*A*S*H* that was the forerunner of the hit TV series.

Several days before it was time to return to Vietnam, the dread of going back started to set in, but what choice was there? I got the address of the girl with intentions of staying in touch, but never did.

Well, R&R is all over now. It was expensive but well worth it. I arrived in Saigon late on the 16th and stayed at Camp Alpha the R&R processing center. The next day I flew to Binh Thuy and looked up Tom Reside. He took the day off and we had a good time talking about old times and exchanging what our old buddies and old girlfriends were doing. The next day he drove me to Can Tho and I got a helo to Vinh Long where the mail truck from Sa Dec picked me up...In some ways of thinking, I can't wait to get back to my boat and see the guys.
(Letter, August 19, 1970)

Tom showed me around the Naval Air base, and I got a close up look at the planes that flew support for us on the river. I discovered that "hundred mile an hour" tape is no joke. The military proper name for what we civilians call duct tape is "olive drab green reinforcement tape." They actually used it to cover bullet holes in the skin of the aircraft!

I got to look inside the cramped cockpit with all its controls. Like most fighter planes, the pilot and copilot don't sit side by side. They sit one in front of the other with the rearward pilot sitting higher than the forward pilot so that he has clear vision over top of the forward pilot. Looking at the controls, I noticed a small rubber, cup-shaped device with what looked like either a tube or wire running downward from the bottom of it. I asked, *"Is that for the guy in the front to talk to the guy in the back?"*

Amused, Tom explained, *"No, that's for the pilot if he needs to take a piss while he's flying"*

I was glad I didn't lift the cup and try talking into it!

CHAPTER 12

MY LAST DAYS IN NAM

My last days in Vietnam, I was caught up in ACTOV, the Accelerated Turnover to Vietnamese. It was clean and paint and transport boats from one place to another. The dull gray hulls were painted black and olive green to camouflage them. Every pipe in the engine room had to be cleaned, painted, and color-coded to make it easier for the Vietnamese sailors to tell fuel, water, oil, and bilge lines from one another. Everything had to be in tip top shape right down to being sure there were exactly six spoons, six forks, and six knives.

It seemed to most of us that it had gotten a little ridiculous just how particular the Vietnamese had become about the condition of the boats when we *gave* the boats to them. It was okay for us to come to their country and fulfill our mission no matter the conditions we encountered. But when they were to take over, they had to have everything in top working order and brand-new bases too!

A few short days after returning from my week of R & R I found out that I was going back to An Thoi—the hellhole I had so desperately wanted to get out of. I do not recall my reaction or my feelings when I heard the news. Perhaps it was made clear to me that we would only be there to prepare our boat for turnover to the Vietnamese Navy and that we would not be on any combat missions. Otherwise, I think I would have been severely upset to learn I would return to the daily dangers of missions and patrols from the forward bases into hostile territory.

Well, guess where I am? An Thoi. PCF 9 picked me up in Sa Dec on its way back from Cat Lo on the 19th. From there we went to Chau Doc and stayed the night. The next day we went to Ha Tien by way of the Vinh Gia canal. The next day we went to An Thoi where we're getting our boat ready to turnover to the Vietnamese on Sept 1. I don't know what they'll do with us then. We're supposed to fly back to Sa Dec and I imagine they'll put us on other boats. By the way, I have now circumnavigated the Delta. Piece by piece I've been all the way around it. Not to mention being all through it.

Wroblowski got railroaded into being an advisor because he didn't get along with Mr. Klinedinst I think. Last I heard he was putting up a hell of a fight about it.
(Letter, August 24, 1970)

***

We're supposed to be making our 5 year old battle worn, sea battered boats look like brand new, but in reality everyone knows that's impossible so we're doing as little as possible. The VNs are very particular about the condition of a quarter of a million dollar boat when you outright give it to them. Supposedly they will refuse to accept them if they don't meet their standards. That takes a lot of nerve if you ask me.

One of the astronauts [Neil Armstrong] *that was on the moon came here today. I didn't see him. I heard that he is trying to have the treatment of our prisoners in N. Vietnam improved and that he's going to prison camps all over the world. The one here on Phu Quoc Island is supposed to have 26,000 prisoners.*

Well, I've got 60 days or less left now and I keep thinking about going home more and more as the time draws near. I can hardly wait. There are so many things I want to do and people I want to see.
(Letter August 29, 1970)

Apollo 11 was the first space flight to land humans on the moon. Americans Neil Armstrong and Buzz Aldrin landed on the moon July 20, 1969. As Neil stepped onto the me moon he spoke what would become historic words: *"That's one small step for man, one giant leap for mankind."*

I returned to Sa Dec today after turning PCF 9 over to the Vietnamese a day early. They turned half of the 8 boats over early because there were two trawlers off the coast that had to have an eye kept on them and they needed extra boats to do it. Orders were, if the trawlers came within the 12 mile limit, to capture or destroy them. Brutal characters aren't we. Haven't heard any further word on it.

I'm being put on PCF 102 tomorrow which is on border patrol near Tan Chau. I certainly have done some traveling around the countryside in the last month by air and water. In the last month I've been from Tan Chau to Sa Dec to Saigon to Nha Be to Saigon to Cho Lon to Saigon to Sydney to Saigon to Binh Thuy to Can Tho to Vinh Long to Sa Dec to Tan Chau to Ha Tien to An Thoi To Saigon to Vinh Long To Sa Dec. I keep track of where I've been in VN on my map and its starting to be one big mess of lines all over the Delta. I probably know more about the geography of the Delta than New Jersey!

It won't be long before almost all of the guys we know will be home. It'll be great.

You wouldn't believe it but in the last 2 months I think I've read more books than in all my life. Espionage being my favorite and war history and politics my second. I've read about a dozen novels and also Airport, Hells Angels,

Coffee, Tea or Me, CIA, The Changing Society of China, Youth Quake, oh I can't remember them all. Right now I'm reading "The United States in World War II." One thing that is imperative if I return to college is that I improve my reading habits and speed and I'm well on my way.

I met a guy the other day who was just like me in high school. All he wanted to do was be a mechanic and his guidance counselor said he could do much better. He went to a 2 year Automotive Engineering School in Boston called Wentworth…He finished school and went back to being a mechanic and then joined the Navy as an Engineman.
(Letter, Sept. 1, 1970)

I would like to know why Coastal Division 13s base at Sa Dec was located where it was. We were all about Swift Boats, logically a base would be right next to the water, so one would think. One can explain why a "Coastal Division" was not on the coast because of the move from coastal patrol to inland waterways. But how do you explain the base in the town (I mean "in the town") of Sa Dec? It was in a compound that had been a French resort complete with tennis courts and all. The chow hall, which was more like a nice old restaurant dining room, was complete with a beautiful large fireplace. Not sure why one would need a fireplace in Vietnam. Our boats were tied up at a small dock on a canal far enough away that we had to take a jeep ride to get back and forth to them.

By some procedure not clear to me, the base had a food allotment for all the men in the division to eat at the base dining room every day. But there was never more than two or three crews on the base at any one time. Nearly all our boats were deployed miles away from the base for weeks at a time. While deployed we lived on our boats and got all our support from the mobile support bases. The result was that the food and the selection of food at Sa Dec was great! I was told that the food is allocated on a point basis, and certain more desirable foods such as steak or seafood cost more points than other foods. The chow hall had more points than it knew what to do with, which resulted in having the best meals in the Delta.

The Navy newspaper, the *Jackstaff News,* did the following write up on Sa Dec dated September 9, 1970:

Spotlight: NSA DET SA DEC
by JO3 Alan J. McKean

The only way to get there, if you drive, is to cross the Mekong River by ferry. Once you reach Naval Support Activity Saigon's detachment in Sa Dec you'll be in another part of Vietnam that echoes back to a quieter, more peaceful period.

While the fields are green and tranquil, Sa Dec city itself appears to be living in Vietnam's colonial past, for it is clean, well-kept area hardly touched by the war.

For a full-fledged detachment, Sa Dec fits right into this mosaic of contentment. Measuring only 104 by 50 feet, it is possibly the smallest NSA activity.

Compact as it is, the base has an interesting history. Now a military complex, the buildings and most of its yard used to be a French athletic club that featured tennis, volleyball and soccer. The courts are now covered with buildings and the soccer field, not part of the base, lies flooded and dormant.

The highlight of Sa Dec has to be the detachment's galley. Among galleys, NSAD Sa Dec's has to be rated among the top 10 anywhere. Part of the old French establishment, the immaculate, walnut-paneled dining area reminds you more of the Ritz than of a messhall... Men accustomed to eating from tin mess trays are treated to porcelain plates, lemon merengue or Boston cream pies, seafood and other delicacies.

***

12 Noon—I just had lunch and as everyone around here says Sa Dec serves the best meals in the Delta. For lunch they had BLTs, grilled ham and cheese sandwiches, baked beans, soup, French fries, tomatoes and bread like you make, cole slaw, macaroni salad, cucumbers, tossed salad, cottage cheese, fruit, pie, ice tea, kool-aid, tea, coffee and milk. The base personnel here are some of the healthiest looking, heaviest people in Vietnam.

Did you hear that the U.S. Navy is now allowed to wear full beards anywhere in the world? So don't be surprised if I come home as such, but I doubt it.

I would like you to make an appointment for me with Dr. Ehlich for sometime around Nov. 5. Anytime around then will do. My teeth are very badly stained and dirty and I want to have them cleaned as soon as possible when I get home. I've gone this far without having the Navy touch them so now I don't want them to as I don't really trust their Dr's and dentists.

My distrust of Navy dentists was based on the discrepancy between two previous exams that had been done. The dentist at NIOTC, in California, examined my teeth before I left. He told me that I had two cavities and needed a cleaning. I was instructed to get my dental work done when I got to my permanent duty station. Lots of luck with that, I never had a "permanent" duty station, I was all over the country.

While we were at the USS *Tutilla* early in March, I had a dental exam and was told that I only had one cavity and desperately needed a cleaning. The dental work was scheduled for a day or two later after the exam. The day of my appointment the generators were down so the dentist did not have electricity to do the work. Then we were back on the river again.

When my teeth were examined at Philadelphia Naval Base before separation from active duty, I was told that I had no cavities but needed my teeth cleaned. Now, I'm no dentist, but I was fairly certain that cavities don't heal themselves.

I also want new glasses made, but I guess I won't need an appointment as far in advance for that.

With only 55 days to go and much more free time on my hands than I used to have, I think about getting home quite often and can hardly wait. On Sept. 15th I should find out exactly what day I leave for the States as that is when the scheduled flight dates are posted.
(Letter, Sept. 3, 1970)

***

Still in Sa Dec waiting for a ride to Chau Duc. Mr Klinedinst has put me in for the Navy Commendation Medal with Combat "V." That doesn't mean I'll get it though. It has to go before a board and be reviewed and O.K.ed. He said he was trying to get me a bronze star but met a lot of resistance. Still haven't heard anything about the one that Mr. Burke put me in for.

I never used to think much of medals and still don't because they give them out for ridiculous things these days if you know the right people. But I feel I've earned mine and I sure would like to have them. Now don't go blabbering all over that your son is a hero, because I haven't got the medals yet and I didn't do anything more than do what I was trained to do and expected to do. (Lots of good stories to tell you when I get home.)
(Letter Sept. 6, 1970)

As my September 6 stated, after turning PCF 9 over to the Vietnamese, I spent a week in Sa Dec waiting for a ride to Chau Duc. There was no air conditioning in the barracks, the base was small and there was nothing to do. There was a large fan in the barracks, the kind that has a large base supporting a pipe, that in turn holds the fan about four or five feet off the ground. The fan was annoyingly loud, but without it, the barracks was stifling.

I did not feel comfortable in the town of Sa Dec and only made one or two trips into the town outside of base. There were only a few guys in the Swift sailors' barracks. Somebody had the Beatles'

Sergeant Pepper tape and played it repeatedly. I spent hours lying in bed, listening to the Beatles' songs on the album over the noise of the giant fan.

My daily routine was get up, shower, have a good breakfast, lie around in the barracks until noon when the enlisted men's club opened, have a drink or two, go to lunch, return to the club for a while, go take a nap, get up for dinner, then back to the club to finish the night off drinking. Boring but relaxing, and no one was shooting at me, so I would endure it. The goal at this point was to stay safe, stay alive, and get home in one piece.

I'm supposed to leave Sa Dec today at 4pm to go to Chau Duc. Of course that's what they said a week ago.

We had a special day yesterday for Labor Day. Pool tournament, barbecue, free booze and band from Saigon. I took movie pictures of the band but don't know if they'll come out because of the light. [I have no memory of this Labor Day event or taking a movie.]

These days I haven't been doing much but drinking and eating ever since R&R.

"Sources" say that Mr. Klinedinst put in a 5 page report on me that was pretty impressive, but they wouldn't disclose what it said. They said that they thought I would probably get a bronze star without a doubt after reading the report even though he put me in for a lesser medal. Sometimes it takes months for these things to get through though. So I may be long home and finished with the Navy before I get it. Boy I wish I could see what he wrote! It impressed my "sources" enough to make them get me staggering drunk two nights ago.

? 49 ? days to go
(Letter, Sept. 8, 1970)

The commendation letter goes on to say that I *unleashed a devastatingly accurate barrage of fire into the enemy's position until his craft received a direct hit.* We had already been hit, and I was unable to return fire until we had gotten the boat untied from the tree and turned about. Evidently, Mr. Klinedinst did indeed write a very impressive report on me. Unfortunately, it was quite a stretch of the truth in regard to the details of the ambush of February 13–14. And it was also a stretch of the truth of my actions on that night. That bothers me a bit, but given my overall service in Vietnam, I think the Commendation Medal was well earned, and it was entirely accurate to have the "Combat V" on it.

To my knowledge, on the night of the thirteenth–fourteenth, only one rocket was fired and hit us, unlike the commendation letter's description of *heavy enemy automatic weapons and rocket fire.* If there were more rounds fired at us, then they must have been fired while I was tangled up in my poncho and headphone cord. The rest of the commendation is reasonably accurate.

COMMANDER
UNITED STATES NAVAL FORCES
VIETNAM

The Secretary of the Navy takes pleasure in presenting the
Navy Commendation Medal to

CHARLES WILBUR HUNT
ENGINEMAN THIRD CLASS
UNITED STATES NAVAL RESERVE

for service as set forth in the following

CITATION

"For meritorious service while serving with friendly foreign forces
engaged in armed conflict against the North Vietnamese and Viet Cong
communist aggressors in the Republic of Vietnam from November 1969
to October 1970. While serving as a gunner on inshore patrol craft
attached to Coastal Divisions Eleven and Thirteen, Petty Officer HUNT
participated in over one hundred sixty combat patrols and engaged the
enemy on thirteen occasions in conjunction with Operations MARKET
TIME, SEA LORDS, SEA FLOAT and TRAN HUNG DAO I. During those patrols,
he boarded and searched numerous junks and sampans, interdicted cross
river traffic, enforced curfew, inserted and extracted friendly forces
in hostile territory and provided fire support for besieged units and
outposts. On 13 February 1970 while set in waterborne guardpost on
the Vinh Te canal, his unit came under heavy enemy automatic weapons
and rocket fire. From his exposed position, he unleased a devastatingly
accurate barrage of fire into the enemy positions until his craft
received a direct hit. He then assisted in patching the damaged hull
and administering first aid to the wounded while his craft proceeded to
a secure area. Petty Officer HUNT's exemplary professionalism, devotion
to duty and courage under fire were in keeping with the highest traditions of the United States Naval Service."

The Combat Distinguishing Device is authorized.

For the Secretary of the Navy

J. H. KING, JR.
Vice Admiral, U. S. Navy
Commander U. S. Naval Forces, Vietnam

*Well, several days ago I jumped on PCF 36 at Sa Dec which
was headed for Chau Doc where PCF 102 is patrolling. An
hour out of Sa Dec PCF36 blew an engine, so we turned
around and went to Dong Tam to get another engine. This
morning we got to Chau Doc and I got on PCF 102. Much
to my dismay I've found that PCF 102 is going to Quin
Nhon soon to be overhauled. We're supposed to pick up the*

88 boat there and bring it back to Cat Lo to be turned over on Oct. 1st. I'm really not looking forward to all this traveling during the end of the monsoon season. Quin Nhon (pronounced KWIN YAN) is way up north, quite a long trip. I'm going to see if someone wants to trade places with me as I'd rather patrol.
(Letter, Sept. 11, 1970)

***

Left Cat Lo 5:30am arrived Cam Rahn Bay about 3pm. Got some frustrating news yesterday. Could be good news. Cos Div 13 is authorized to send me home anytime within 30 days from the day they're supposed to. But I'm not going to be back in Cos Div 13 headquarters again until after Oct. 1st, so I won't be able to request an early flight date until I get back there. At the best I don't think I'd get home until maybe the 2nd week of Oct. At worst, last week of Oct.

I don't like the officer on this boat (PCF 102). He is a chronic worrier and he doesn't seem to trust his crew. To someone like me who's been over here for almost 11 months and been all over and in some tight spots, he's a real pain in the ass because what we're doing now is just a boring ordeal to me. If I weren't leaving soon I would request, in fact insist, upon being removed from this boat, but I'll stick it out for a few more weeks.

It's getting so close to when I'll be home that I think about how great it'll be all the time. I keep thinking, "What will I do first?" I think I want to go home and put on some civilian clothes and talk to you two for a while first and then listen to my stereo gear and maybe look at some of my slides and then drive a car *again and start visiting people. Dick first, I guess and see about getting a car (Corvette). Then B.A. & family (of course Anna as soon as she's home), Grandmom, Housels, Deys and then the others that I actually feel more obligated to visit than really want to. And of course most of my friends around town can be located at the Wayside Inn nights. Then in the next couple weeks I'll make arrangements like buying a car and insurance, looking into colleges and going back to work. I particularly want to visit the Deys and Housels as they have been so great to me.*

It'll be great to sleep in a clean fresh bed and shower whenever I feel like and have clean clothes that fit right and be sure of being able to get a good home cooked meal and be my own boss and not have to worry about a boat before all other things.

Putting in 8 hours a day, 5 days a week may be a little difficult after such a scrambled way of life for a year. And actually I haven't done that much actual work, patrolling doesn't consist of much but being there ready to be shot at. And I haven't even done much of that lately.

I don't think anyone will ever know what this year has been like. Some will think it was much worse than it really was and others will never realize that it wasn't that good either. No one will ever know, but I don't really expect them to. Parts of it were bad and parts of it were good. I've had hundreds of buddies and friends, but even more important I think the year has done a lot to improve my character and awareness of the world we live in. It's made me more independent and self-confident than I've ever been. Of course I don't think I was lacking too much in those areas anyhow. But this was a final proving ground of manhood I think. I think in time to come I'll be glad I spent a year over here. It gave me time to do a lot of thinking about a lot of things. And it forced me out of my blind little self-centered world I resided in—in Titusville, N.J. I don't think that you'll find I've changed that much though.

I'd like to move out of the house, but I can think of as many reasons to stay as I can to leave. There's nothing wrong with you two or our home, but I've got that urge to be on my own. Maybe college will present that opportunity.

Let you know as soon as I know anything about getting home.
(Letter, Sept. 18, 1970)

***

Guess what??? The news you've been waiting for. Here it is - are you ready? Are you sitting down? My flight out of Saigon leaves on October 6th at 5:10am. After we turnover PCF 88 on Oct. 1 I'll have to hurry back to Sa Dec, pack my gear and head for Saigon. I should arrive at Travis Air Force Base in Calif. Then I go to Treasure Island for separation from active duty. Then I want to look Tony up. Maybe 3 days or so at T.I. and then a day or two with Tony so I should hit the east coast around the 12th maybe. No promises. The Navy may hang me up at T.I. with red tape as its been known to do.
(Letter, September 25, 1970)

***

So you heard about the Navy's beards. Well, I've got one and can't make up my mind whether to wear it home or not. The commander of Cos Div 11 is flying back to the states on the same flight with me and 5 or 6 of my buddies. He is the greatest commander I ever met. Every man in his division likes him and he knows everyone of them by sight and most of them by name. His men would sail on Hanoi in a minute if he gave the order. He's down to earth, but still has authority and respect. And he respects everyone of his men for the job they do. The commander of Cos Div 13 couldn't hold a candle to him. Cos Div 11 as of Oct. 1st will no longer be. What's left of it has been transferred to Cos Div 13 and already they're hollering that they want Dung Island which is the only hot spot in Cos Div 13. When I get out of the Navy I want to write a letter to his higher ups telling them what kind of man he is.

305

As I get close to coming home and I realize I'll probably never have to "shoot it out" again, I think of the poor guys down at Sea Float. All the boats down there are VN now and they've been losing boat after boat. Things are getting worse there. I wish somebody would do something about that place. It's made a lot of heroes and a lot of dead men and accomplished nothing in my estimation. The bad part is that nobody understands what it's like down there until they've been there. No amount of explaining will get the message across. There's nothing down there, nothing but the VN Navy and God knows how many VC. (and billions of mosquitos) Now NVA elements are moving in with better weapons and getting bolder and bolder because there's less and less Americans there. But it's such a small piece of land compared to all the other world's problems that no one ever hears about it. Also there's nothing terribly valuable or important down there. Before U.S. patrol boats pulled out of there they should have dropped in about 1000 U.S. Marines and cleaned the place out a little.

I am enclosing a Chu Hoi pass which guarantees the enemy safe passage in surrendering. The U.S. drops them all over the country by helicopter. The enemy (if he turns himself in of his own free will) is repatriated and trained to fight for S.V.N. or is taught a trade to become productive.

I think tomorrow I'll go into Vung Tau and see if I can't find something to bring home for my nephews and niece.
(Last letter home, Sept. 26, 1970)

Chu Hoi Pass

From Vung Tau I flew to Saigon for my flight home. As usual we had extra days to get there, leaving a day or two in Saigon before the day of our flight. A few of us who had come to Vietnam together were leaving together. Rather than stay at the provided military barracks, we took off for a big hotel in Saigon and spent our last time together partying and telling stories.

We were authorized to wear civilian clothes home. I had a short-sleeved button-up shirt, a pair of slacks, and a pair of loafers that had spent most of the year in a locker at one base or another, other than when I went on R & R. Our flight was leaving out of the civilian airport that was right next to Ton Son Nhut Air Base. I went into the men's room at the civilian airport to change. My jungle boots and greens were so disgusting that I just dropped them on the floor as I changed and left them there. I was appalled at how filthy the civilian restroom was. I thought they would keep a civilian airport clean. I needed to use a toilet, and everyone one of them was clogged and overflowing, so I made a long walk across a field to use the restroom at Ton Son Nhut Air Base.

Finally, it was time to board the "freedom bird" for the long flight home. One last takeoff in a country where someone might try to shoot you down. A few more tense minutes as the plane climbed to a safe altitude. Then that sense of relief.

Home, for my heart still calls me;
Home, through the danger zone;
Home, whatever befalls me,
I will sail again to my own!
[from "Homeward Bound" by Henry Van Dyke]

CHAPTER 13

HOME

I don't remember much about the flight back to the United States. I know we took the southern route back as opposed to the flight to Vietnam that had taken the northern route. The southern route made brief stops at Guam and Hawaii before landing at Travis Air Force Base in California. From there, a bus took us to the Navy base at Treasure Island for separation from active duty. Treasure Island sits in San Francisco Bay and is a beautiful setting.

Everything looked so clean! America looked so good! I was so used to living in filth that I was taken aback by how clean things were. Upon arrival at Treasure Island, we were advised that the base was overwhelmed with sailors waiting for separation from active duty, so we were allowed to request separation at any other Navy base that handled separations. I requested Philadelphia and got it. My original plan to visit Tony Amoruso was abandoned for the chance to get home earlier. After a day at Treasure Island, I had the paperwork to be separated at Philadelphia and got a ride to San Francisco International Airport. Looking at the landscape go by on the ride to the airport once again was amazing. The roads, the streets, homes—everything looked so good.

Being in civilian clothes, I did not encounter any of the bad treatment so many returning Vietnam veterans had experienced. I went into the men's room and was almost startled at how all the porcelain and stainless steel shined so brightly. Funny how I cannot remember much about a long flight back to the United States that took nearly a day, but I can remember how bright and clean the men's room was at the airport. Clean things in the United States are so clean. If you live here all your life and never experience anything else, you don't realize how clean things are.

Likewise, if you live in a free nation that is free of war within its borders, you likely don't realize how great freedom is because you've never experienced life without freedom, nor do you realize how precious peace is if you have never lived in a country torn by war. I believe this fact is the reason for what has been called the "Greatest Generation." Millions of men and women went off to World War II and experienced countries that had been torn by war and peoples that had lost their freedom. Those men and women came home with a deep sense of how blessed this country has been with a value system that had stressed what is important in life. Many Vietnam veterans have come home with the same life lessons learned, but their stories are rarely told. The media prefers to tell stories of men suffering from posttraumatic stress disorder (PTSD), alcoholism, drug abuse, homelessness, and acts of violence.

I called ahead and arranged to have my best friend Dick Rogers pick me up at the airport. In order to fly with a military discount in the United States, I had to be in uniform. I was in dress blues. The excitement, happiness, and relief of approaching home were mixed with the awkwardness of being out of the environment that I had become accustomed to in Vietnam. We made the turn onto Bear Tavern Road from Washington Crossing–Pennington Road, and home was only a quarter mile away down an old familiar stretch of road that was like home itself.

Dick was a salesman at Coleman Oldsmobile and was driving one of the dealerships used cars, a Chrysler. As he straightened out the car, he pressed hard on the accelerator and headed for home. When he let off the accelerator pedal to begin slowing for the approach to the driveway, the engine continued to race; the accelerator did not return. Thinking quickly, he turned off the ignition, placed the shifter into neutral, and we coasted to the side of the road immediately in front of my home as the engine made awful noises and gradually quit.

Puzzled as to what had happened to make the accelerator stay floored, we lifted the hood to take a look. At this point, I had not even made it into the house. I stripped off my jersey and was under the hood. I didn't even make it completely home, and I was already under the hood of a car again.

Back in the days of carburetors, before the cars of today that all have fuel injectors, it was common to secure the air-cleaner housing by means of a threaded rod that screwed down into the center of the carburetor. The air-cleaner housing had a hole in the center of the top that the rod passed through when the air cleaner housing was placed on top of the carburetor. A wing nut was fastened onto the protruding threaded rod to hold the housing in place.

On our ride home, the threaded rod had come unscrewed from the carburetor, and when Dick had accelerated hard, the rod fell down and blocked the throttle plates in the wide-open throttle position. Now with a flashlight and a pair of pliers, I was fishing the rod back out of the throttle plates and threading it back into place. I had repaired cars for class members a year ago back in NIOTC, repaired engines and systems on Swift Boats for a year, and now before even getting in the back door at home, I was fixing a car again already. It was just part of my lifelong occupation of repairing things, mostly cars.

For the first few days, all I wanted to do was be home. *Home—* just one simple word, but it means so much. Out on the side of the barn my father had placed a large sign that read, *"Welcome Home, Charles."*

I had ordered a high-end Pioneer stereo receiver and two large speaker cabinets. For a couple days, all I did was lie on the living room floor and listen to my stereo. No doubt part of the lying around was recovering from the traveling halfway around the world and part was just drinking in being home. That time on the living room floor was like a two-day exhale. Shortly after returning home, my parents threw a "welcome home" party for me and invited many friends and relatives. Unlike so many veterans that had come home with little recognition of a job well done, I was warmly received home by many people.

Dick knew I wanted some type of muscle car and had a 1967 Oldsmobile 442 waiting for me at the dealership. As I trusted him completely; I just said I would buy it "sight unseen." Dick brought it to me, and the deal was done. So much for all the talk about buying a Corvette.

Returning veterans were eligible to collect unemployment, so I went to Trenton to apply. Trenton had been the scene of race riots; the streets were blocked off to vehicles, and access to the city was limited. I parked in a lot just outside the center of the city and walked up to the first barricade where a police officer questioned me as to my destination and warned me about the dangers of entering the city. Having faced worse than a riot in Vietnam, I answered in a manner typical of an overconfident young man, "What have you got in the city that would scare me, I just came home from Vietnam!"

I only stayed unemployed for one week, but did not return immediately to the job I had left behind. Federal law required my previous employer to give me my job back upon release from active duty. In 1970, General Motors had a sixty-seven-day strike. Business was slow for all GM products including Oldsmobile. When I approached the dealership about returning to work, they agreed to take me back, but due to business being so slow, they would have to lay off another mechanic who was married and had two children. Not wanting to cost a married man his job, I agreed to wait to return until business picked up. Another of my friends had just opened a gas station in Trenton, so I went to work with him, but that developed into working for him while he partied rather than working *with* him, so I quit after a couple months.

Some months after returning home, I was informed by the Navy that I was to be awarded the Navy Commendation Medal with Combat Distinguishing Device. I was given the option of receiving the medal in a formal awards ceremony or just having it sent to my home. I elected to just have it delivered, but my parents would not hear of it; they wanted the ceremony. Early in 1971, I donned my Navy "dress blues" and went with my parents to the Reserve Center to be awarded the medal. To my surprise, my parents had invited a couple of dozen people who had been influential in my life to be present. In front of rows of young first year reservists and the invited guests, I stood at attention as the citation was read aloud and the medal pinned on my chest.

PROUD MOMENT: Seen at the ceremony at which Charles W. Hunt of Titusville, second from left, received the Navy Commendation Medal, are, from left: Mr. and Mrs. Wilbur E. Hunt, the recipient's parents, of Titusville, and the presenting officer, Captain R. F. Howarth of the U.S. Naval Reserve Center in Trenton.

Gets Commendation Medal

Charles Wilbur Hunt, son of Mr. and Mrs. Wilbur E. Hunt of Bear Tavern Rd., Titusville, has been presented the Navy Commendation Medal. Hunt, who now is employed at Coleman's Oldsmobile in Trenton, served as an Engineman Third Class with the United States Naval Reserve.

The citation, which accompanied the medal, states: "for meritorious s e r v i c e . . . in armed conflict against the North Vietnamese and the Viet Cong communist aggressors in the Republic of Vietnam from November, 1969, to October, 1970." The citation goes on to read:

"While serving as a gunner on inshore patrol craft attached to Coastal Divisions Eleven and Thirteen, Petty Officer Hunt participated in over one hundred sixty combat patrols and engaged the enemy on thirteen occasions in conjunction with Operations Market Time, Sea Lords, Sea F l o a t and Tran Hung Dao I. During those patrols, he boarded and searched numerous junks and sampans, interdicted cross river traffic, enforced curfew, inserted and extracted friendly forces in hostile territory and provided fire support for besieged units and outposts. On 13 February, 1970, while set in waterborne guardpost on the Vinh Te

canal, his unit came under heavy enemy automatic weapons and rocket fire. From his exposed position, he unleashed a devastating accurate barrage of fire into the enemy positions until his craft received a direct hit. He then assisted in patching the damaged hull and administering first aid to the wounded while his craft proceeded to a secure area. Petty Officer Hunt's exemplary professionalism, devotion to duty and courage under fire were in keeping with the highest traditions of the United States Naval Service."

Hunt is a 1966 graduate of Hopewell Valley Central High School.

The strike at General Motors was still on, and business had not picked up at the dealership. The one area of automotive repair that I had no experience in was automatic transmissions, so I volunteered to work for free at a privately owned transmission shop. I spent a month working six days a week removing and replacing transmission and cleaning parts. The shop owner took me on test drives and explained what he was listening for and feeling, then he would tell me what the likely cause of the malfunction was. He did give me a little cash from time to time. After work, I would read shop manuals and taught myself how transmissions work. After a month at the transmission shop, the dealership was ready for me to return. Years later, when I had become the shop foreman at a local Ford dealership, my mentor from the transmission shop would come to me for technical assistance on Ford transmissions.

The warnings were correct. It seemed that things at home had changed a lot while I was gone. Some friends had gotten married and weren't hanging out at the bars anymore. Some were away at college. Others had moved away. A lot of the guys that had not served treated me differently than they had before. They sort of kept their distance. And of course, I had changed.

On weekends and a few nights a week, I frequented two of the local bars. I wanted to find someone that would understand what I had been through. Even if I talked with a Vietnam veteran, none of them had been where I was, doing what I was doing. The local VFW and American Legion urged me to join, but I felt no connection with them. Their membership was mostly old World War II veterans, and it seemed to me (perhaps incorrectly) that all they did was have meetings and drink beer. After about a year, I decided that no one would ever understand, and it was time to put aside my experiences in Vietnam and move on with life.

I recall in the mid-70s there were a few occasions when I would start to talk about Vietnam with a fellow employee that I had befriended. When the conversations ended, I realized that I was all wound up inside—my heart was pounding, and I was feeling extremely nervous. These were not good feelings, so I decided not to talk about it anymore.

Years later, I was able to talk about Vietnam and not get so wound up inside, but there are still some times and topics that affect me in other ways. Nowadays, it is more that certain topics trigger tears and fight them as I may—they just come. Usually, the triggers are stories of heroism or sacrifice, often not even directly related to Vietnam. For instance, I was asked to give a eulogy at the funeral service for one of my uncles. He was one of my mother's five brothers who all had served in World War II. When I got to the part saying that all five had served, the tears came. How embarrassing—standing in front of a room full of people and crying because all five uncles had served.

For a long time, civilians aggravated me because they are so unprepared for emergencies. I had learned to be alert at all times and be ready to react. Seeing people stand around and do nothing when someone needed help angered me. Eventually, I guess, I calmed down and became a "civilian" again.

Besides working a regular forty-hour a week job as a mechanic, I worked part-time at a liquor store just to save up some extra money.

Lieutenant Calley, the My Lai Massacre

On March 29, 1971, Lt. William L. Calley was convicted of the murder of twenty-two South Vietnamese civilians in what had become known as the My Lai Massacre. He was sentenced to life imprisonment at Fort Leavenworth. At the time, many of my fellow Vietnam veterans and I felt that Lieutenant Calley was taking the fall for a lot of things that went very wrong in Vietnam. In response, my good friend and fellow Vietnam veteran Dan Breese and I organized a letter, obtained the signatures of thirty-one fellow Vietnam veterans from Hopewell Valley, and had it printed in local newspapers.

A lot of what fueled us at the time was the negative attitude so many people had about us Vietnam veterans. I think we were tired of being painted in a negative light by the media and wanted to defend one of our fellow vets. Years later, as I viewed the details that were presented about, My Lai, I think he may actually have been guilty.

LETTERS To The EDITOR

Lt. Calley

Editor, The Packet:

We the undersigned, as members of your community and veterans of the Viet Nam conflict urge you not to stand by while another American life is lost for Viet Nam. William Calley's life will be wasted if the American people don't exercise their right to let their will be known.

If Lt. Calley is guilty then there are several thousand pilots that should go on trial, and possibly a few of the undersigned also. We don't feel that he should have been court martialed. We contend that Lt. Calley is being used as a scapegoat for all Viet Nam atrocities.

We urge you to write to the men who are responsible for carrying out your will and let them know that you want pressure to be applied in the proper areas to correct this wrong. If it seems like too much of an effort - think of the lives it cost for you to have and maintain this right.

Charles W. Hunt
Dana L. Breese
J. Peter Klein

Vincent Dombroski
Paul Van Noy
Thomas R. Reside Jr.
John E. Martancik
John A. Vaccarino
Roger W. Anderson
Angelo Tormina
William L. Stewart Jr.
Brian Fillebrown
William B. Meytrott
John J. Vorgang III
Dennis P. Kitzel
Charles A. Holcombe
John W. Holcombe
John R. King
John C. Abbott Jr.
R. William Shaub
David Hackett
Joseph H. Kamrad
Jeffrey D. Stewart
Timothy C. Housel
Daniel F. Flynn
John K. Wolfarth
Kenneth C. Ruth
R. Kirk Seaton
D. Craig Stevens
Jesse S. Branham Jr.
Irwin W. Moran

Withdrawal and Betrayal

In January 1973, representatives of the United States, North and South Vietnam, and the Viet Cong signed a peace agreement in Paris, ending the direct U.S. military involvement in the Vietnam War. Its key provisions included a cease-fire throughout Vietnam, the withdrawal of U.S. forces, the release of prisoners of war, and the reunification of North and South Vietnam through peaceful means...

Even before the last American troops departed on March 29, the communists violated the cease-fire, and by early 1974 full-scale war had resumed.[32]

---

[32] *History.comStaff* March 29, 1973: U.S. Withdraws from Vietnam

In a shocking betrayal of the Vietnamese people, of America's 58,000 war dead, and Americans shattered by their war experience, Congress voted on June 4th, 1973, to block funds for any U.S. military activities in Indochina.

On April 30, 1975, after the communists overran the country. The remaining Americans and some of their South Vietnamese allies were evacuated just ahead of the Communist forces.[33]

It was sad and sickening to me to see the images on television of the Vietnamese people trying to get on the last helicopters as they lifted off from the roof of the American embassy in Saigon. Then the waste as helicopters were pushed over the side of the US ship at sea. How could we, the American people, allow this to happen? How could we do this to the people we had promised to help? How could we just leave and allow thousands of our allies be slaughtered?[34]

God, Family, Country

In December of 1971, I met the young woman who would become my wife. By next February, Claire and I spent every free minute together and got engaged. We married in May of the same year and moved into a small apartment. Claire was pregnant before the year was out, and as her delivery date approached, she insisted that we could not raise a child in an apartment and that we had to have a

---

[33]. Weymouth D. Symmes, *War on the Rivers pg 232-233*

[34]. Desbarats, Jacqueline. "Repression in the Socialist Republic of Vietnam: Executions and Population Relocation", from *The Vietnam Debate* (1990) by John Morton Moore. "We know now from a 1985 statement by Nguyen Co Tach that two and a half million, rather than one million, people went through reeducation...in fact, possibly more than 100,000 Vietnamese people were victims of extrajudicial executions in the last ten years...it is likely that, overall, at least one million Vietnamese were the victims of forced population transfers."

home of our own. With less than two thousand dollars to our names, we managed to get both a demand loan and a mortgage to buy our first small home. Douglas Charles Hunt was born on May 5, 1972, just eight days short of our first wedding anniversary. Now we were a family. I had our three mouths to feed and a mortgage payment to make. I had changed jobs shortly after we had met, and now I was working long hours, six days a week.

In February of 1973, I received my honorary discharge from the Navy, my full six-year obligation had been met.

On Veterans Day, November 11, 1975, our second child, Stacy Anna Hunt, was born. Our pastor would visit occasionally, and the desire to have our second child baptized was cause for another pastoral visit. We were not regular church attendees, but Pastor Shaub was the pastor of the church that I had been raised in, and he had married us. Bill, as everyone called the pastor, was also a Vietnam veteran. He was a very mild-mannered and polite man, hardly the image of an Army combat veteran. Years later, I would hear the story of his self-less actions as an Army Chaplain, winning himself numerous medals that included a Silver Star and a Purple Heart in the heat of battle. On every visit, Bill would encourage me to reenlist in the Reserves, and he would go on in detail about all the benefits of staying in the military until retirement.

After my experience in Vietnam, I wanted no part of a chance to be sent to another war not of my choosing. When leaving Vietnam, I had passed up the opportunity to return to Cambodia as an advisor to some irregular forces. That job offered very lucrative pay, but I had had enough of being shot at, and additionally, I had no desire to be in combat with anyone but US forces. Finally, I asked Bill, *"What is a reserve unit?"*

Bill gave a nice description of what reservists do on weekend drills, but that was not the answer or point I was getting at. I reworded my question and delivered it again, *"What is the purpose of a reserve unit?"* Again I did not get the answer I was trying to dig out of him. So I answered my own question, *"Reserves are a reserve fighting force! I will serve my country again if they really need me, but the next time it will be my choice, I will decide if it is a war I want to fight in."*

In order to show a degree of connection or commitment to the church, we attended Sunday worship a few times prior to Stacy's baptism. Something strange, uncomfortable, and puzzling was happening to me during church services—I kept getting the urge to cry, but I had no idea why.

The baptism was in the spring of 1976, and afterward, we had a party at our house. That afternoon, I listened in on a conversation between my sister and my mother. They were talking about things in the Bible, and I wondered, "Since when does my sister know about all this stuff in the Bible?"

During one of the pastor's visits to our home, Claire shocked me when she told Bill that she wanted to recommit herself to the Lord, and the two of them prayed about it right then and there. I did not know where that came from; that was not something that we had even discussed, and I did not know what to think of it.

I reached a point where I had a lot of questions. I was bothered by the urge to cry when in church, I did not understand my sister's sudden knowledge of the Bible, I was not in tune with my wife's renewed interest in spiritual matters, and tucked away in the back of my head was the memory of the previous pastor at Titusville, waking on February 13, 1970, and praying for my safety while I was in trouble in the Vinh Te Canal on the other side of the world.

My mind could not process all these things. I had always considered myself what I called a realist—I only believed in what I could see, hear, or feel. Now there were things that had happened and things that were happening that I could not explain or fully understand. I called Bill and arranged to meet and talk with him in his office at the church. The evening that we met, I sat and laid out these things that were bothering in the form or questions. Included in my list of questions was, *"Why does God let innocent civilians and babies die in wars?"* At the top of my list was (1) what did it mean and (2) how does it happen that a pastor here in Titusville prays for me on the other side of the world when I was in trouble? Bill listened patiently and intently. Rather than attempt to have an answer for each question, he addressed what was at the heart of my perplexity. Bill explained how God reaches out to draw people to Him. God by his Holy Spirit can work on people's hearts, causing them to have unexplained tears when in His presence.

God, by his Holy Spirit, can move a pastor to feel that one is in danger half way around the world. The pastor's belief was that God used things that I could not understand to draw me to Him and let me know how much he loved me.

Bill went on to tell me that he felt I needed to accept Jesus into my life by praying for that. He patiently went on, word by word, to explain how to say that prayer. When he finished, there was this awkward silence. I said, *"Do you mean right now?"*

He replied, "Yes."

Together, we prayed the prayer, confessing myself to be a sinner, acknowledging Jesus as the son of God who died for my sins, and asking Him to come into my life.

When we were done, Bill encouraged me to start reading the Gospel of John in the Bible. Immediately, I started making excuses as to how slow a reader I was and how difficult it was to read the Bible. In the days that followed, I did start to read the Bible and to my amazement, it made sense—I understood it. No longer was it just a lot of dos and don'ts as I had thought it to be.

In the years to follow, Claire and I served the Lord in many different ministries within the church. I was bolstered by the knowledge that I served a God who had reached around the world to let me know he cared for me. The story is not that we accepted the Lord and did a lot of service in the church. The story is that we accepted the Lord and the knowledge of His love and grace changed our hearts and our lives.

In 1978, our third child Susan Janet Hunt was born.

The movie *Apocalypse Now* came out in 1979. Finding out that the movie was about Vietnam and a river patrol boat was in the movie, I was eager to see the movie. I was severely disappointed. The movie angered me because of how it depicted Brown Water Sailors. It was bad enough that we Vietnam veterans were already dimly viewed, this movie made us look even worse. It is true that we Vietnam vets displayed no "spit and polish" while out in the "boonies." It is also true that there was a relaxing of military protocol for us river patrol people. But to portray us as high on drugs and having little to no control of our firepower was an insult.

The Boat People

For years after the fall of Saigon, thousands of South Vietnamese people fled the country in small boats. Boat people had to face storms, diseases, and starvation, and elude pirates.[35] Estimates of the number of Vietnamese boat people who died at sea can only be guessed. According to the United Nations High Commission for Refugees, between 200,000 and 400,000 boat people died at sea.[36] By June 1979, there were 350,000 boat people in refugee camps in Southeast Asia and Hong Kong.[37]

Why would people risk what the boat people risked to get out of the only home they had known? They wanted to escape the same thing we Americans and the South Vietnamese had been fighting to prevent for the past ten years: the forced (and I really mean forced) acceptance of Communist rule and the loss of freedom.

Nguyen Co Tach was the foreign minister of Vietnam from 1980 to 1991. He was quoted in a 1985 statement as saying,

> that "two and a half million...people went through reed-ucation...in fact, possibly more than 100,000 Vietnamese people were victims of extrajudicial executions in the last ten years...it is likely that, overall, at least one millions Vietnamese were the victims of forced population transfers.[38]

---

[35] *Associated Press*, June 23, 1979, *San Diego Union*, July 20, 1986

[36] Nghia M. Vo, *The Vietnamese Boat People* (2006)

[37] *State of the World's Refugees, 2000* United Nations High Commissioner for Refugees, pp. 83, 84

[38] Desbarats, Jacqueline. "Repression in the Socialist Republic of Vietnam: Executions and Population Relocation," from *The Vietnam Debate* (1990) by John Morton Moore

A total of more than 1.6 million Vietnamese were resettled between 1975 and 1997... with the United States resettling 402,382 refugees.[39]

Refugee camps were set up in a few of the countries where the boat people fled. Living conditions were overcrowded and poor. Many refugees lingered in these camps for years. To get into another country, refugees needed to have a sponsor in the host country. Sponsors could be individuals or organizations. Sponsors had to promise to provide food, clothing, and shelter until the refugees became self-sufficient and help find employment, register children into schools, and other adjustment details.

Our church, First Presbyterian Church of Titusville, sponsored a Vietnamese family in 1980. Deacon Arlene Maressa took the lead in organizing church members to meet the needs of the Tran family for their first few months in the United States. Phuoc and his family had escaped Vietnam in a small boat and made a dangerous, six-day and six-night trip to Galang Island in Indonesia.

There were two hundred people squeezed onto three-deck levels. The boat was so overcrowded that they had to spend the trip squeezed together, sitting in a squatting position unable to stand. Muoi, Phuoc's wife, sat with one of their two young daughters on either side and her baby in her lap. There was no bathroom on board, so when nature called, they had to make their way through the others to the aft part of the boat and relieve themselves over the side. Pirates attempted to stop the boat, but somehow, they eluded them.

There was no dock or pier to disembark the boat when they reached Galang Island, so they had to jump into nose-high water and make their way to the island. It was a struggle with two young girls and a baby to keep them all afloat. During the several months they were in the refugee camp at Galang, their baby died. They were

---

[39.] Robinson, *Terms of Refuge,* Appendix 1 and 2

transferred to Kuku refugee camp on Jemaja Island where they spent eighteen months before being able to get to the United States. Living conditions in the camp were poor, and there were reports of horrible treatment by Indonesian soldiers.

Phuoc's wife, Muoi, arrived in the United States with a lung infection and pregnant. None of the family spoke English. The church provided the first few months of rent for a modest apartment and stocked their refrigerator and cupboards to get started.

Phuoc was a mason by trade and found work soon after arrival. Not yet having a driver's license, he got up early every morning and rode a bike to the job site, did masonry work all day, and then rode home on his bike. Muoi walked to work at a local laundry. Members of the church took turns driving Phuoc and Muoi to English lessons and babysitting while they were in class. In a matter of two or three months, they were self-supporting. Their new son Vinh George Tran was born an American citizen. Phuoc worked six and seven days a week in addition to attending night classes to learn English. It wasn't long before he knew enough English to pass his driver's written test and get a license. He quickly earned enough money to buy a used car. Phuoc and Muoi had been Buddhists but converted to Christianity. In time, the Trans purchased a modest home in Trenton.

As the years passed, other Vietnamese family members and friends migrated to the United States and settled in the Detroit area and also nearby in Canada. The Tran family moved to Michigan to join them and opened a restaurant. From the restaurant business, Phuoc moved on to purchase and operate a used car lot.

The Tran family's story was the epitome of what anyone could hope for in a refugee family's melting into our American society. The work that was done by the church members to sponsor and support them was rewarding and refreshing.

The successful acclamation of the Tran family into American life was like a small victory over Communism that we never had in Vietnam.

As of this writing, there are hundreds of thousands of Syrian refugees awaiting sponsorship in other countries. It is heartwarming to see that there are Vietnamese families in Canada working to sponsor Syrian refugees in their communities.[40]

[40.] Toronto Star Touch, Dec. 16, 2015, *Vietnamese Refugees Prepare to Sponsor Syrian Families*

EPILOGUE

The Vietnam era was a negative period in our nation's history. The war was unpopular and nearly tore our country apart. Those of us who served in it did not return to victory parades and national celebrations. We returned almost embarrassed to say that we had gone to Vietnam. The media focused on everything that had been or might have been negative about the war. Yet those of us that served in the Brown Water Navy knew we had gone and done the job we were sent to do. We had made things better. We had accomplished the mission we were sent to do. And in the process, we had paid the price it cost to get it done. No doubt there were veterans in other units that had done the same.

Authors John Forbes and Robert Williams wrote several volumes entitled *The Illustrated History of The Vietnam War*. In the volume *Riverine Force*, they presented an accurate and positive assessment of what was accomplished by the riverine forces in the Delta. It deserves to be told and I have copied a portion of the last chapter entitled "Last Act of a Tragedy."

> *The completion of the Sea Lords barrier...was the result of one of the most remarkable naval campaigns in history.*
>
> *A region that was an enemy stronghold was turned around to the extent that it was the last significant area of South Vietnam to fall to the Communists.*
>
> *A vast area of land had been captured and held by the world's greatest blue-water Navy. The ocean going might of nuclear submarines, battleships, and giant aircraft carriers had been abandoned for small boats in small channels,*

winning countless tiny skirmishes, waiting in ambush for pajama clad platoons in the brown waters 100 miles from the sea.

It was a supreme example of the flexibility of sea power, made possible by the adaptability and open-mindedness of US Navy personnel at all levels, but above all by the bravery and fortitude of the men at the cutting edge of the battle.

The very nature of the war for the boat crews was that it had to be fought in small teams. Loyalty to the team proved to be a very effective motivator in combat. Morale was also helped by the knowledge that the overall strategy was working and their resources were superior. The inland barrier patrols forced the Communists to respond, and gave the Navy boat crews the tactical advantage of defending their own turf.

The Navy's successes left the Saigon government in a controlling position in the Mekong Delta, the most vital single area for a viable South Vietnam, when President Richard Nixon launched his Vietnamization program.

The key to keeping the Communists out of the Delta was the Sea Lords barrier, which offered, for the only time in the Vietnam War, the real prospect of long-term security. Behind that barrier the Viet Cong were visibly losing the war; behind that barrier prosperity was visibly growing. These visible trends were bound to have a powerful effect on morale, both among the peasants and among the men fighting to protect them.

They had most dramatic effects in the deep south of the Ca Mau peninsula, a remote backwater that was one of the VC's biggest resources of support and revenue in the Delta before Sea Lords.

The fact that these achievements were to be sacrificed at the negotiating table is part of the tragedy of Vietnam.

Swift Boat Sailors Association

Approximately twenty-three years after the United States withdrew from Vietnam, two separate efforts began that led to the formation of the Swift Boat Sailors Association, which now maintains a website, has an elected board of officers, and holds biennial reunions. Weymouth Symmes and his wife attended a reunion of PBR sailors in Las Vegas and came away feeling the need for an organization for Swift Boat sailors. They started collecting names and reaching out to ascertain interest. Meanwhile, others were attempting to have a reunion. *"As this went on, a separate effort, led by Wade R. Sanders, Deputy Assistant Secretary of the Navy, and Senator John F. Kerry, both of whom served on Swifts during the war, was going on in Washington, D.C. They had located two of the three last remaining Swift Boats, which were then in the Panama Canal, and arranged to have them brought to Washington, D.C."[41]*

One of the two recovered Swift Boats was dedicated on June 17, 1995, at the Washington Navy Yard. Senator John F. Kerry was one of the speakers that day, and he did a wonderful, eloquent job of relating what life on the Swift Boats was like. I wish I had been there that day. The following is a large portion of his speech:

> *And we exalted in the beauty of a country that took us from glorious green rice paddy, black water buffalo caressing the banks of rivers, children giggling and playing on dikes, sampans filled with produce—that suddenly took us from innocence and tranquility deep into the madness of fire fights, chaos reigning around us, 50 calibers diminishing our hearing, screams for medevac piercing the radio waves, fish-tailing rockets passing the pilot house - suddenly to be replaced by the most serene, eerie beauty the eye could behold. We lived in the daily contradiction of living and dying.*

---

41. Weymoth D. Symmes, *War on the Rivers*

EPILOGUE

In a great lesson for the rest of this country in these difficult times, we never looked on each other as officer or enlisted, as Oakie or Down Easterner. We were just plain brothers in combat, proud Americans who together with our proud vessels answered the call.

We were bound together in the great and noble effort of giving ourselves to something bigger than each of us individually, and doing so at risk of life and limb. Let no one ever doubt the quality and nobility of that commitment.

The specs say Swifts have a quarter-inch aluminum hull—but to us it was a hull of steel, though at times that was not enough. It was hospital, restaurant, and home. It was sometimes birthplace and deathbed.

It was where we lived and where we grew up. It was where we confronted and conquered and where we found courage. It was our confessional; our place of silent prayer.

We worked these boats hard. No matter the mission, no matter the odds, we pushed them and they took us through violent cross-currents of surf, through 30 ft. monsoon seas, through fish stakes and mangrove, through sandbars and mudflats.

We loved these boats, even if we abused them of necessity, and the truth is—they loved us back. They never let us down.

We made mistakes. Sometimes we bit off more than we could chew. We didn't just push the limits, we exceeded them routinely and still the boats came through. There were our partners on a grand and unpredictable adventure.

Mines exploded underneath us, and—for the most part—the boats pressed on.

The Marines made amphibious landings and took the beachheads—so did we.

The Army conducted sweeps and over-ran ambushes— so did we.

The regular Navy provided shore bombardment and forward fire control—so did we.

The Coast Guard intercepted weapons and gave emergency medical care—so did we.

The nurses and Red Cross saved lives and delivered babies—so did we.

The SEALS set ambushes and gathered intelligence—and so did we.

But the power and strength was not just in the boats. It was in the courage and the camaraderie of those who manned them.

In the darkness and solitude of night, or parked in a cove before a mission, or in the beauty of a crimson dawn before entering the Bay Hap, or the My Tho, or the Bo De, or any mangrove cluttered river—we shared our fears and, no matter what our differences—we were bound together on an extraordinary journey the memory of which will last forever.

On just routine patrols, these boats were our sanctuary—our cloister, a place for crossing divides between Montana, Michigan, Arkansas and Massachusetts.

The boats occupied us and protected us. They were the place we came together in fellowship, brotherhood, and ultimately in love to share our enthusiasm, our idealism—our youth.

Some were not as lucky as we were. They did not have the chance to grow up as we did. They did not get to see their children. They did not have the chance to fulfill their dreams, and we honor their memory today.

But, because of the nature of the war we fought we came back to a country that did not recognize our contribution. It did not understand the war we fought, what we went through, or the love that held us together then. It did not understand what young men could feel for boats like these and men like you.

This is really the first time in 30 years that we've been able to share with each other the feelings we had then, and the feelings we have now. They are deeply and profoundly personal feelings. They are different for each of us, but the memories are the same—rich with the smells and sounds of the rivers and the power of the boats—punctuated by the faces of the men with whom we served and the thoughts we shared.

To all who served on these boats, I salute you. May God bless you and your families.[42]

It is hard to believe that these words in 1995 came from the same John Kerry that in 1971 joined the Vietnam Veterans against the War, asserted before a Senate foreign relations committee that US forces daily committed war crimes and atrocities in Vietnam, joined in antiwar demonstrations, and threw his medals over the White House wall in protest. The news media ate this up, and it served to further besmirch the reputation of the millions of veterans who served honorably in Vietnam. Furthermore, John O'Neill and Jerome Corsi, in their 2004 best-seller *Unfit for Command* assert that *the record shows that Kerry and the VVAW consistently coordinated their efforts with Communists, both foreign and domestic, represented the Communists positions, and repeated their grossly exaggerated claims of American atrocities.*

I have been to the Washington Navy Yard a couple times since the dedication to see the Swift Boat that is on display there—once with my wife on the way home from a vacation south of Washington and again with my two grandsons in 2012. Neither visit was impressive. The first time the Swift was just sitting in a cradle at the end of a Navy Museum building near the water. The second time we nearly did not get to see the Swift as we arrived close to closing time. Only after I explained to a guard that I was a Swift Boat veteran and I wanted my grandsons to see the type of boat that I had served on did he allow us in for a few minutes to see the boat. We were not allowed on either occasion to board the boat.

---

[42]. Ibid pp. 252–254

Once the Swift Boat Sailors Association got organized and running, I joined and enjoyed receiving the quarterly newsletter and visiting the website occasionally.

Swift Boat Veterans for Truth and the 2004 Presidential Election

John Kerry stood on the deck of the USS *Yorktown* on September 2, 2003, and announced his candidacy for president. When he made mention of his Vietnam service, veterans across the nation began to worry about the possibility of the former war protester becoming the Commander in Chief. Those especially concerned were the Swift Boat veterans who had served with him and the POWs whose suffering was increased due to John Kerry's words and actions.

In March of 2004, Senator Kerry won the Democratic primaries. In response, Admiral Roy Hoffman, former commander of all Swift Boats in Vietnam, began calling and e-mailing former Swift Boat sailors. He requested any person who had firsthand knowledge of John Kerry's service to contact the retired admiral with the information. In addition, the opportunity to sign on for Kerry to stop calling us his "band of brothers" and for him to release all his service records was extended.

A small gathering followed in Texas. The members of the fledgling group possessed an amazing pool of talents but would need much more to accomplish their mission. These few men would need something near a miracle to get their message out to the American people. What they got was more like a chain of miracles. What emerged was the *Swift Boat Veterans for Truth*. They began a barrage of news conferences, interviews, newspaper articles, and a web page. Donations to support the group poured in, and television ads were produced and released.

Admiral Hoffman contacted me and enlisted me to join the group. I agreed to sign on to the request letter to John Kerry. As the television ads rolled out, I became uncomfortable with the attacks against Kerry's record, so I contacted Admiral Hoffmann by e-mail on August 14, 2004, to express my concerns about attacking one of our own Swift Boat veterans. I requested verification of the accusations that were being made about Senator Kerry. Admiral Hoffman replied immediately by phone and by e-mail.

> *Dear Charles:*
>
> *First and foremost, the Navy is us. Official records are what we submit from spot reports, after action, accidents, exercises and a myriad of other reports and letters. They are all dependent upon the truthfulness and accuracy of the reporting individual. You must make the decision. Do you believe Larry Thurlow, Dick Pees, Chenoweth, Van O'Dell and a dozen more direct witnesses, or Kerry/Rassmann? That decision is yours, not mine.*
>
> *I suggest you go to the library or buy two books:* Tour of Duty, *Kerry's biography by Douglas Brinkley, and* Unfit for Command *by John O'Neill and Jerome Corsi. Read* Unfit *first. It is well documented and analytical.* Tour *is more like a novel...*
>
> *Finally, I respect your opinion and foremost, honor your combat experience and service to our Navy and Country.*
>
> *Respectfully,*
> *Roy F. Hoffmann*
> *Friday, August 20, 2004 America Online: Guest*

I contacted my retired pastor Bill Shaub, who is a retired Army lieutenant colonel and Vietnam veteran, to get his thoughts on the whole Kerry issue and my continued involvement with the SBVT. He surprised me with his reply, *"Have you read the book* Unfit for Command? *I have, and I find it very believable, and I also financially support the group. Would you like to borrow the book?"*

I borrowed and read his copy and became convinced that John Kerry was egotistical and self-promoting. Furthermore, I believed that he had dramatically exaggerated his experiences in Vietnam. I hesitate to use the strong word *lie*, but in at least one case, he either lied or had a serious memory fault regarding being in Cambodia illegally on Christmas Eve and Christmas Day. After reading the book through the eyes of one who had been there and knew how things were done there, I decided to go "all in" with the Swift Boat Veterans for Truth.

On the weekend of October 8–10, 2004, the SBVT held a conference in Washington DC. The main task of the weekend was to video several large group television advertisements entitled *They Served.* Approximately seventy-five Swift Boat veterans and several former POWs gathered at Atlantic Studio. I was in the back row and barely seen in the video. Having never attended a Swift Boat veterans' reunion, I enjoyed the opportunity to be with this group and exchange stories.

George W. Bush defeated John F. Kerry by a narrow margin. Many people believe that the campaign by the SBVT made the difference and credited the organization for keeping John Kerry out of the highest office in the land.

> *President Bush may be celebrating victory today, but he owes it to a group he never acknowledged during the campaign. I'm talking about the Swift Boat Veterans for Truth. They are responsible for keeping Bush in the White House—or, more precisely, keeping John Kerry from snatching it from him.*
>
> *There is no doubt in my mind this was the difference in the race. The vets did Bush's dirty work. They took Kerry on and told the American people the truth about this fraud, this liar, this deceiver. Just enough Americans got the message to preserve a win for Bush...*
>
> *It is impossible to overstate just how significant the impact of* Unfit for Command, *the best-selling book by John O'Neill and Jerome Corsi, was in this campaign...*[43]
>
> *"...the effect of the Swift Boat Veterans' ad was to neutralize Kerry's record as a combat veteran as a campaign*

---

[43] *Credit the Swiftboat vets* by Joseph Farah. WorldNetDaily. November 3, 2004

advantage. Across the month of August Kerry slowly sank in the polls,... The marketing of the Swift Boat message was extraordinarily sophisticated, with Swift Boat spokesmen popping up on all the news and talk shows, particularly on cable and AM radio, and with a best-selling book released within days of the original ad... [44]

Sadly, what the SBVT accomplished for truth in 2004 quickly became a negative term. Rather than "Swift Boating" being used to describe a campaign to uncover untruths, it is now used to describe an unfair or untrue smearing of a political person or party. Although we swayed enough people away from John Kerry to cost him the election, it seems that the majority of people, or at least the majority of the media, thought that we were lying. The negative use of the term angers me.

No doubt there were some large donations from individuals that were more concerned about promoting the Republican party and getting George Bush elected than exposing the truth, but in a statement released November 3, 2004, Admiral Roy Hoffman stated, *"Our SBVT grassroots effort produced donors in every state in the nation and raised more than $26 million, with more than $7 million in online contributions."*

In addition, the SBVT campaign created enough dissent amongst the members of the Swift Boat Sailors Association (a separate organization) to lose some members in spite of the SBSA's attempt to separate itself from the SBVT. The pursuit of truth ended up just like our service in Vietnam; we threw ourselves into an endeavor to do what was right and came out the bad guys. After a while, you almost get accustomed to things turning out that way in life.

---

[44] *Public Profiles/Private Lives; the Strengths and Limitations of the Modern American Presidents.* by Holder, Moretta and Olivares. Published by Abigail Press in 2005

Agent Orange

Between 1961 and 1972 the United States dropped nineteen million gallons of herbicides over 4.5 million acres of land.[45] A lot of the area along the Cua Lon and Bo De Rivers in the Ca Mau peninsula was defoliated by Agent Orange. The land was defoliated to make it safer for us. The enemy could not hide very well in a defoliated area, so we usually breathed a little easier while passing by these areas. (Even so, we were ambushed once from a bunker built in a defoliated area.)

In the years after Vietnam, a lot of veterans were diagnosed with various types of skin rashes and cancers. For a number of years, the chemical companies and the government denied any connection between Agent Orange and the ailments of the Vietnam veterans. In 1979, a class action suit was filed on behalf of 2.4 million veterans that had been exposed to Agent Orange. Five years later, there was an out of court settlement with chemical companies followed by a number of challenges. Eventually in 1991, President George H. W. Bush signed into law the Agent Orange Act, which mandates that some diseases associated with defoliants be treated as result of wartime service.[46]

In 1983 Elmo Zumwalt III was diagnosed with lymphoma, a cancer of the lymphatic system.[47] Elmo III was an officer on a Swift Boat and operated at Sea Float and Ha Tien in the same period that I was there. At the time, his father Admiral Elmo Zumwalt, Jr. was the Commander of Naval Forces in Vietnam and had ordered the step up of the use of defoliants around Sea Float for security reasons. The irony of the story in the book that they coauthored *My Father, My Son* is that father ordered the use of a defoliant that caused the cancer in the son, but the son does not hold any ill feelings toward his father for the decision he made to use the defoliant. On August 14, 1988, Elmo Zumwalt III lost his battle with cancer.

[45.] History.com Staff, *Agent Orange*, retrieved from www.history.com

[46.] ibid

[47.] *My Father, My Son*. Admiral Elmo Zumwalt Jr. and Lieutenant Elmo Zumwalt III 1986

In September of 2011, I was diagnosed with prostate cancer. After thirty-nine radiation treatments, follow-up testing indicated, to the amazement of my urologist and oncologist, the cancer was not eradicated. Injections to inhibit the cancer were started, and I was referred to the specialists at Memorial Sloan Kettering Hospital in New York City. A program of monitoring and testing was begun. In July of 2013, I was diagnosed with bladder cancer, which was treated and cured, but now requires a regular cystoscopy to monitor for reoccurrence. In April of 2014, a biopsy revealed cancer in my right pelvic lymph node. Surgery was discussed but not recommended. A program of shots to inhibit the cancer and regular monitoring was begun. I was offered and agreed to be in the care of the prostate cancer research program at Sloan Kettering.

Prostate cancer is one of the cancers that research suggests may be caused by exposure to Agent Orange.[48] Like Lt. Elmo Zumwalt III, I spent a lot of time in defoliated areas. Thanks to the battles for VA assistance by thousands of Vietnam veterans before me and the expertise of the county Veterans Affairs officer, I had no difficulty in obtaining veterans benefits for prostate cancer.

Like many other veterans, it seems the war, or its effects, will not be over for me in this life.

[48.] The American Cancer Society medical and Editorial content team, *Agent Orange and Cancer,* retrieved from www.cancer.org/cancer/cancercauses/agent-orange-and-cancer

Way of the Warrior

(excerpt)
...But the warrior never forgets...
Any battle won or lost
For when he lays his sword down he's still a man
Who knows...that everything comes at a cost.

Louisa

AFTERWORD

Imagine that your family, parents, grandparents, wife, and siblings all talked you into saving and scrimping, working two jobs, giving up your hobbies all in order to pay for someone else's medical expenses and welfare. For years, you do just that because you believe this person can be healed and restored to a healthy life. Then after years, your family begins to argue and disagree about continuing to give this assistance. Finally, they insist that you stop providing the aid to this other person despite the fact that they had promised to see them through their journey. The person in need slowly loses ground while your family looks on but feels the cost to continue assisting is too high and they need to take care of themselves. Eventually, the battle for health is lost. Not because you failed but because of your family's decisions. Imagine how you would feel about the sacrifices you had made that had been allowed to be wasted.

Well, men and women leaving their homes and families, giving up a part of their lives, suffering hardships, risking being killed, captured or wounded, watching their buddies die and then your country decides to quit and withdraw leaving an inadequate and underfunded defense system to weaken and fail due to your country's failure to keep its promise to its ally—this is the same thing as the aforementioned analogy. How would you feel?

I gave up a year of my life, risked all that, paid the price for freedom and came home to a seemingly ungrateful country that was no longer willing to fight for freedom for others. Right now, the mantra and signs in the streets and on the news is "Black lives matter." Well, those lives we sacrificed in Vietnam mattered. The lives of the Vietnamese that died in that conflict (that no one wanted to call a war), those lives mattered. The lives of the Vietnamese people that we turned our backs on mattered. Our promise to another country of human beings to stand with them for freedom should matter.

The Vietnamese people were betrayed by the American people, and we who served were betrayed by our own people. Watching helicopters leaving desperate people behind to fall into the hands of a vengeful enemy force in 1975 was a disgrace. Seeing helicopters pushed over the side of a US Navy ship was further disgrace. Failing to hold the North Vietnamese to the provisions of the Paris Peace accords was a show of weakness. How could we stomach thousands of Vietnamese drowning while trying to escape by sea in overcrowded small vessels because we abandoned them? How did we allow this? Sadly, I know. If I could insert one of those faces that you can put in text messages, it would be a sad one with tears.

Year after year of American sons and daughters, fathers and mothers, brothers and sisters shedding their blood and dying was more than our quick-fix/easy-win populace wanted to continue. Their eye was on the continuing cost, not the sought-after goal. Stopping the pain outweighed our concern for other's freedoms. The media's slanted reporting played a big part in turning our people against the war. From their perspective, they could not see the progress we had made. Whole areas previously controlled by the Viet Cong forces had been pacified by the time I was there, but no one reported that. We had bombed North Vietnam just about to its knees and then backed off.

So who was right? Those who believed we were bound to keep our promise or those who decided the price was too high? No doubt you could argue forever about that. We will never know for sure.

Surely a determining factor in a person's view is the degree to which they feel an obligation to be your brother's keeper. I believe for most of us who paid the price, we wanted to see the mission completed. We did not want our sacrifices or our fellow countrymen's sacrifices to be wasted. For those who faced what it may cost them or their loved one, the cost outweighed the goal they did not see being accomplished.

Although I have written about these feelings and events, I have learned that it is not healthy to dwell on them. For me, a reluctant warrior, I know that I went and I served honorably. I know that the US Navy, especially the brave men of the Brown Water Navy, were extremely successful at accomplishing the mission we were tasked with in the Mekong Delta. I learned a lot about life and how precious it is. I learned that we can endure and push way beyond what we think our limitations are. I learned to be thankful to God that he never left me and even gave me a sign that would eventually draw me to surrender to His love in the form and person of his son Jesus Christ.

The topic of sacrifice for others can hardly be talked about without thinking of the sacrifice that Jesus made for each of us. God sent his Son to pay the price, to make the sacrifice for freedom from the penalty of sin for all who would turn to him and accept the gift of salvation. The price Jesus paid was his body and blood for the debt we have for our sins. Just like we too often take freedom for granted, we also take the free gift of eternal life through faith in Jesus Christ for granted too often. Beyond that imagine how God feels when His sacrifice is wasted by those who refuse to believe. Gary S. Paxton authored a song titled "I Wonder if God Cries." I think He does.

Paxton also wrote and recorded "He Was There All the Time."

The verses say that while we are caught up searching for fulfillment in our earthly pursuits, Jesus is waiting for us to turn to Him. The chorus goes on:

He was there all the time, He was there all the time;
Waiting patiently in line, He was there all the time.

The first time I heard the song, it spoke directly to my heart and soul.

In the Book of Revelation Jesus says,

Here I am! I stand at the door and knock. If anyone hears my voice and opens the door, I will come in and eat with him, and he with me.

The sudden realization that through all I had been through, Jesus was patiently knocking and waiting for me to open the door of my heart to Him brought me to tears. It is difficult cognitively to grasp the depth of love and patience that God has for us. When one gets just a glimpse of it, our heart melts, and we fall in love with Him. It is one thing to mentally make a decision to believe that Jesus is the Son of God who died and rose again to purchase salvation for each one of us. It is a vastly different experience to become aware of the depth of His patience and love for us. Therein lies the power that changes lives.

I started off this book talking about freedom and choices. I am ending on the same topic. Each one of us has the freedom to choose what we will believe and the path we will take in life. The most important choice you can make is to choose Jesus and follow him. Jesus says to those who believe him, *"Hold to my teaching... Then you will know the truth, and the truth will set you free"* (John 8:31–32).

GLOSSARY

ACTOV. Accelerated Turnover to the Vietnamese, a program to train and equip the Vietnamese to take over the role of US forces in Vietnam.

APL. Auxiliary Personnel Lighter. A barracks barge, not self propelled. Used to house and feed troops.

ARVN. Pronounced "arvin." Army of the Republic of Vietnam (South Vietnamese regular Army).

B40. A type of rocket propelled grenade used by the communist forces.

Beach. as used in this book—any place where the land meets the water, be it ocean, sea, river, or canal.

Brass. The empty shell casings expelled from weapons after firing.

Brown-water Navy. A proud term to distinguish inland water craft from ocean going ships in blue water. Named brown-water Navy because the water of the delta was often brown from the monsoon rain and storms.

BM. Boatswain Mate is the rate in the Navy responsible for all matters regarding the deck maintenance, hull, lines, anchor, etc.

Charlie. Viet Cong insurgent.

Chart. Navy's term for a map.

CO. Commanding Officer

COSDIV. Coastal division

Crocodile. The Vietnamese used this as a slang verb meaning to kill.

Cumshaw. Procuring goods or materials through questionable means.

Didi Mau. Vietnamese: "go quickly."

Drifty. A person who acts in a disorganized or haphazard manner, lacking full awareness.

Dung Lai. Vietnamese: "halt."

EN. Engineman.

Fix. A geographic location generally identified by grid coordinates on a chart.

Friendlies. Military slang for friendly troops.

General quarters. Naval term for the order for everyone to immediately go to battle stations.

GM. Gunners' Mate.

HE. High explosive.

Illumination. Vietnam: hand held "pop" flares fired by removing the top cap reattaching to the bottom end of the flare and smacking the bottom. The flare is launched skyward, then "pops" (ignites) and deploys a small parachute to hold the burning flare in the air for short period of time to light up an area. Also mortar rounds that deploy a much larger flare and parachute.

In country. In Vietnam

KIA. Killed in action

Kit Carson Scouts: Former Viet Cong soldiers that came over to our side and acted as scouts for ground forces.

Lai day: "Come here."

LTJG. Lieutenant junior grade. Second step up from entry level officer. Most officers on the Swift Boats were LTJG.

LST. Landing Ship Tank, often referred to as a T. Created during WWII to support amphibious operations by carrying vehicles, cargo, and landing troops directly onto unimproved shore. Had doors that opened in the front and a ramp dropped down to load and unload. Used in Vietnam to support riverine craft—380 feet long and 65 feet wide.

LZ. Landing Zone for helicopters

Medevac. A helicopter used to evacuate wounded from combat zones

MRF. Mobile Riverine Force. Known as Task Force 117, it was an assemblage of modified smaller WWII landing craft used to carry troops into enemy held territory and slug it out.

NVA. North Vietnamese Army

OIC. Officer in Charge. Designation given to those in command of a Swift Boat. Equivalent to the captain of a ship.

Operation Market Time. Task Force 115 the US Navy mission to conduct surveillance, gunfire support, board and search, and other operations along the 1,200-mile coast of South Vietnam in order to detect and prevent Communist infiltration from the sea.

Port side. Left side.

PBR. Patrol boat river. Task Force 116 used these thirty-three-foot fiberglass boats designed to conduct riverine operations

PCF. Patrol Craft Fast—official name of a Swift Boat.

PG. Patrol Gunboat, 164-foot US Navy craft equipped with radar controlled three-inch gun and 40 mm cannons.

Psyops. Psychological operations. For Swift Boats, pysops meant riding along the waterways blasting a prerecorded message to the enemy to surrender to us and promising rewards for those who did. There are more facets to psyops but that was our part in them. For us it was like broadcasting way ahead that we were coming, which gave the enemy time to get a good ambush setup.

QM. Quartermaster—Navy rate for person responsible for charting and checking the course, navigation, taking the helm, record keeping and the pilot house.

R & R. Rest and recreation (or relaxation). In Vietnam, it was a week away vacationing in one of several locations.

Radarman. Navy rate for person responsible for watching and maintaining the radar. On a Swift Boat, he often served as a gunner when at general quarters. Radarmen and Radiomen were used interchangeably on swifts.

RPG. Rocket-propelled grenade such as the B40 rocket usually launched from a handheld launch tube by enemy forces.

Rules of engagement. Standing orders as to how to engage or respond to the enemy in given situations, often changing depending on the area of operation.

Sapper. In Vietnam, riverine warfare, an enemy swimmer who sets mines or other explosives.

SEAL. Named SEALs because of their ability to operate from sea, air, or land. The US Navy special operations group often used for clandestine operations directed more toward gathering intelligence by means of forward observation and body snatches. Their tactics and reputation struck fear in the hearts of the enemy.

Seawolf. US Navy helicopter gunship armed with mini guns and rockets

SEALORDS: Southeast Asia Lake, Ocean, River, and Delta Strategy. A US Navy operation begun in November 1968 using Swift Boats, PBRs, and the River Assault Group boats. The objective was harassment of Viet Cong strongholds in the Mekong Delta and interdiction of supplies infiltrated from Cambodia.

SERE. Survival evasion resistance, and escape training.

Short. Very few days left before going home.

Starboard side. Right side

Swifty. A Swift Boat sailor. Often known for a certain degree of devil-may-care, lack-of-discipline attitude when it came to lesser important military order and courtesy. Also known for courage as they were sent anywhere, anytime to perform any task assigned to them.

Tet. Major Vietnamese holiday

The world. Used when speaking about getting out of Vietnam, as in, "I can't wait to get back to the world."

UDT. Underwater Demolition Team

VC. Viet Cong. Communist insurgents fighting the government forces of South Vietnam.

WPB: Water Patrol Boat, an eighty-one-foot US Coast Guard boat.

Waterborne guardpost. the practice of positioning a boat in a river or canal at night to detect and stop movement or infiltration of enemy forces and supplies.

Z-grams. A term coined using the first letter of Admiral Elmo Zumalt's last name and grams as short for telegrams. Z-grams for operation orders from him as COMNAVFOR—Commander of Naval Forces Vietnam.

Related Reading

Cutler, Thomas J. *Brown Water, Black Berets.* Annapolis, Maryland: United States Naval Institute, 1988.

Daly, Dan. *White Water Red Hot Lead.* Cambridge, MA: Harvard Book Store, 2015.

Forbes, John and Williams, Robert. *Riverine Force.* Bantam Books, 1987.

Gugliotta, Yeoman, Sullivan. *Swift Boats at War in Vietnam.* Guilford, Connecticut: Stackpole Books, 2017.

Marolda, Edward J. *The U.S. Navy in the Vietnam War* (original title, *By Sea, Air, and Land*). Washington, D.C.: Naval Historical Center, Dept. of the Navy, 1994.

Means, William. *Letters from a Swift Boat.* 2016.

Scheffer, Jason. *The Rise and Fall of the Brown Water Navy.* Fort Leavenworth, Kansas: U.S. Army Command and General Staff College, 2005.

Symmes, Weymouth. *War on the Rivers.* Missoula, Montana: Pictorial Histories Publishing Company, Inc. 2004.

Zumwalt, Elmo, Jr. and Elmo III. *My Father, My Son.* New York: Macmillan Publishing Company, 1986.

Websites

www.pcf45.com by Robert B. Shirley
www.swiftboats.org, Swift Boat Sailors Association
www.swiftboats.net by Larry Wasikowski

About the Author

Charles W. Hunt dropped out of college early in 1967 and joined the Navy Reserves in hopes of staying out of combat in Vietnam. In 1969, the Navy sent him to South Vietnam where he spent 345 days as Engineman and aft gunner on a fifty-foot patrol boat. Petty Officer Hunt was awarded the Navy Commendation Medal with Combat "V" for courage under fire.

He returned home and honed his technical skills repairing automobiles. During the course of his career, he accumulated numerous certifications including Ford senior master technician and ASE/ASIA world-class technician. Competing in numerous technical skill challenges, he placed first in the Ford Philadelphia District in 1987 and first in the Eastern Region in 1989. In 2002 and 2007, he qualified as a Ford Ultimate Master Technician.

In 1972, he married his wife Claire and began their family. God blessed them with three children in the years to come. They became foster parents for other children from time to time and later raised two of their own grandchildren.

In 1976, Charles accepted Jesus Christ as his Lord and Savior. He went on to serve at his local church as Sunday school teacher, youth group leader, elder, and worship leader.

In 2011, he was diagnosed with prostate cancer and then, in 2013, bladder cancer. Radiation and chemotherapy slowed the prostate cancer but failed to eradicate it. In 2014, the cancer had advanced to stage four, and treatment continues. Charles is currently receiving full benefits from the Veterans Administration as the Agent Orange defoliant used in Vietnam is believed to be the likely cause of his cancer.

After retiring in 2015, he spends his time gardening and caring for the family homestead that has been in the family for generations. Charles still serves the Lord through various mission trips and ministries in the local church. His special ministry is fixing cars and equipment for those in need or persons serving in full-time ministry.